Does History Matter?

Making and debating citizenship,
immigration and refugee policy in
Australia and New Zealand

Does History Matter?

Making and debating citizenship,
immigration and refugee policy in
Australia and New Zealand

Edited by Klaus Neumann and Gwenda Tavan

ANU
THE AUSTRALIAN NATIONAL UNIVERSITY

E PRESS

ANU
E PRESS

the Australia and New Zealand
School of Government

Published by ANU E Press
The Australian National University
Canberra ACT 0200, Australia
Email: anuepress@anu.edu.au
This title is also available online at: http://epress.anu.edu.au/immigration_citation.html

National Library of Australia
Cataloguing-in-Publication entry

Title:	Does history matter? : making and debating citizenship, immigration and refugee policy in Australia and New Zealand / editors Klaus Neumann, Gwenda Tavan.
ISBN:	9781921536946 (pbk.) 9781921536953 (pdf)
Series:	ANZSOG series.
Subjects:	Citizenship--Australia.
	Citizenship--New Zealand.
	Refugees--Government policy--Australia.
	Refugees--Government policy--New Zealand.
	Australia--Emigration and immigration--Government policy.
	New Zealand--Emigration and immigration--Government policy.

Other Authors/Contributors:
Neumann, Klaus, 1958-
Tavan, Gwenda.

Dewey Number: 323.63

Cover design by John Butcher

Funding for this monograph series has been provided by the Australia and New Zealand School of Government Research Program.

John Wanna, *Series Editor*

Professor John Wanna is the Sir John Bunting Chair of Public Administration at the Research School of Social Sciences at The Australian National University and is the director of research for the Australian and New Zealand School of Government (ANZSOG). He is also a joint appointment with the Department of Politics and Public Policy at Griffith University and a principal researcher with two research centres: the Governance and Public Policy Research Centre and the nationally-funded Key Centre in Ethics, Law, Justice and Governance at Griffith University.

Table of Contents

Foreword

Malcolm Fraser

This collection is a useful contribution to the debate on the vexed question of Indigenous rights but more particularly on the complex issues concerning immigration, refugee and asylum-seeker policy.

If the attitudes and the tenor of public debate that prevailed in Australia during the Howard years and which appear to be continuing had been dominant in the late 1940s, the 1950s, the 1960s and the 1970s, mass immigration, which has contributed so much to Australia's cultural and physical wealth and to its development generally, could never have occurred. Political parties would have competed on the issue of race, appealing to the worst, rather than the best, of our natures.

We underestimate the restraint that was shown in 1954 when the Menzies Government acceded to the Refugee Convention, and during the years in which the White Australia Policy was slowly being whittled away and ultimately abolished.

Certainly a majority, but not all, of the new citizens coming to Australia in those years were from Europe but the original promise of concentrating on people from Britain and Ireland was never capable of achievement.

The debate now has been given an added significance because many of the world's refugees are Muslims and from countries that have not been natural sources of immigration for Australia. These changes have made it both easier and more dangerous for the issues to be politicised. It became possible to play on fears of the unknown, of people alleged to be different, and to suggest that such people would not make a positive contribution to Australia.

When we accepted a large number of refugees from Indochina at the end of the Vietnam War—a decision that was warmly and generously accepted by a great many Australians—I thought we had reached a turning point for the better. I believed we would never go back to the narrow, introspective days when our population was overwhelmingly of British origins, that we would now accept people for what they were, for what they could contribute to this country. Unfortunately, the way in which the refugee issues have been handled in the past dozen or so years has dashed those hopes.

In the Howard years, there were even attempts to ban the use of the term 'multicultural', but no other word was offered in its place. They came to nought because the debate over the benefits of multiculturalism had passed its time. One only needs to walk down the streets of Sydney or Melbourne to know that this is a multicultural society, with people from many different countries settling here. The evidence overwhelmingly, so far, has suggested that Australians support these developments and also that Australia's new citizens over the past half-century have overwhelmingly contributed very strongly to the country's physical and cultural development.

The debate over Australia's response to refugees has involved many falsehoods. The previous government defamed refugees from Afghanistan who were fleeing the Taliban. It said that such people were different, they would become criminals, drug runners, prostitutes and would obviously be a very bad influence on Australian society. The government could much more accurately have said that such people had shown initiative in trying to find a better future for their children. Many refugees are from countries that have become archaic and quite impossible. For example, young girls would not have anything like a reasonable life in Afghanistan and many tried to flee to find a country where they also could be normal citizens. People who are prepared to pull up stakes and go to a new land—that is clearly going to be different for them—are resourceful and enterprising and will make good citizens for their new country.

The debates about these issues showed how easy it was to cause concern, even fear, among a great many Australians. They show how easy it is to attract the red-necked element in our society—an element that exists in every country in the world. In earlier times, our objective as a nation was to sideline such people, to make as many as possible, and the group themselves, believe that their views were indeed disreputable. Such views, which had been regarded as disreputable, narrow or racist, were made respectable.

While the current government has made some welcome changes, it has not done enough to reverse earlier damage.

We are often told that we live in a globalised world where everything we do has an implication for other people or other countries. This is certainly true in economics; it is perhaps even more true in relation to the environment. If we do live in one world in these senses, we need to understand that our attitudes to people must also grow and change and develop productively.

While people come from widely differing backgrounds and circumstances, they have similar aspirations: they want to be able to look after their families, to feed and educate their children and to give them an opportunity for a better life than they themselves had. The values embraced in such desires are not particular to Australia or any other country; they are universal. These issues should be more widely recognised.

I hope the chapters in this book and the academic analyses involved will promote a wider understanding of the reality that we do in fact live in one world. Where there is disadvantage, there is an obligation on the wealthy and the powerful to help and to assist. How we act on these issues will be the ultimate determinant of what kind of nation we in Australia are and what kind of nation we become.

Contributors

Ann Beaglehole

Dr Beaglehole is the author and co-author of six New Zealand histories. Her work focuses on immigration policy, refugee settlement and ethnic relations. Dr Beaglehole has held various roles in the New Zealand Public Service. They include senior analyst positions in the Ministry of Maori Development and in the Office of Ethnic Affairs. She is at present undertaking research for the Waitangi Tribunal.

Rt Hon Malcolm Fraser AC CH

Malcolm Fraser served as Prime Minister of Australia from 1975 until 1983. He regularly comments on public affairs, particularly in the area of human rights policy. He is a professorial fellow at the Australia Pacific Centre for Military Law at the University of Melbourne.

J. Olaf Kleist

J. Olaf Kleist has published several papers about social memory in Australia and edited a collection of articles (in German translation) by Moishe Postone. He is currently completing doctoral research about social memories in Australia and Germany at the Otto-Suhr-Institut of Berlin's Freie Universität.

Amy Nethery

Amy Nethery is a PhD candidate in the Centre for Citizenship and Human Rights at Deakin University. Her research interests include political responses to forced migration, the history of administrative incarceration and theories of bureaucracy and governance relating to national boundaries. She has a longstanding interest in the treatment of refugees in Australia and has been active in establishing networks of researchers in the field to inform government policy.

Klaus Neumann

Klaus Neumann is a professor in the Democracy and Justice Program of the Institute for Social Research, Swinburne University of Technology. He is the author of five books, including most recently the award-winning *In the Interest of National Security* (2006). He is currently completing research on the history of refugee and asylum-seeker policies in Australia and New Zealand.

Glenn Nicholls

Dr Nicholls is the author of *Deported: A history of forced departures from Australia* (2007) and a regular commentator on immigration policy. He is an adjunct research fellow at the Institute for Social Research at Swinburne University of Technology and works in academic support at Deakin University.

Roderic Pitty

Dr Pitty is an associate professor in International Relations at the University of Western Australia, teaching global governance and human rights. He is an editor of *Global Citizens: Australian activists for change* (2008) and contributed chapters to *Facing North: A century of Australian engagement with Asia* (2001, 2003). His research interests include cosmopolitan politics and international law, including the recognition of Indigenous rights in Australia and New Zealand.

Gwenda Tavan

Dr Tavan is a senior lecturer in Australian politics at La Trobe University. Her research interests include the history and politics of immigration, national identity and race. She has published several articles and the multi-award winning book *The Long, Slow Death of White Australia* (2005). She is currently working on a biography of Arthur Calwell.

Acknowledgments

Does History Matter? is the result of a lengthy process that began with an invitation, issued by Paul 't Hart and Tim Rowse, to run a workshop on the role of the past in immigration policy making under the umbrella of the Governing by Looking Back conference at The Australian National University in December 2007. We would like to thank Paul and Tim for prompting our interest in the issues canvassed in this volume.

The Politics and International Relations Program at La Trobe University and the Institute for Social Research (ISR) at Swinburne University of Technology have provided a congenial environment for our work. The Australian Research Council has funded part of this project through a Discovery Grant administered by Swinburne University.

We would like to thank the individual contributors for patiently responding to our queries and suggestions and for bearing with us while we were negotiating the publication of their papers. We are grateful to John Butcher for timely advice and for seeing the project through to its completion and to the volume's five anonymous reviewers for their comments. A big thank you goes to David Hudson at the ISR, to the ANZSOG series editorial team and to staff at ANU E Press for assisting us in the final stages of the publication process.

Abbreviations and acronyms

ABC	Australian Broadcasting Corporation
ALP	Australian Labor Party
ANZ	Archives New Zealand
ASIO	Australian Security Intelligence Organisation
CPD	*Commonwealth Parliamentary Debates*
MP	Member of Parliament
NAA	National Archives of Australia
NT	Northern Territory
NZIS	New Zealand Immigration Service
NZPD	*New Zealand Parliamentary Debates*
SAS	Special Air Service (Regiment)
SIEV	suspected illegal entry vessel
UN	United Nations
UNHCR	United Nations High Commissioner for Refugees

Introduction

On 15 April 2009, the Australian Navy intercepted a boat carrying some 50 suspected asylum-seekers near Ashmore Reef, a group of three small uninhabited islands about halfway between the Australian mainland and the Indonesian island of Roti. In accordance with the government's policy, the boat was to be escorted to Christmas Island where the asylum-seekers were to be detained while security and health checks were carried out and their asylum claims processed. The next day, an explosion sank the boat, killed six of its passengers and badly injured dozens of others. The explosion was apparently caused when fuel that had been poured onto the deck, possibly to compel the Navy to take the boat's passengers to Australia, was accidentally ignited. The boat was the sixth so-called suspected illegal entry vessel (SIEV) to arrive in Australian waters since the beginning of the year.[1]

For several days, questions arising from the tragedy preoccupied politicians, journalists and the Australian public. Many of these questions were about possible parallels with events in 2001 after the Australian Government's refusal to let the Norwegian container ship *Tampa* land more than 400 asylum-seekers on Christmas Island (see Chapter 5). The perspectives of politicians and commentators were influenced by memories and histories of the Tampa affair and its aftermath. For example, the government's information management strategy was informed by an analysis of the 'children overboard' affair of 2001, when the Liberal-National Coalition Government of John Howard claimed—wrongly, as it turned out—that asylum-seekers aboard SIEV 4 had thrown their children overboard in a callous attempt to force the Australian Navy to abandon its plan of towing the boat back to Indonesian waters.[2] The Opposition too was looking to 2001: several of its members—including former Howard Government ministers Kevin Andrews, Philip Ruddock and Alexander Downer—seemed to believe that a line that had won them an election eight years earlier could save them once again.[3] In editorials, journalists were asking how the situation in 2009 differed from that in 2001, with several commenting on the need to avoid a repeat of the hysteria that had beset the country eight years earlier.[4]

It is safe to assume that the government carefully analysed the events of 2001 also to gauge the potential of being perceived as weak on border protection. One day after the explosion aboard the SIEV, Prime Minister, Kevin Rudd, identified those ultimately responsible for it: the people smugglers, 'the vilest form of human life' who 'should rot in jail, and in my own view, rot in hell'.[5] His shrill outburst was arguably both a ploy to deflect any criticism levelled at the government and to identify a party that could be held responsible not only for the tragic events of 16 April but for the arrival of 'boat people' more generally, and an attempt to avoid doing what Howard and his government had done in 2001—namely, blaming refugees for embarking on perilous journeys to Australia.[6]

It is likely that Rudd and his ministers saw parallels between the response of the Liberals and Nationals in 2009 and Labor's response in 2001. In both cases, the Opposition was divided and its leadership indecisive. In both cases, the government pounced on this weakness. In both cases, the Leader of the Opposition was compelled to adopt a stance that appeared to be counterintuitive: in 2001, Labor leader, Kim Beazley, eventually sided with the government for fear that he would be seen as weak, while in 2009, Malcolm Turnbull let himself—at least temporarily—be drawn into the corner of Liberal Party hardliners who were barracking for a return to the asylum-seeker regime that had been introduced by Howard and his Minister for Immigration, Philip Ruddock, and dismantled from 2005 onwards, initially at the urging of a small number of government backbenchers.[7]

While politicians and journalists turned to history to interpret the situation at hand, images of badly burnt victims arriving in hospitals in Perth and Darwin prompted memories that were seemingly unrelated: of the recent Victorian bushfires and, more significantly, of the 2002 Bali bombing when many of those injured in the blast had been evacuated to Darwin and from there transferred to burns units in other capital cities.[8] These memories also shaped the public's response to the tragedy: notwithstanding the suspicion that the explosion had been caused by those aboard the asylum-seeker boat, it was the Bali bombing that provided the most enduring prism through which the arrival of injured 'boat people' was interpreted.

How are history and memory implicated in policy making and political debate? What processes of remembering and forgetting do political leaders utilise when making or defending policy decisions? Does the use of history and public memory enhance or inhibit the policy making process? These are the central questions that have shaped the contributions to this volume.

The broad questions addressed here are not new. Political scientists and historians have paid close attention to the use of historical analogy in policy making.[9] In recent years, they have explored, for example, to what extent the international community's response to the genocide in Rwanda in 1994 was predetermined by the failed intervention in Somalia,[10] or how Ronald Reagan's response in the mid-1980s, when seven US citizens were taken hostage in Lebanon, was shaped by his reading of the Iranian hostage crisis of 1979–81, which had paved the way for his emphatic election win in November 1980.[11] The case that has perhaps more than any other attracted political scientists interested in the use of historical analogies is the American response in the Cuban missile crisis, which relied heavily on particular readings of the past (see also Chapter 2).[12]

Most of the scholarship on the use of the past in policy making has focused on issues of crisis management and/or on foreign policy. In moments of crisis, policy makers act in a climate of uncertainty and are more likely to perceive the need for a *proven* solution. They cannot have recourse to making incremental changes to existing policy measures but are in need of a response that—in terms of its significance and momentum—corresponds to the dramatic departure from the norm they experience. Furthermore, during a crisis, policy making has to rely on a comparatively large degree of conjecture. That is particularly true for natural disasters and international crises. In both instances, there is a pronounced sense of unpredictability. The forces of nature and foreign actors (be they governments or terrorist groups) are perceived as capricious because of a lack of reliable intelligence about their behaviour. In such cases, policy makers turn to history, not least to be reassured.

Crises also present themselves as potential lessons. While, for example, the fight against the 2009 Black Saturday bushfires in Victoria was informed by lessons learnt during, and from, the Black Friday fires in January 1939 or the Ash Wednesday fires in February 1983, the catastrophe was also perceived as an opportunity to gain knowledge that could be applied during similar emergencies in the future. Crises therefore prompt policy makers to look back, towards useful pasts, and to look ahead, towards a future when the present has itself become a useful past.[13]

The papers assembled in this book have a specific focus. Drawing on memory studies and policy studies, their authors reflect on the complex interrelationship between past and present issues and concerns and the political and policy dynamics it creates in immigration, refugee and asylum-seeker, and citizenship policy. They are concerned only peripherally with crisis management and explore domestic policy issues that usually do not feature in a literature that is preoccupied with foreign policy crises and natural disasters.

Scholars analysing the use of historical analogies have also neglected these areas of policy making because history does not seem to feature prominently in the deliberations of policy makers dealing with immigration, refugee or citizenship issues. Immigration policy, in particular, is an inherently contemporary and future-focused enterprise; policy makers determine the levels and types of entry on a year-by-year basis according to present circumstances (for example, the need to fill labour shortages or respond to a pressing refugee crisis) and/or future planning. This present/future focus extends to migration settlement policy. In Australia and in New Zealand, strongly integrationist—and, previously, assimilationist—cultural assumptions have encouraged a view among policy makers that migrants should abandon their old histories, identities and loyalties and begin their lives afresh. The histories and experiences of migrants up until their disembarkation in the new country are denuded of meaning or relevance.

At its most obvious, this enforced rupture between past and present circumstances is manifested in the official neglect of new settlers' prior skills and qualifications. It extends to the neglect of individual and collective migrant histories and their place in the national story.

In the areas that interest us here, policy making is also strongly influenced by political circumstances, further problematising any substantive attempt to deal with the past when determining policy. The political sensitivities surrounding immigration in Australia and New Zealand have generally been contained through the maintenance of political bipartisanship. The presentation of a united front by the major parties and the general support of major pressure groups have provided legitimacy to immigration decision making. At the same time, however, it might have had the effect of discouraging rigor in policy debates or the questioning of policy fundamentals. When this political consensus has been threatened (for example, by then Liberal leader John Howard in Australia or by New Zealand First leader, Winston Peters), the highly charged circumstances of these threats have not encouraged reasoned debate and analysis either.

Finally, immigration is formulated according to a bureaucratic structure and culture which demands transparency, consistency and adherence to rules, and in which a variety of political interests are constantly balanced. As Charles Lindblom points out, this tends to encourage an incremental, reactive and ad hoc approach whereby policy making is formulated and administered as a continuum, with only gradual change evident over specific time frames.[14] This incremental approach, combined with the practical and political concerns that surround immigration, deters policy makers from any substantive engagement with past practices and attitudes in determining solutions to present-day concerns.

Australia's Department of Immigration and the New Zealand Immigration Service (NZIS) have shown a remarkable lack of interest in their own pasts. Neither has commissioned or otherwise funded a substantial historical analysis of the development of immigration policy. The following anecdote illustrates the lack of interest that seems to prevail among those responsible for Australia's immigration policy. A few years ago, the Department of Immigration privatised its archives. In the rush to hand over to the private operator, the long-serving departmental archivists must have left without passing on their considerable institutional memory. One of the immediate consequences of that loss epitomises the consequences of the lack of interest evidenced by the new arrangements: while the majority of the department's policy files were deposited with the National Archives of Australia, the department retained the only copy of a subject index for those files—but, following the privatisation, had to be reminded of its existence and precise location in the basement of the department's head office.

Department of Immigration and NZIS policy files document incremental developments and dramatic policy shifts. New Zealand's and Australia's immigration histories contain several examples of decisive policy and paradigm changes that substantively changed the character, politics and public representation of immigration policy. Australian examples include the launch of the mass immigration program in the immediate aftermath of World War II, the decision to set up the Department of Immigration, the shift to continental European immigration in 1947, the end of the White Australia Policy between 1966 and 1973, the birth of multiculturalism during the 1970s, the introduction of mandatory detention for unauthorised boat arrivals in 1992 and the hardline approach to asylum-seekers adopted by the Howard Government between 1999 and 2001, which was encapsulated by temporary protection visas and the so-called 'Pacific Solution'. New Zealand's immigration history had fewer dramatic turns than Australia's, but there, too, the composition of the migrant intake changed significantly as a result of momentous policy decisions. New Zealand's refugee resettlement regime underwent a complete transformation: from a case-by-case admission of people who were sponsored by the churches, to a quota system that no longer relied on sponsorship. Dramatic changes too have tended to reinforce a view of complete rupture from past attitudes and practices. They have discouraged a search for policy analogies, the assumption being that the past offers nothing of relevance or value for dealing with new circumstances.

The neglect of history is evident in another aspect of immigration: the public political debates that surround it. This neglect partly reflects the broad marginalisation of immigration history in both countries. While immigration is acknowledged as fundamental to the creation of the two settler states, its history does not enjoy significant status or popularity because its importance is constrained by the cultural and ideological interests that surround immigration and ensure immigration history matters only in so far as it relates to the nation-state more broadly. Far less central to the national story are the individual and collective migrant histories and the history of the agencies administering immigration, of which the history of immigration is also constituted. The failure of Australians and New Zealanders to know this history except in superficial and statist-nationalist terms undoubtedly influences the tenor and dynamics of public political debate. Immigration debates—be they about the size and composition of the migrant intake or the admission or deportation of individuals—occur regularly in both countries but are generally characterised by the absence of informed opinion and of a tangible conceptual and historical framework for understanding contemporary issues and events. The political interests and practical concerns surrounding immigration that we have outlined above reinforce this historical vacuum.

There is a sense, however, in which history clearly does have a tangible presence in immigration discourse and is self-consciously used by politicians for practical, political and/or ideological purposes. This representational and strategic use of history has become more prevalent in recent years, facilitated by the historical vacuum that surrounds immigration, allowing political leaders to shape and create immigration narratives as they see fit. A range of narratives has developed in both countries in the past few decades and is used actively in public discourse. In both countries, it includes the claim that 'we' are a humanitarian nation with a long history of accommodating refugees. In Australia, there is the additional claim that 'we' are a multicultural nation with a long and successful record of welcoming and settling people from around the globe. Such stories are key ingredients of a unifying narrative for the nation-state—something that is common to all nations perhaps, but arguably has more relevance in a settler society where it offers reassurance of social cohesion, unity and identity despite the disparate histories and cultures of the population.

Patriotic narratives of 'our' generous welcome to newcomers rely on a highly selective process of remembering and forgetting the past. Governments variously fashion, employ and draw on them to explain and legitimate specific policy actions or to deflect attention and criticism from controversial decisions. Such narratives can provide short-term political advantages for politicians but they can have significant constraining effects. They discourage any substantive engagement with the complexity of historical process. They tend to reinforce the view of migrants' histories as beginning at disembarkation and having relevance only in so far as they fulfil specific contemporary statist-nationalist needs. The selective use of the past means policy makers forgo the opportunity to actively learn from the historical record.

The chapters presented in this volume provide insights into three dimensions of the relationship between immigration and citizenship policy on the one hand, and history on the other: policy making (Glenn Nicholls, Roderic Pitty, Klaus Neumann and Gwenda Tavan), public debate (Neumann, Amy Nethery and Olaf Kleist) and history making (Kleist, Ann Beaglehole and Tavan). All seven authors are directly or indirectly responding to a 2004 article by Annika Brändström, Fredrik Bynander and Paul 't Hart in which they developed a typology of historical analogies.[15] Drawing on two case studies—the decision by EU leaders in 2000 to impose sanctions against Austria after the party of the ring-wing populist Jörg Haider became the junior partner in a coalition government, and the so-called Hårsfjärden incident in 1982 when the Swedish Navy tried to hunt down a Soviet submarine that had supposedly entered Swedish territorial waters—Brändström et al. identify six mechanisms determining the use of historical analogies, which in turn result in six distinct enabling or constraining impacts.

In the papers assembled here, the focus is on the failure to employ historical analogies in the first place and on the constraining effects of history and memory. All contributors would respond with an emphatic 'yes' to the question 'does history matter?' and deplore the fact that policy making and public debate are rarely informed by a nuanced understanding of the past. The arguments put forward in the following chapters, however, go beyond such a critique and explore the reasons for and implications of the failure to harness and employ historical knowledge. While identifying a—sometimes surprising—disregard for detailed historical analysis, however, the authors of the following chapters agree that the past looms large when Australians and New Zealanders make and debate immigration, refugee and citizenship policy. It is one of the central aims of this book to draw attention to the presence the past has in the present.

Endnotes

[1] Arup, Tom and Nicholson, Brendan 2009, 'Sabotage fear on boat blast', *Age*, 17 April 2009; Jackson, Andra and Arup, Tom 2009, 'Blast warning revealed as Rudd declares war on "vile" people smugglers', *Age*, 18 April 2009.

[2] Grattan, Michelle 2009, 'Rudd must resist being spooked', *Age*, 17 April 2009. For the events of 2001, see Marr, David and Wilkinson, Marian 2003, *Dark Victory*, Allen & Unwin, Crows Nest.

[3] Kerr, Christian 2009, 'Pacific solution effective: Downer', *Weekend Australian*, 17–18 April 2009; Grattan, Michelle 2009, 'Return arrivals, says Andrews', *Age*, 22 April 2009.

[4] For example, Grattan, Michelle 2009, 'There and back again on refugees', *Age*, 17 April 2009; Marr, David 2009, 'Who's afraid of the "r" word?', *Age*, 18 April 2009; 'Trickle of asylum seekers stirs old fears of flood', Editorial, *Age*, 18 April 2009.

[5] Quoted in Kerr, Christian 2009, 'Rudd rhetoric blows Turnbull tirade to hell', *Weekend Australian*, 18–19 April 2009.

[6] See also Craven, Peter 2009, 'PM plays game of morality', *Australian*, 24 April 2009.

[7] For the dismantling of Ruddock and Howard's asylum-seeker regime, see O'Neill, Margot 2008, *Blind Conscience*, UNSW Press, Sydney.

[8] Munro, Catherine and Liston, Gail 2009, 'Bali experience helps hospitals swing into action', *Sydney Morning Herald*, 17 April 2009, <http://www.smh.com.au/national/bali-experience-helps-hospitals-swing-into-action-20090416-a8x3.html>; Miles, Janelle and Cavanagh, Rebekah 2009, 'Boat blast victims to be treated in Brisbane', *Courier-Mail*, 17 April 2009, <http://www.news.com.au/couriermail/story/0,23739,25345847-953,00.html>

[9] For detailed studies, see, for example, Neustadt, Richard E. and May, Ernest R. 1986, *Thinking in Time: The uses of history for decision makers*, Free Press, New York; Yuen Foong Khong 1992, *Analogies at War: Korea, Munich, Dien Bien Phu, and the Vietnam decisions of 1965*, Princeton University Press, Princeton, NJ.

[10] Brunk, Darren C. 2008, 'Curing the Somalia syndrome: analogy, foreign policy decision making, and the Rwandan genocide', *Foreign Policy Analysis*, vol. 4, no. 3, pp. 301–20.

[11] Hemmer, Christopher 1999, 'Historical analogies and the definition of interests: the Iranian hostage crisis and Ronald Reagan's policy toward the hostages in Lebanon', *Political Psychology*, vol. 20, no. 2, pp. 267–89.

[12] See, for example, most recently: Tierney, Dominic 2007, '"Pearl Harbor in reverse": moral analogies in the Cuban missile crisis', *Journal of Cold War Studies*, vol. 9, no. 3, pp. 49–77.

[13] See Boin, Arjen, McConnell, Allen and 't Hart, Paul (eds) 2008, *Governing After Crisis: The politics of investigation, accountability and learning*, Cambridge University Press, Cambridge.

[14] Lindblom, Charles E. 1959, 'The science of muddling through', *Public Administration Review*, vol. 19, no. 2, pp. 79–88.

[15] Brändström, Annika, Bynander, Frederik and 't Hart, Paul 2004, 'Governing by looking back: historical analogies and crisis management', *Public Administration*, vol. 82, no. 1, pp. 191–210.

1. Gone with hardly a trace: deportees in immigration policy

Glenn Nicholls

In 1910, Winston Churchill, the British Home Secretary, sought information on deportation practices in order to coordinate them across the empire. J. A. Stalking, Acting Secretary of Australia's Department of External Affairs, made a note on Churchill's letter, indicating that the matter was of marginal relevance to Australia and would become important only 'should our present powers of deportation be increased by legislation or more extensively availed of in practice'.[1]

This note was remarkable for completely ignoring the extensive use that the Australian Government had made of deportation since Federation. Just two years earlier, in 1908, the government had concluded a mass deportation campaign against Pacific Islanders, the basis for which was laid in one of the first acts passed by the Commonwealth Parliament, the *Pacific Island Labourers Act 1901*. Under the act, more than 4000 Islanders were deported, mainly to the New Hebrides, Solomon Islands and Fiji. The Commonwealth Government's power to do this was challenged in the first deportation case heard by the High Court, *Robtelmes vs Brenan* (1906). The challenge was unanimously dismissed and the Commonwealth's deportation power established in resounding terms. In a statement almost prescient of John Howard's 2001 election slogan, 'We will decide who comes to this country and the circumstances in which they come', Chief Justice Samuel Griffith declared that the Commonwealth had untrammelled power 'to determine the conditions under which aliens may be admitted to the country, the conditions under which they may be permitted to remain in the country, and the conditions under which they may be deported from it'.[2]

This chapter argues that those formulating Australian deportation policy have consistently failed to learn from the past. This is because deportation decisions have been driven by policy imperatives such as national security and immigration control, rather than focusing on whether or not individuals should be deported. Immigration policy makers in particular have seen themselves as being responsible for managing incoming migration; from this perspective, deportation is simply a consequence of someone not being entitled to stay in the country. No lasting policy has been developed to take individuals' circumstances into account or to examine factors militating against deportation.

When called on to justify deportations, policy makers have invoked their duty to uphold national security, law and order or immigration controls and have portrayed deportees as a group who abuse Australia's hospitality by overstaying their welcome, committing crimes or being associated with Australia's enemies (whether by choice or not). After World War I, the backbencher John Leckie justified his government's deportation of more than 6000 German-Australians with the claim that 'they were unworthy of Australia's hospitality', although many were long-term residents of the country and were given no opportunity to put their case to stay.[3]

The mass deportation program after World War I followed large scale internment (see Chapter 4 of this volume) and has rightly been called 'the destruction of the German-Australian community' at that time.[4] Deportation frequently removes not only the people concerned but traces of their pasts in the country—an erasure that facilitates forgetting. There are no public memorials to deported peoples in Australia and few works of art on the theme—an exception is a 1991 novel by Joan Dugdale, which is fittingly called *Struggle of Memory*, about a German-Australian family after World War I.[5] The former presence of deported individuals and groups is often retrieved from obscurity only later. This chapter examines various examples from the past, but also endeavours to analyse current deportation policy in this light. It argues that current policy misses opportunities for positive change that could be gleaned from past knowledge and experience. Deportation policy today turns a blind eye to the personal histories of individuals facing deportation and also to the knowledge built up by courts, tribunals and officials who have dealt with deportation cases in previous decades.

Activism against deportation by Pacific Islanders

The Pacific Islander episode provides an instructive first example because the Islanders briefly managed to make their cause a prominent concern for Australia's politicians and achieved changes in government policy. In 1905 and 1906, with the deadline for deportation looming at the end of 1906, Islanders launched energetic protests, although their weak legal position had been confirmed by the *Robtelmes* case. They succeeded in being granted an audience with Prime Minister, Alfred Deakin, and eventually won important exemptions from deportation for people who were long-time residents of Australia, were too old or infirm to travel, had locally born spouses or children or who had a spouse from another island, which was thought to make the prospect of return fraught with conflict. These exemptions allowed 2500 Islanders to stay in the country legally. An estimated further 1000 stayed unlawfully but lastingly since staying on was easier amid a sizeable remnant community.[6] These concessions did not, however, become part of any developed deportation policy. Neither did the fact that a community of Islanders remained in Australia after the deportation program began command any attention in government policy. These were the 'forgotten people', as historians Clive Moore and Patricia Mercer wrote in 1978.[7] In 1993, the Keating Labor Government asked the Human Rights and Equal Opportunity Commission to collect statistics on the community, since not even the number of people who identified as Islanders was known.[8]

At the time of the Islanders' deportation, Senator Henry Dobson criticised his colleagues in Parliament for learning nothing from the mistake of legislating for the wholesale removal of Pacific Islanders in 1901. Speaking in December 1905 as Islanders were mounting their protests, Dobson stated that in the *Pacific Island Labourers Act 1901* 'we absolutely ignored the principles of humanity and Christianity. We made no provisions for exceptions.'[9] He argued that Parliament was making the same mistake again in 1905 when amending the *Immigration Restriction Act 1901*. The amendments tightened restrictions on Chinese immigrants and made no allowance for individuals who had made their homes in Australia, or had left the country intending to return but now found their re-entry blocked.

The exemptions won by Islanders represented an acknowledgment that the mass deportation program against them was unjust, but afterwards the same blanket measures came to be applied again—for example, against people who were deemed to be enemy aliens, or unsuitable or unauthorised immigrants, or who had overstayed their period of allowed residence. Time and again, groups and individuals resisting deportation from Australia have raised the same arguments in their defence: their commitment to their country of residence, length of residence, compassionate circumstances and the perils that exist in the destination state. Sometimes governments have accepted these arguments and exempted individuals or groups from deportation, only to forget the exemption categories immediately afterwards, so that later groups have to argue again for the same exemption categories from scratch. Governments have established firm criteria to select immigrants for settlement, but have been reluctant to lay down lasting criteria exempting people from the threat of deportation.

Immigration control and deportation

The Department of Immigration was created in 1945. As its first minister, Arthur Calwell gave no quarter to individuals resisting deportation. He was committed to building up a system for controlled immigration within the parameters of the White Australia Policy and enforcing the departure of prohibited immigrants. He maintained an uncompromising position on deportations. As Gwenda Tavan explains, Calwell believed that allowing people to avoid deportation on the basis of their individual circumstances 'would threaten the whole administrative apparatus upon which effective immigration control depended'.[10]

In October 1948, Calwell introduced the Aliens Deportation Bill into Parliament. It established a specific process for the deportation of non-British aliens regardless of their length of residence in the country. Calwell explained that it targeted 'those aliens whose character and conduct is such that they should not be allowed to continue to reside here'. There was criticism in Parliament about the breadth of powers conferred by the act, but the only amendments accepted by the government were technical and the Act came into force on 18 January 1949.[11] Calwell stated that the act was the first time that a law on deportation had been made using the aliens power of the Commonwealth Constitution rather than the immigration power. This was incorrect: it again overlooked the Pacific Islanders. As we saw earlier, the High Court rejected the Islanders' legal challenge to deportation with reference to the Commonwealth's power over aliens.

Shortly after seeing the *Aliens Deportation Act 1948* come into force, Calwell had to deal with a threat to his deportation powers on another front, involving one of the few occasions in which the High Court found against the Commonwealth in a deportation case. In *O'Keefe vs Calwell* (1948), the court quashed a deportation order against Annie O'Keefe, a wartime evacuee from Indonesia who had married a local man. This was because she had not been formally given the status of a prohibited immigrant when she was allowed to enter Australia with a certificate of exemption, so the expiration of the certificate did not make her liable to deportation as a prohibited immigrant. Nor could she be declared a prohibited immigrant more than five years after being allowed into the country. The decision threatened Calwell's determination to force the departure from Australia of non-Europeans who had been allowed into the country during World War II. Although most such arrivals departed Australia voluntarily after the war ended, approximately 800 sought to stay permanently and at the time of the *O'Keefe* decision there were a number of similar cases either before the courts or being debated in public.[12] In an infamous speech, Calwell claimed that the *O'Keefe* case opened the floodgates to a 'mongrel Australia'.[13]

After the *O'Keefe* decision, Calwell moved to not only restore but strengthen the Commonwealth's deportation powers further. First, he amended provisions in the *Immigration Act* to overcome the procedural problems exposed by the court's decision. The original draft of this amendment was breathtakingly broad, giving the minister the power to deport anyone who had entered Australia after 1901. Legal counsel advised that the very breadth of the draft made it vulnerable to legal challenge and the amendment was pared back to apply specifically to certificates of exemption.[14] Henceforth these would be valid even if the individual concerned had not formally been given the status of a prohibited immigrant when he or she entered the country. This amendment restored the situation that the cancellation or expiration of certificates of exemption led to deportation.

In addition to this amendment, Calwell introduced the War-Time Refugees Removal Bill 1949, which was designed specifically to enable the deportation of every person who, as in the O'Keefe situation, had arrived in Australia during World War II and stayed afterwards without being an approved immigrant. The Act came into force on 12 July 1949 and empowered the minister to force any person to depart the country who had been allowed to enter as a result of the war and had not since left.

The success of Calwell's moves in shoring up and strengthening the Commonwealth's deportation powers was seen in the next deportation case before the High Court, *Koon Wing Lau vs Calwell*. This involved 43 individuals from Hong Kong who had been granted entry to Australia during the war and who fought deportation after Calwell's legislative changes. They argued that the changes were not a valid exercise of the Commonwealth's power. The court dismissed their appeal. Chief Justice John Latham was most emphatic in upholding the government's powers. He found that the Commonwealth could make laws providing for deportation for any reason it thought fit. He gave an array of criteria that the Commonwealth could use to order deportations and then added a catch-all to dispel any doubt: 'age, sex, race, nationality, personal character, occupation, time of arrival or on the order of a Minister or of an official.'[15]

Calwell did not get to capitalise on this vindication of his legislation. Eleven days before the judgment in *Koon Wing Lau* came down, the Chifley Government lost power. The incoming Minister for Immigration in the Liberal Government, Harold Holt, took a more accommodating approach to the groups targeted by Calwell and accepted the refugees still in Australia as a 'wartime legacy'.[16] Calwell's strengthening of the Commonwealth's deportation power in fact went further than his successors needed. Neither the *War-Time Refugees Removal Act 1949* nor the *Aliens Deportation Act 1948* was used by Holt or later by Alexander Downer, senior. They relied on the deportation powers in the *Immigration Act*.

The long reach of the deportation power in Australian law

Calwell's moves to shore up the deportation power in immigration legislation had two lasting effects. The first arose from his insistence that people who had the status of non-British aliens should be liable for deportation on the basis of poor character or conduct no matter how long they had been settled in Australia. This principle, inscribed in the *Aliens Deportation Act 1948*, was incorporated into the *Migration Act 1958*, the legislation that still forms the basis of Australia's immigration policy. As we will see later in this chapter, the principle lives on today.

For the moment, it is instructive to touch on one case from 1961—that of Antonio Panozzo. He arrived in Australia from Italy in 1952 with his wife and infant son as part of the postwar immigration program. Panozzo struggled to make good during his first decade in the country and, on several occasions in 1959 and

1960, he was convicted of earning income from premises used for prostitution—namely, the back room of his shop and his house in Carlton, Melbourne. After serving his sentence, Panozzo and his family moved into a new house. They seemed to be rebuilding their lives when, nine months later, Panozzo was summoned to a deportation hearing because he was a non-British alien who had engaged in conduct that indicated that he 'should not be allowed to stay in the country'.[17] The hearing, held before Commissioner F. R. B. Martin, was farcical in that it focused entirely on the respective roles of the commissioner and the minister in dealing with Panozzo's convictions. Panozzo's pleas that he was remorseful and had reformed, supported by his wife and his priest, were totally ignored. The hearing reduced his life in Australia to the rude fact of his convictions, casting a shadow over his entire existence in the country.

As Chief Justice Latham concluded in the *Koon Wing Lau* case, the Minister for Immigration could use any one of a range of criteria to issue a deportation order. In this case, Panozzo was deported because the minister concurred with the commissioner that Panozzo's convictions proved that his conduct was such that he should not be allowed to stay. The fate of Panozzo's wife and son is a blank spot in the history of deportation. Mrs Panozzo told the commissioner she was committed to her new country and did not wish to leave if her husband were deported, but it is not clear from archival records whether or not the family left with Panozzo.

The second of Calwell's changes that resonates with more recent times was his use of the term 'removal' in the *War-Time Refugees Removal Act 1949*, instead of 'deportation', as used in the *Aliens Deportation Act 1948* or, 10 years later, the *Immigration Act*. 'Deportation' implied a legal process, typically the issuing of a formal deportation order and a hearing before a court, tribunal or commissioner. 'Removal' on the other hand suggested that procedures before any court, tribunal or commissioner could be dispensed with. Under the act, wartime refugees were simply to be 'removed' from the country because they had stayed on after the war ended; they would have no opportunity to put their case to stay in any hearing.

Calwell's scheme refused to countenance that individuals might have reasons to stay. His attitude to those who sought to stay was summed up in his characterisation of those people as 'a recalcitrant minority'.[18] This characterisation recalled John Leckie's justification for mass deportation after World War I because it implied that the people concerned had abused Australia's hospitality by stubbornly overstaying their welcome. Calwell, however, did not look to the past. He failed to recognise that exemptions to deportation had been made without detracting from overall immigration controls. For example, the exemption categories won by the Pacific Islanders were relevant to wartime refugees with locally born spouses, but Calwell feared that any exemption would open the floodgates. He was determined to hurry the wartime refugees on by the expeditious process of removal.

The *War-Time Refugees Removal Act* was shelved after the government changed in 1949, and it slipped into obscurity. Fifty years later, however, 'removal' began to be revived. This was no conscious act of remembrance or recovery, but it did begin with another government trying to dispense with deportation hearings, reviews and processes.

Mandatory deportation and removal

In 1989, the Hawke Labor Government was in its third term and was concerned with the increasing number of visa overstayers. The growing unemployment rate and fears about overstayers working illegally heightened its concerns. The Minister for Immigration, Robert Ray, introduced a draconian law for the 'mandatory deportation of illegal entrants', targeting visa overstayers: 'they are liable to be deported mandatorily', Ray stated, and his justification for the law resonated once again with the notion of Australia's abused hospitality. 'Those who choose to stay and impose themselves on Australia's generosity will feel the full weight of its laws,' he warned.[19] There was, however, no indication that the minister was aware of the earlier statements he echoed, and the mandatory deportation policy failed to make allowance for even the exemption categories that the Pacific Islanders had won.

Mandatory deportation applied to visa overstayers no matter how long they had been in Australia. Their pasts in the country counted for naught against the fact that they had overstayed their visas. Labor Senator Jim McKiernan made clear that the law applied even to well-settled individuals and families: 'in some instances they will be leaving behind a home in some sort of fire sale', he told Parliament. 'Furniture and other possessions will have to be disposed of...There are also the difficulties associated with children's education.'[20]

Like Calwell's legislation, the Labor Government's hardline measure in 1989 was not fully implemented, so community protests did not gather steam. Among other things, the government's focus shifted in 1989 to the reappearance of 'boat people' on Australia's shores and to the large number of Chinese students in Australia promised sanctuary after the crushing of the Tiananmen Square protests on 4 June 1989. Nonetheless, the law about the 'mandatory deportation of illegal entrants' signalled a return to the idea that people should be removed from the country if they had no permission to stay and that this should occur as a simple matter of course, not as a result of a deportation decision against an individual after a hearing or review of their case.

In 1992, 'mandatory deportation' was superseded by 'removal' under Section 189 of the *Migration Act 1958* and the act set out a fully fledged removal system directed against people in Australia without authority. This required that any people lacking a valid visa should remove themselves from the country or face being put in detention and removed by the Immigration Department. A parliamentary committee described the nature of the new system:

> Unlike the power to order deportation, which is discretionary, removal is an automatic consequence for every unlawful non-citizen. Non-citizens who do not hold a valid visa must be detained under s.189 of the Act and removed (ie expelled) under s.198. Mandatory removal was introduced to simplify the procedures for removing persons who had no legal authority to remain in Australia. It reinforces the principle that such persons have 'no right to stay in the country'.[21]

The final phrase quotes an instruction from the Immigration Department to its officers as to who they should remove from the country.[22] Under the removal system, officers were required to check the visa status of non-citizens in the community to identify unlawful non-citizens (such identifications were called 'locations') and to see that any unlawful non-citizen was removed from the country via a 'monitored removal', 'supervised removal' or plain 'removal'.

The removal system led to a significant increase in the number of enforced departures. In the 1980s, approximately 1000 deportations occurred from Australia each year. Since 2000, the Immigration Department has recorded more than 10 000 removals annually.[23]

There have been a number of controversial cases under the removal system. These include the removal to China in 1997 of a heavily pregnant woman whose near-term baby was aborted a week after her arrival, the threatened removal of a Somali man in 1998 and, most prominently, the threatened removal of Cornelia Rau to Germany in 2004–05 and the unlawful removal of an Australian citizen, Vivian Alvarez, to the Philippines in 2001—a scandal that came to light only in 2005 after the Cornelia Rau case.[24]

There are three features of the removal system that merit comment. The first is the parallel between the current system and Calwell's earlier legislation, whereby there is no decision on an individual's particular circumstances but they face removal simply by virtue of being in the country beyond their permitted stay. A recent report by the Refugee Health Research Centre in Melbourne has summarised how this can lead to individuals' circumstances being neglected:

> [T]here is no formal decision to remove someone. This means there is no pre-removal assessment of the whole of an individual's situation, including medical issues or issues regarding children and family ties, that may bring to light significant reasons to delay or reconsider removal.[25]

The Vivian Alvarez scandal provided a stark illustration of these problems. An Australian citizen of Filipino background, Alvarez had suffered mental health problems for five years before she went missing in February 2001, having failed to pick up her son from child care in Brisbane. She was found, although not identified, six weeks later in Lismore, New South Wales, and was hospitalised for physical and mental health problems. She was in no position to present evidence of citizenship status in Australia and, when immigration officials were called in on 3 May 2001, they acted on the assumption that she was an unlawful non-citizen. Alvarez had no hearing before an independent authority and no legal representation. The traditional function of a deportation hearing—primarily to verify the identity and citizenship status of the person—does not occur under the removal system. Instead, officials concentrated on making the arrangements for Alvarez's removal, which occurred on 20 July 2001. What happened to her was fully revealed only in 2005 when she was located in a hospice in the Philippines and an inquiry into her case was launched. The investigator, Neil Comrie, noted that '[t]here is no record of an actual decision to remove Vivian—if one was made' and criticised the perfunctory medical check certifying her as fit to travel. Comrie concluded that, quite apart from being unlawful because she was an Australian citizen, Alvarez's 'removal was effected with undue haste and without adequate consideration of her welfare'.[26]

The second point about today's removal system is that it turns its back on knowledge available from earlier decisions on deportation cases. Under administrative law reforms in the 1970s, deportation decisions became reviewable by the Administrative Appeals Tribunal. The tribunal published its decisions and built up a valuable corpus of knowledge about how to ensure that deportation procedures were fair and flexible. For example, in the case of Drago Sajatovic in 1985, it was prepared to endorse the minister's decision to issue a deportation order on the grounds of his criminal record, but noted that his country of birth, Yugoslavia, was not facilitating his return after virtually a lifetime away. The tribunal noted that 'it is undesirable that the execution of a deportation order should be delayed for any considerable time; circumstances relevant to the appropriateness of the deportation may have changed in the meantime'. It therefore recommended that the deportation order be revoked. If it subsequently became possible to carry out the deportation, the tribunal concluded, the case should be reconsidered in the light of all the circumstances at that time.[27]

In the case of John Kirakos five years later, in 1990, the tribunal followed a similar line. It noted that he had already been held in prison for 10 months after the expiration of his sentence while immigration officials sought to finalise his deportation. Kirakos was born in Syria to Armenian refugees from Turkey, but had no civil registration in Syria, in the absence of which Syrian officials refused to accept him. Noting the long delay already, the tribunal set a deadline of a further four months for officials to arrange for his departure. If they were unable to do this, the tribunal recommended that the deportation order should be revoked, rather than Kirakos continuing to languish in incarceration.[28] These decisions evince a far more flexible approach than is available under the removal system whereby individuals can be held for indefinite periods in immigration detention while immigration officials make the arrangements for removal.

The Administrative Appeals Tribunal developed a strong position in reviewing cases involving long-term Australian residents facing deportation. The key case was the drawn-out saga of Luigi Pochi, who was issued with a deportation order in 1978 after serving a year in prison for his part in cultivating marijuana. Pochi had been in Australia for nearly 20 years, was married and had three Australian-born children. In these circumstances, the tribunal's president, Gerard Brennan, found that a compelling case was required to proceed with deportation:

> When an alien has been resident in this country for many years, when his roots are deep in Australia and the ties which bind him to Australia are strong, a clear case will be required to persuade the decision-maker that it is in the best interests of Australia to banish him from our shores.[29]

Pochi's case dragged on through the courts for another four years, but, ultimately, he was not deported. In 1983, the Hawke Government in its first term tackled the issue of long-term residents facing deportation after a criminal conviction. It introduced legislative amendments whereby the liability to deportation on grounds of criminal conviction ceased after 10 years' residence in Australia (excluding prison time) and it introduced a specific criminal deportation policy.[30]

The final point to note about the removal system is that it has turned the clock back to the days when individuals could be expelled on the grounds of criminal conviction despite having lived in the country for decades. The 10-year rule has been rendered ineffective by means of the *Migration Legislation Amendment (Strengthening of Provisions Relating to Character and Conduct) Act 1998*, which was introduced by Philip Ruddock. Its provisions allow the Minister for Immigration to cancel a person's visa regardless of how long that person has lived in Australia and disallows reviews to the Administrative Appeals Tribunal in cases where the minister personally has cancelled the visa. There are no hearings on such matters—the cancellation is made on the recommendation of a departmental briefing paper. This new power came to supersede the traditional criminal deportation process, which fell into disuse.[31]

Between 1 July 2002 and 30 June 2005, the Howard Government removed 233 permanent residents on the grounds that they had been sentenced to imprisonment of one year or more and were therefore deemed to be of bad character.[32] Many had lived in Australia since childhood and were removed to places they barely remembered. The guidelines for cancelling visas gave little weight to length of residence and ties to Australia were downgraded.

The starkest case was that of Stefan Nystrom. He was born in Sweden when his mother visited there from her new home in Australia. Nystrom himself arrived in Australia as a twenty-seven-day-old baby, and grew up and was educated in Australia. He did not leave the country until he was removed as a thirty-three-year-old after his permanent residency was cancelled because of his criminal convictions. Nystrom was sent back to Sweden although he spoke no Swedish and had only distant relatives there. He told a journalist who spoke to him there that 'I am Aussie, I don't give a stuff about Sweden, I never have and I never will'.[33] The High Court of Australia had been called on to decide Nystrom's case and it affirmed the minister's power to remove him and other long-term permanent residents.[34] Others in a similar situation included Tayfun Ayan, removed to Turkey despite having arrived in Australia as a six-month-old child and being, in the words of a Federal Court judge, 'an Australian...in every respect, except citizenship', and Toni Morgani, removed to Italy in 2003 notwithstanding that, as representatives of the Italian Government observed, 'culturally, psychologically, educationally, he's Australian'.[35]

Conclusion

Today's removal system contains the two key elements of Calwell's deportation regime after World War II. Like Calwell's *Aliens Deportation Act 1948*, the removal system gives the minister imposing powers to expel people with alien status on the grounds of character and conduct, regardless of their length of residence in the country and local ties. And, like Calwell's *War-Time Refugees Removal Act 1949*, today's removal system replaces traditional deportation hearings and decisions with automatic action against people in the country without valid documentation.

Today's removal policies were made with no consciousness of Calwell's legislation, which had long been forgotten. Nor do today's policies pay attention to lessons set down by the Administrative Appeals Tribunal in its deportation decisions in the 1970s and 1980s, as we have observed. The Department of Immigration asserts that Australia's policies are forward looking. In 2004, the department claimed that it had achieved 'world's best practice' in identifying and dealing with people without a visa and that the rest of the world was trying to catch up.[36]

There is some truth to this claim. Other countries have implemented removal systems that seek to minimise legal procedures and achieve expeditious expulsions of undocumented immigrants. The United States introduced 'expedited removal' in 1996 in the *Illegal Immigration Reform and Immigrant Responsibility Act*. Canada completely overhauled its immigration enforcement bodies in 2003 to provide more vigorous execution of removals. And in the United Kingdom officials have established a 'tipping point' target, whereby the number of asylum-seekers being removed from the country exceeds the number of rejected asylum applications.[37]

While these international similarities are important, we have seen that there is a distinct national lineage underpinning Australia's removal system today. This lineage is grounded in the imposing powers of the Commonwealth Government, endorsed time and again by the High Court, to control the entry, stay and departure of people with alien status, now usually called non-citizens. Calwell drew on these powers in strengthening deportation laws after the *O'Keefe* defeat when he reinforced the legal framework for deporting aliens even after decades in the country and for removing individuals in the country without valid documentation. These powers were hardly used at the time, but elements from Calwell's legislation survived in the *Migration Act 1958*, and in 1961 Antonio Panozzo felt the brunt of the minister's power to deport an alien on the basis of his bad character. In 1989, Ruddock strengthened the character test in the *Migration Act* and used it to remove hundreds of non-citizens with criminal convictions. He did this regardless of the fact that many had lived in Australia virtually their whole lives.

Under Ruddock, the removal system was at its most unrelenting. In 2002–03, nearly 14 000 people were removed from the country: rejected asylum-seekers, visa overstayers, illegal workers and 'bad character' criminals.[38] The nether side of this heavy-handed action was the Cornelia Rau and Vivian Alvarez scandals and more than 200 individuals held in immigration detention centres for more than two years, whose cases were investigated by the Commonwealth Ombudsman after 2005. Ruddock's rigid application of the removal system had no time for the principles of flexibility that the Administrative Appeals Tribunal worked out when it dealt with deportation cases involving inordinate delays. The tribunal's assumption in such cases was that it was in no-one's interest to leave the individuals concerned languishing in limbo for years awaiting deportation. The position was principled and practical, but it was forgotten under Ruddock's regime of being tough on crime and border control.

In the face of protests about particular cases, policy makers have justified deportation with the argument that the regime serves to maintain immigration controls and keep the floodgates shut, and to uphold law and order and guarantee Australia's national security. As we have seen, these justifications have been accompanied by the argument that deportation is directed against those who have abused Australia's generosity by overstaying their welcome or endangering national security or law and order (see Chapter 3 for further discussion of the notion of Australian generosity). A range of policy makers over the years has invoked this argument without awareness of one another. Nor have policy makers been aware of exemption categories accepted in earlier times—for example, those exemptions won by the first group to face mass deportation: Pacific Islanders in Australia at the time of Federation. Policy makers have not viewed deportation as an area of decision making in its own right and with its own history, but as a footnote or follow-up to policies on immigration control, law and order and national security. Consequently, no lasting policy has been developed to take individuals' circumstances into account or to examine factors militating against deportation. Today, non-citizens without a valid visa face automatic removal from Australia without any decision on their particular circumstances.

Pacific Islanders were the first group to face mass deportation from Australia but they won a series of exemption categories. Unfortunately, these categories were forgotten afterwards. The dominant factor driving policy makers has been maintaining immigration controls, especially on non-European migration, and not allowing exemptions that will weaken controls. In addition, mass deportations after the two world wars were driven by hysteria about national security and wartime animosity. At these times, policy makers ordered the mass expulsion of people born in countries that had become Australia's wartime enemies or were descended from citizens of those countries. This happened regardless of individuals' pasts in Australia and of their prospects in the destination country. An Australian embarkation officer who raised concerns in 1946 about atrocious conditions on a deportation ship to Japan was told that 'the responsibility of the Australian army would cease at the gangway', reflecting the official desire to get individuals out of sight and mind.[39] Australia's Japanese community was deported en masse after World War II. No exemptions were allowed and no traces of their presence were preserved.

Policy makers today could improve Australia's deportation practices by developing a policy that is not merely an afterthought to rigidly upholding immigration controls. Such a policy would insist on careful decision making on each deportation case and would allow exemptions based on individuals' pasts in the country and on their likely fate in destination countries. Today, only the Minister for Immigration can grant an exemption along these lines in exceptional circumstances. It is time to make these exemption categories the basis of a specific deportation policy that focuses on individuals' circumstances.

Endnotes

[1] J. A. Stalking, Note, 23 December 1910, National Archives of Australia [hereafter NAA], A1, 1912/11862.

[2] *Robtelmes vs Brenan* [1906], 4 CLR 395, p. 420. For a more detailed discussion of this and other cases referred to in this article, see my book: Nicholls, Glenn 2007, *Deported: A history of forced departures from Australia*, UNSW Press, Sydney.

[3] *Commonwealth Parliamentary Debates* [hereafter *CPD*], vol. 88, 10 July 1919, p. 10636.

[4] Fischer, Gerhard 2000, 'Integration, "negative integration", disintegration: the destruction of the German-Australian community during the First World War', in Kay Saunders and Roger Daniels (eds), *Alien Justice: Wartime internment in Australia and North America*, University of Queensland Press, St Lucia, pp. 1–27.

[5] Dugdale, Joan 1991, *Struggle of Memory*, University of Queensland Press, St Lucia. A recent novel by Linda Jaivan (2006, *The Infernal Optimist*, Fourth Estate, Pymble) concerns a deportation case but focuses mainly on conditions in one of Australia's immigration detention centres.

[6] Corris, Peter 1972, '"White Australia" in action: the repatriation of Pacific Islanders from Queensland', *Historical Studies*, vol. 15, no. 58, pp. 237–50.

[7] Moore, Clive and Mercer, P. M. 1978, 'The forgotten people: Australia's immigrant Melanesians', *Meanjin*, vol. 37, no. 1, pp. 98–108.

[8] Human Rights and Equal Opportunity Commission 1992, *The Call for Recognition: A report on the situation of Australian South Sea Islanders*, Human Rights and Equal Opportunity Commission, Sydney, p. 91.

[9] *CPD*, Representatives, vol. 30, 12 December 1905, p. 6673.

[10] Tavan, Gwenda 2005, *The Long, Slow Death of White Australia*, Scribe, Melbourne, p. 62.

[11] Arthur Calwell, 22 October 1948, Deportation of Aliens Bill, Second Reading, House of Representatives; and Senator Armstrong, 2 December 1948, Second Reading, Senate, NAA, A446, 1964/46109.

[12] Neumann, Klaus 2006, 'Guarding the flood gates: the removal of non-Europeans, 1945–1949', in Martin Crotty and David Roberts (eds), *The Great Mistakes of Australian History*, UNSW Press, Sydney, pp. 186–202.

[13] *CPD*, vol. 201, 9 February 1949, p. 66.

[14] J. B. Tait, Memorandum of counsel, 25 May 1949, NAA, A432, 1949/472.

[15] *Koon Wing Lau vs Calwell* [1949], 80 CLR 533, pp. 561–2.

[16] Frame, Tom 2005, *The Life and Death of Harold Holt*, Allen & Unwin, Sydney, p. 67.

[17] Section 14 of the *Migration Act 1958* empowered the Minister to order the deportation of an alien whose conduct 'has been such that he should not be allowed to remain in Australia'. (*The Migration Act 1958*: An investigation by a Commissioner Pursant to Section 14 of the Act of the Case of Antonio Panozzo, Transcript of Proceedings p. 10A, NAA A446 1961/66437).

[18] King, John 2005, 'The creation of a "recalcitrant minority": a case-study of the Chinese New Guinea wartime refugees', *Journal of the Royal Australian Historical Society*, vol. 91, no. 1.

[19] Ray, Robert 1989, 'Minister Ray hails start of new era in immigration', *Ministerial Document Service*, 18 December 1989, p. 4238.

[20] *CPD*, Senate, vol. 140, 10 October 1990, p. 2833.

[21] Parliament of the Commonwealth of Australia 1998, *Deportation of Non-Citizen Criminals*, Joint Standing Committee on Migration, Canberra, p. 71, para. 7.1.

[22] Migration Series Instruction 5, 31 October 1996.

[23] Parliament of Australia 1990, *First Report: Illegal entrants in Australia—balancing control and compassion*, Joint Standing Committee on Migration Regulations, p. 23, Table T5; Department of Immigration and Multicultural Affairs 2001, *Annual Report 2000–01*, Canberra, <www.immi.gov.au/about/reports/annual/2000-01/report19.htm>; Department of Immigration and Multicultural and Indigenous Affairs 2004, *Annual Report 2003–04*, Canberra, p. 89; Department of Immigration and Multicultural and Indigenous Affairs 2005, *Annual Report 2004–05*, Canberra, p. 124.

[24] Senate Legal and Constitutional References Committee 2000, *A Sanctuary Under Review: An examination of Australia's refugee and humanitarian determination process*, June, Senate Printing Unit, Canberra, pp. 203–35, 268–96; Palmer, M. 2005, *Inquiry into the Circumstances of the Immigration Detention of Cornelia Rau: Report*, 6 July 2005, Commonwealth of Australia, Canberra; Comrie, Neil 2005, *Inquiry into the Circumstances of the Vivian Alvarez Matter*, Commonwealth Ombudsman, Canberra.

[25] Sampson, Robyn, Correa-Velez, Ignacio and Mitchell, Grant 2007, *Removing Seriously Ill Asylum Seekers from Australia*, Refugee Health Research Centre, Melbourne, p. 51.

[26] Comrie, *Inquiry into the Circumstances of the Vivian Alvarez Matter*, pp. xiii, 60.

[27] *Re: Drago Sajatovic and Minister for Immigration and Ethnic Affairs*, Administrative Appeals Tribunal Decision No. V85/275.

[28] *Re: John Arsene Kirakos and Minister for Immigration, Local Government and Ethnic Affairs*, Administrative Appeals Tribunal Decision No. V90/83.

[29] *Re Luigi Pochi and the Minister for Immigration and Ethnic Affairs* [1979], 36 FLR 482, 491.

[30] *CPD*, Representatives, vol. 131, 4 May 1983, pp. 166–9.

[31] Turner, Ray 2002, 'Ridding the country of "bad aliens": the operation of the character and conduct provisions in the *Migration Act 1958*', *Immigration Review*, vol. 6, pp. 7–10.

[32] Senate Legal and Constitutional References Committee 2006, *Administration and Operation of the Migration Act 1958*, Senate Printing Unit, Canberra, p. 293.

[33] Medew, Julia 2007, 'Aussie rapist deported to Sweden on a technicality to do even harder time', *Age*, 24 February 2007.

[34] *Minister for Immigration and Multicultural and Indigenous Affairs vs Nystrom* [2006], HCA 50, 8 November 2006.

[35] *Ayan vs Minister for Immigration and Multicultural and Indigenous Affairs* [2003], 126 FCR 152, 154. Panichi, James and Pascucci, Maurizio 2003, 'Arrivederci, padre: an Aussie becomes an alien', *Age*, 17 November 2003.

[36] Department of Immigration and Multicultural and Indigenous Affairs 2004, Tracking of visa overstayers world's best practice, Press statement 074/2004, Canberra, 19 July 2004.

[37] Konet, Dawn and Batalova, Jeanne 2007, 'Spotlight on immigration enforcement in the United States', *Migration Information Source*, Migration Policy Institute, 22 March 2007; Fraser, Sheila 2003, Citizenship and immigration—Canada faces a growing backlog of removal orders and does not know how well its immigration border controls are working, Media release by the Auditor-General of Canada, 8 April 2003, Ottawa, <www.oag-bvg.gc.ca/domino/media.nsf/html/20030405pr_e.html>; United Kingdom Border and Immigration Agency n.d., *Our Targets*, London, <www.ind.homeoffice.gov.uk/aboutus/ourtargets>; United Kingdom House of Commons Home Affairs Committee 2003, *Asylum Removals*, Stationery Office, London.

[38] Department of Immigration and Multicultural and Indigenous Affairs 2003, *Annual Report 2002–03*, Canberra, <www.immi.gov.au/about/reports/annual/2002-03/report34.htm>

[39] Nagata, Yuriko 1996, *Unwanted Aliens: Japanese internment in Australia*, University of Queensland Press, St Lucia, p. 204.

2. The unfinished business of Indigenous citizenship in Australia and New Zealand

Roderic Pitty

Australia and New Zealand are cognate societies characterised by a partial, lopsided engagement. There is regular and extensive interaction in the realms of business and the law, so much so that a recent Australian parliamentary report on harmonising legal systems in both countries was promoted in the *New Zealand Lawyer* under the heading 'moving to a closer union with Australia'.[1] There is no harmony in sporting contacts between the societies, but these have become a routine, weekly occurrence. Meanwhile, those who see beyond corporate profits and parochialism encourage the creation of a profoundly closer union, based on a mutual awareness of similar problems. Michael Kirby, who served as judge of the Australian High Court from 1996 to 2009, once proposed a two-state solution for New Zealand's inclusion within a Federation of Australasia, but has accepted such 'constitutional matrimony' is politically impossible. He has argued, however, that 'something new, imaginative and different' should be created in the political interchange between Australia and New Zealand in the lead-up to the ANZAC centenary in 2015. He suggests that this trans-Tasman engagement should be a broad and enlightening process, one that is not limited to economics and contributes to an enhanced understanding of how both societies can resolve similar challenges.[2]

One challenging area in which mutual learning between Australia and New Zealand should be enhanced concerns how these states have dealt with Indigenous peoples. The history of colonisation in both countries has been subject to extensive research and some public debate. In both cases, however, government policies towards Indigenous peoples have hardly ever been developed and scrutinised in the light of a critical assessment of the failures of past policies. Instead, political uses of the past in this area have tended to be occasional and opportunistic, influenced by a search for immediate justifications of existing policy rather than by an understanding of historical legacies. Comparative insights rarely intrude into such immediate uses of history, although it is occasionally acknowledged by politicians that public policy failures—for example, in not improving Aboriginal health in Australia—are worse than in comparable societies such as New Zealand.[3] This predominant mode of the political use of history has reflected mythical traditions of national memory, such as the rhetoric of Australia as a land of the 'fair go'.[4] By ignoring comparisons, it has limited the public space for developing policies that would enable Indigenous peoples to achieve a position of genuine equality with respect for cultural difference in Australia and New Zealand.

This chapter reviews examples of the political use of history that concern relations between the State and Indigenous peoples in Australia and New Zealand, arguing that the crucial issue is whether a political use of history constrains or facilitates adequate public policy. First, a framework for analysing how politicians use the past to justify present policies will be considered, focusing on the scope for political distortion of the past. Then the problem of Indigenous exclusion from effective participation in policy making will be outlined, principally with reference to issues of 'unfinished business' regarding recognition of Indigenous rights in Australia. Three Australian examples of the use of history by politicians when discussing Indigenous peoples will be analysed. These are the official apology to the Stolen Generations given by Prime Minister, Kevin Rudd, on 13 February 2008 and speeches by Rudd as Leader of the Opposition and by then Prime Minister, John Howard, on 27 May 2007, on the fortieth anniversary of the 1967 referendum on Aborigines. The tension between these examples will be compared with the impact in New Zealand of the illusory rhetoric of uniform citizenship used in 2004 by Don Brash, leader of the opposition National Party. I aim to show that a comparative understanding of the unfinished business of Indigenous citizenship in Australia and New Zealand would enhance public policy in both states, and help to foster an enabling rather than a constraining use of history by politicians.

Crisis management and political distortion of the past

In an era of dramatically improved communications technology, expectations about the temporal awareness of policy makers have grown. In 1997, then UN Secretary-General, Kofi Annan, said that 'policy-makers and concerned publics know more about the possible ways in which today's actions or inactions might shape the state of things to come'. He suggested this awareness had partly eroded 'the very distinction between present and future for policy purposes'.[5] This preoccupation with managing perceptions of the future also affects political uses of the past. One way to examine this is to analyse different dimensions of using the past in political decision making. Concerning the use of historical analogies in crisis management, the three 'continuums' identified by Brändström et al. are particularly useful. These are: 1) whether the past situation is remembered deliberately or spontaneously; 2) whether past events are used cognitively to understand the present or politically to justify a current policy; and 3) whether the impact of a use of history is 'constraining' or 'enabling'—that is, whether the range of relevant policy options assessed is thereby reduced or enlarged.[6] While all three dimensions are significant, it is most important to consider how the third dimension is affected by one or both of the others—that is, why and how a particular historical comparison enhances or diminishes consideration of good policy options.

This analytical framework provides insight into the use of history in a context of crisis by decision makers, who must respond to a novel situation under pressure of immediate time constraints. In such circumstances, the quality of analogical reasoning is most critical. The importance of an appropriate analogical 'filter' or lesson, which helps decision makers to accurately interpret the character of the crisis and see possible pitfalls, can be decisive in enabling a crisis to be resolved, not escalated with catastrophic consequences.[7] Probably the most important example occurred during the Cuban missile crisis, when US President John F. Kennedy and his brother Robert avoided a cataclysmic surprise attack on Russian missiles in Cuba in favour of a negotiated solution, partly because the case of Pearl Harbor made them realise how illegitimate such an attack would seem, and that it would be likely to provoke a disastrous Russian response.[8] This episode shows something else, however, about how key decision makers often use history politically. The real process through which the crisis was resolved was kept top secret and was deliberately obscured in order to create the misleading impression that Soviet leader, Nikita Khrushchev, had backed down in the face of American pressure, rather than reached an agreement to withdraw Russian missiles from Cuba in exchange for Kennedy's secret commitment to withdraw US missiles from Turkey, as well as his public commitment not to attempt another invasion of Cuba.[9]

This historic case of crisis management highlights the importance of how politicians can misrepresent their experience of resolving a crisis as history. It also shows how they can use historical analogies as a weapon or a tool for political persuasion. During a crisis, such an opportunist use of history might be 'enabling', in the narrow and 'value-neutral' sense of facilitating the *process* of decision making.[10] Crisis management is not, however, a technical procedure. It involves choices between values that have critical consequences, so it is inadequate to study the process of decision making without considering whether a particular decision is defensible in terms of certain values and consequences. Olaf Kleist's analysis of the Tampa crisis (Chapter 5) illustrates this point well. The Howard Government's rhetoric of border protection *enabled* a speedy, militarised resolution of a manufactured 'crisis', but this rhetoric *constrained* any proper consideration of an appropriate response to the plight of onshore refugees. Artificial crisis management in that case contributed to a narrowing of policy making.

An important implication of these two cases is that it should not be presumed that the opportunistic use of historical analogies by politicians to persuade audiences should be characterised as 'enabling'—that is, as *widening* the horizons of decision makers.[11] Indeed, the mystification of the Cuban missile crisis suggests a different hypothesis. One consequence of the misrepresentation of that crisis, as a case of who blinked first, was to accelerate the build-up or vertical proliferation of nuclear weapons. A critic of the Western strategic mind-set that contributed to that outcome has called that mind-set (created before the Cuban missile crisis, but reinforced after it) a 'deterrence dogma', which pervasively *constrains* sensible policy.[12] The alternative hypothesis about the opportunistic use of historical analogies can be stated as a general presumption and a limited exception. While this use might occasionally be enabling if it helps to resolve an uncertainty that obstructs the process of policy making, usually good policy will result from a use of history that is based on an appropriate analogical filter or lesson. For a use of history to enable good policy, it must not only facilitate a real (rather than artificial) resolution of a policy problem, it must not create other, larger problems.

Indigenous citizenship as unfinished business

The claims made by Indigenous peoples in Australia and New Zealand for a distinct yet equal form of citizenship within these states pose major challenges for politicians leading, or aspiring to lead, those states. History is an important aspect of those claims. In Australia, this is reflected in the regular use of the phrase 'unfinished business' to refer to the outstanding agreements that are needed to achieve a national reconciliation.[13] The need for such agreements has been emphasised by Pat Dodson, the first chair of the Council for Aboriginal Reconciliation during the 1990s. Responding to the Howard Government's intervention in the Northern Territory in 2007, Dodson called again for Australia's 'unfinished business' with Indigenous peoples to be resolved through a 'political settlement', which would become 'a formal symbol of our shared history'. He claimed that, whereas a 'political settlement approach to Indigenous relationships' had been adopted in recent decades in New Zealand and Canada, the reassertion of assimilation by the Howard Government highlighted the 'perennial crises' that have engulfed the Australian nation over its unreconciled relationship with Indigenous peoples.[14]

Such crises reflect the exclusion of many Indigenous people from participation as full citizens, with opportunities to achieve not just formal equality (that is, the same rights as other citizens) but substantive equality (a similar capacity to exercise those rights). The crucial distinction between formal and substantive equality is related to a parallel distinction between what Baubock has called 'nominal and substantial citizenship'.[15] Nominal citizenship is little more than nationality, or access through a passport to the State's protection beyond its borders. Substantial citizenship is much more important, because it concerns people's capacity to enjoy human rights living within their state. The crises of everyday life for Indigenous people are experienced as an absence of that capacity. There is disagreement about how to respond effectively to those crises, yet agreement among Aborigines about the widespread lack of substantial citizenship. Cape York Aboriginal leader Noel Pearson, when diagnosing the problems in his community, used the term 'nominal citizenship' to describe the problem of 'passive welfare'—that is, bureaucratic dependence on a neo-colonial state. He said this had stopped Aborigines from experiencing 'the true meaning of citizenship'.[16] Pearson's Aboriginal critics, such as Megan Davis, dispute the wisdom of his political actions during the dotage of the Howard Government, but they also argue forcefully that the crises experienced by Indigenous people result from an absence of full citizenship.[17]

This absence is obscured if citizenship is conflated, as it often is in Australia, with a dominant idea of a culturally homogenous nation, not linked to political participation and protecting human rights. David Pearson has noted that conflating citizenship with nationality prevents the creation of new, inclusive forms of citizenship for Indigenous peoples in Australia and New Zealand.[18] A similar conflation has existed in many modern societies, because nominal citizenship has 'generally depended on membership in a national community'.[19] Maintaining a distinct national identity is, however, made increasingly difficult by global changes, such as the diminishing capacity of states to protect citizens' welfare, greater cultural interchange and more diverse sources of migration.[20] Reacting to those changes, some politicians in Australia and New Zealand have reasserted ideas of exclusionary citizenship, using the rhetoric of formal equality to deny real cultural differences and the legacies of colonisation. As Paul McHugh has noted, such rhetoric promotes a false dichotomy by proposing a choice between equality for all and difference for some.[21] Genuine equality, however, requires substantial citizenship, not cultural uniformity. In a society that is structured by Indigenous dispossession, there is a pressing need for what Baubock has called 'differentiated collective rights for socially unequal groups'. He has argued that for Indigenous peoples to really participate in the broader society, 'some rights have to be unequal in order to equalize the worth of citizenship'.[22]

In reality, rights of citizenship within nation-states (and globally) have always been 'deeply *differentiated*'.[23] The structure of contemporary societies means that, as in George Orwell's *Animal Farm*, some people are 'more equal' than others. Rhetoric of formal equality can be used to maintain such a situation. A clear example occurred in 1988 when John Howard, as Leader of the Opposition, responded to Prime Minister Bob Hawke's promise of a treaty with Australian Indigenous peoples by rejecting this as an 'absurd' idea, which 'denies the fact that Aboriginal people have full citizenship rights now'.[24] In 2000, Howard dismissed a call for a treaty by reducing Indigenous difference to just cultural uniqueness and social disadvantage, thus ignoring the legacies of dispossession.[25]

His claim that Aborigines already were full citizens was based on the narrow, legal concept of citizenship as a formal or administrative notion. This has been used as a means of exclusion and disregards the normative concern for achieving substantive equality.[26] Indigenous people reject this narrow view of citizenship for various reasons. These include the fact that formal citizenship rights do not enable political participation in a context of welfare dependency and the fact that, for first peoples, 'citizenship is not predicated on the same basis' as for everyone else.[27] In normative terms, citizenship involves 'a political bargain between the individual and the state', so the nature of this bargain will reflect the particular history between these two types of actors.[28] It will be affected by the fact that Indigenous people identify themselves first with reference to their tribal community, then as individuals within the Australian nation.[29]

The significance of continuing tribal affiliations for understanding the citizenship of Indigenous peoples in Australia has often been underestimated. During the era of assimilation, as a declared aim of government policy, in some states, such as Western Australia, the only way Aborigines could be recognised as citizens was by separating themselves as individuals from their ancestral communities. More broadly, access to nominal Australian citizenship (and potentially to substantial citizenship) was used by the State as a means of control, while it curtailed civil rights and repressed Indigenous political identity.[30] The experience of the Stolen Generations shows the totalitarian extent of such control.[31] For some administrators, such as A. O. Neville, the Protector of Aborigines in Western Australia from 1915 until 1940, this was motivated by the genocidal aim of destroying Aborigines as distinct peoples.[32] Neville's 'long range plan', elaborated at a 1937 conference, was to 'merge' Aborigines 'into our white community' and so ensure that Australians would 'eventually forget that there ever were any Aborigines in Australia'.[33] This was an example of a powerful official trying to rewrite history and engage in social engineering on a massive scale, with disastrous consequences. The failure of the assimilation policy to produce such amnesia, despite breaking up Aboriginal families, has implications for understanding Indigenous citizenship.[34] Neville presumed that white citizenship was the measure of Aboriginal equality, just as Howard later did, but Aborigines did not have exactly the same relationship with the State as other Australian citizens.[35] The Commonwealth Parliament's apology to the Stolen Generations on 13 February 2008 provided an opportunity for a different history of first peoples in Australia to be recognised and understood.

Australia turns a new page: the apology

The official Apology to Australia's Indigenous Peoples was delivered as the first item of business of the new Parliament elected with the defeat of the Howard Government in November 2007. The apology was widely received positively as part of a process of healing. This was because its text was negotiated with

Aboriginal leaders of the Stolen Generations, rather than with the Opposition Leader, Brendan Nelson, who rather grudgingly accepted the need for this act of healing, which Howard had denied for more than 10 years. It was also because the rhetoric of the apology spoke about transforming relationships between Indigenous and non-Indigenous peoples, so 'that this new page in the history of our great continent can now be written'. There was a direct link between 'acknowledging the past and laying claim to a future that embraces all Australians', one 'based on mutual respect, mutual resolve and mutual responsibility'.[36]

The apology was presented by Prime Minister Rudd as a response to public demands, based on 'universal human decency', that the Australian nation 'now step forward to right a historical wrong'.[37] He called forth a new and changed Australia, one that could finally 'bring the first two centuries of our settled history to a close, as we begin a new chapter' by embracing 'with pride, admiration and awe these great and ancient cultures we are truly blessed to have among us'.[38] It was this rhetoric of change, linked to an open acknowledgment of the abuses suffered by the Stolen Generations, which helped to make the apology a unifying experience. The radical Aboriginal leader from Brisbane, Sam Watson, who had been sceptical about the timing of the apology, said after hearing it that 'that moment will then close the door on one era in Australian history'.[39] Rudd started his speech by referring to the need 'to deal with this unfinished business of the nation, to remove a great stain from the nation's soul'.[40] The apology's success depended on an appreciation that healing a divided society required a direct acknowledgment of, and learning from, the past.

Although there was no specific mention of citizenship in the apology or in Rudd's speech, the idea of equality of participation in Australian society was central to the rhetoric of change. The apology envisioned 'a future where all Australians, whatever their origins, are truly equal partners, with equal opportunities and an equal stake in shaping the next chapter in the history of this great country'.[41] It essentially expressed the ideal of substantive, rather than merely formal, equality. As with other official apologies, a central purpose of the Australian apology was 'to change the terms and meanings of membership in a political community'—that is, expectations of how Aborigines and Torres Strait Islanders could participate in Australian society.[42] Rudd said that the apology was 'aimed at building a bridge between Indigenous and non-Indigenous Australians—a bridge based on a real respect rather than a thinly veiled contempt'.[43] He emphasised that historical recognition was central to the apology, both by telling the story of a member of the Stolen Generations, Nanna Nungala Fejo, and by calling on Australians to help 'transform the way in which the nation thinks about itself'.[44]

While not discussing the question of genocide, which had been raised in the *Bringing Them Home* report, Rudd rejected the claim that the forced separation of Aboriginal children had been benevolent. He said the fact that senior officials such as Neville had tried to eliminate Aboriginality must be faced, not ignored.[45] Apart from lacking an accompanying public education campaign, the main thing missing in his speech was an acknowledgment that compensation for the forced separation of Aboriginal children from their families was legitimate, as recommended by the *Bringing Them Home* report and accepted for similar practices in Canada.[46] Rudd acknowledged, however, the cultural and historical differences 'between those who emerged from the Dreamtime a thousand generations ago and those who, like me, came across the seas only yesterday'.[47] He promoted the ideal of a partnership between Indigenous and non-Indigenous Australians as the only decent way to deal with the unfinished business of the past and embrace the future.

As well as the discussion of the suffering of the Stolen Generations, there were two other significant historical references in Rudd's speech. One of these was a general point about the fact that 'most old approaches' have failed to help bridge the appalling gap in life expectancy, educational achievement and employment opportunities between Indigenous and non-Indigenous Australians. Rudd called for 'a new beginning which contains real measures of policy success or failure' and for 'a new partnership' that has 'sufficient flexibility not to insist on a one-size-fits-all approach for each of the hundreds of remote and regional Indigenous communities across the country'.[48] The key reference to a new partnership with Indigenous peoples suggests a new process of policy making, informed by what Pat Dodson has called a renewed 'formal dialogue' between the government and Indigenous peoples. Dodson has stressed that 'the crisis in Aboriginal Australia' cannot be resolved 'solely by intervention by government authority', especially as implemented by a 'dysfunctional bureaucratic machinery'. He argues that 'partnerships cannot be constructed by legislation or by schemes that involve the coercive use of public funds', but only 'through a process of engagement based on mutual respect, trust and a deep understanding and commitment to agreed objectives'.[49] While such a process is compatible with Rudd's rhetoric in his apology speech, he did not clearly espouse it. Instead, he proposed merely a 'joint policy commission' involving the Opposition, which has since foundered.[50] No Aboriginal representative institution has been created to replace the Aboriginal and Torres Strait Islander Commission abolished in 2004, and the lack of a formal process of dialogue with Indigenous representatives remains a major cause of unaccountable government policy.

The other historical reference Rudd made was to the 'unfulfilled spirit of the 1967 referendum'. He said there was a need for politicians to 'move beyond our infantile bickering, our point-scoring and our mindlessly partisan politics and elevate this one core area of national responsibility to a rare position beyond the partisan divide'. He linked this objective to a new partnership with Indigenous peoples, which puts 'an absolute premium on respect, cooperation and mutual responsibility as the guiding principles' of cooperative action.[51] This accurately summarises the purpose of the 1967 referendum, which was seen by those who campaigned for its success for more than a decade as designed to achieve substantive equality for Aborigines and Torres Strait Islanders.[52] The referendum was not an attempt to achieve nominal citizenship for Indigenous people, but an attempt to create a constitutional basis that could facilitate efforts towards equalising substantial citizenship, by giving the Federal Government authority to create special laws for Aborigines when needed by them. There is much debate about the constitutional significance of the referendum, but importantly, Rudd referred to its unfulfilled spirit as a guiding principle of a cooperative partnership with Indigenous peoples, which requires a completely new process of policy making.

Australia spurns a new page: the intervention

The optimism created by the apology contrasts markedly with the widespread confusion and disappointment surrounding the Rudd Government's continuation of the Howard Government's ad hoc manner of intervening in the lives of many remote Aboriginal communities in the Northern Territory. While the new government has made some changes, such as to reinstate permits required for most outsiders to access Aboriginal land and to restore a community training program, the paternalistic nature of the intervention has been maintained. The new government ignored calls for the intervention to be urgently reviewed from Mick Dodson, the Oceania representative to the UN Permanent Forum on Indigenous Issues, and Tom Calma, the Aboriginal and Torres Strait Islander Social Justice Commissioner.[53] These and other critics called for the intervention to be transformed by negotiating with communities about how to improve basic government services such as education, health, housing and policing. Calma has highlighted 'the danger of unilateral action' by governments, which 'is reflected in processes that treat Indigenous peoples as passive recipients of policy rather than active agents for change'.[54] He noted that justifications for the ad hoc intervention relied on 'the appeal and seductive charm of embracing new approaches and breaking from the past', without being informed by any historical analysis of past government failures.[55] Professor Larissa Behrendt made a similar criticism, pointing out that service delivery should never require that people surrender their rights, particularly when the people who are losing their rights are defined only by race.[56]

How has the Rudd Government come to adopt a paternalistic form of intervention that is not only by definition racist, because it suspends the *Racial Discrimination Act 1975*, but which is clearly inconsistent with the spirit of partnership in which the apology was offered and received? There could be various reasons, but ignorance of what a suitable policy would be is not one of them. In his apology speech, Rudd explicitly endorsed the need for 'flexible, tailored, local approaches to achieve commonly agreed national objectives that lie at the core of our proposed new partnership'.[57] This is what critics of the paternalistic nature of the NT intervention have been calling for, yet the government has been slow to signal its willingness to create partnership in practice. To understand why, it is useful to examine what Howard and Rudd said in the lead-up to the intervention. The intervention was announced at a press conference on 21 June 2007—ostensibly as a response to the failure of the NT Government to act on a report about child abuse in Aboriginal communities. The background to this policy fiasco, however, occurred at a ceremony in Old Parliament House on 27 May 2007, Their Spirit Still Shines, which was held to mark the fortieth anniversary of the 1967 referendum and particularly the achievements of those who campaigned for it.

Because of the nature of the event and the audience, comprising campaigners for the referendum and many critics of Howard's policies, it was not easy for him to appeal to those present at that ceremony. This was particularly so in comparison with Rudd, who used the occasion to announce his commitment to saying sorry, in order to make 'new beginnings possible'.[58] What Howard did, apart from an initial gesture to 'the power of myth', which he said was central to 'the larger meaning of the referendum', was to claim the referendum meant the *opposite* of what those who had campaigned for it intended—that is, federal government responsibility for the failure of Indigenous Australians to enjoy the same opportunities as other Australians.[59] Howard claimed that, in overwhelmingly endorsing the referendum, the Australian people had wanted to end Aborigines' 'alienation from mainstream society'.[60] He said 'for indigenous success to shine through sometimes, frankly, it demands *less from government* and more from indigenous civil society'.[61] The main change from 1967 was to give the Commonwealth authority to make special laws for Aborigines when required. This was meant to ensure Aborigines could access Commonwealth government resources, yet Howard claimed the main responsibility for overcoming Indigenous poverty and community violence rested with Indigenous people themselves. His aim was to deny government responsibility for their exclusion from opportunities in Australian society. He could never convince his audience to change their view of the referendum, but by recalling 'the bipartisan spirit in which it was carried', and by his actions a month later, he created a policy wedge that outlasted his government.[62]

Much analysis of Howard's ad hoc intervention in the Northern Territory has focused on its episodic and hasty origins.[63] This was clear from the lack of any provision in the 2007 Federal Budget for what became substantial public expenditure.[64] The crisis of family violence in remote Aboriginal communities, to which the intervention was a belated response, had been publicised several years earlier, in 2003, by Aboriginal leaders such as Jackie Huggins and Mick Dodson.[65] This does not mean, however, that Howard's intervention lacked cunning. It did not achieve a rise in the opinion polls, which, according to Alexander Downer, had been anticipated by the government;[66] but that was not Howard's only purpose. He was responding to a challenge that Rudd had made at the end of his speech on 27 May. Rudd said political leaders should focus not 'on what we disagree on in this critical area—so central to our national soul—let us instead focus on what we can agree on', as a basis for unity.[67] Rudd began his speech by noting that Aboriginal people had been entirely excluded when the Commonwealth Parliament first met in Canberra in 1927 and he ended with an affirmation of 'an enduring spirit of reciprocal partnership'.[68] Howard ignored the historical exclusion of Indigenous peoples and rejected the idea of partnership, but he responded to Rudd's practical challenge about forging 'a common program' with his paternalistic intervention.[69] While in government, Howard could still determine the character of that program.

The most revealing feature of Howard's justification for the intervention was that he did not attempt to place the social problem of child sexual abuse in remote Aboriginal communities in any historical or policy context. Some policies with no connection to stopping child abuse, such as resuming control of Aboriginal land, were justified as a response to a national emergency, which was compared with a natural disaster such as a cyclone.[70] Thus, the historical responsibility of government policy for the crisis in Aboriginal communities was minimised.[71] Howard accused the NT Government of a tardy response to the *Little Children Are Sacred* report by Pat Anderson and Rex Wild, yet he completely ignored its recommendations for action based on consultation with Aboriginal communities.[72] The day before the intervention was announced, Mick Dodson had summarised the key elements of successful policy projects in Aboriginal communities as being: intense community involvement with local decision making and control of resources, combined with respectful support by non-Indigenous parts of the community.[73] All these elements were disregarded by the top-down nature of the intervention, which abandoned consultation with Indigenous people and ignored relevant statistical and historical research.[74] Howard asserted that the intervention would be non-discriminatory and Rudd was prepared 'to give him the benefit of the doubt' by assuming that the bureaucratic controls applying only to Aborigines could be classified as 'positive measures'.[75] In practice, the intervention was inherently discriminatory, and no attempt was made by either Howard or Rudd to explain how measures that reduced Aboriginal autonomy could benefit Aborigines.

There is a deeper reason why the paternalistic intervention in the Northern Territory reflects a use of history that constrains rather than enables effective public policy in Aboriginal affairs. This relates to the legal debate about whether the 1967 referendum altered the terms of the constitution so that racially discriminatory laws were no longer valid in Australia. That was the aim of those who campaigned for that referendum and most probably the view of the overwhelming majority of electors who supported it. It is the opinion of Michael Kirby, though not a majority opinion of his former fellow High Court judges. His reasoning is that after the referendum it is now ambiguous as to whether the 'race power' authorises laws that discriminate *against* rather than *for* the benefit of people of any race, so the issue must be resolved according to Australia's international treaty obligations, which clearly forbid detrimental discrimination.[76] Those obligations are inconsistent with paternalism and the racially discriminatory legislation underlying the intervention. A real partnership with Indigenous peoples requires that the 'race power' must be only beneficial, so that any law that affects only Indigenous people is negotiated together with their representatives, not imposed against their will. Howard, however, used a distorted view of the referendum to justify changes that amounted to a return to assimilation. The intervention was defended with vague rhetoric about 'breaking from the past', but there was little discussion of the causes of past policy failures or how the changes proposed would help to reduce child abuse. Such deliberate ignoring of past policies constrains rather than enables effective policy formulation. This was hardly a novel approach to Indigenous policy. It had been tried previously in New Zealand by a conservative party that, like Howard's, was languishing badly in the opinion polls.

The mythology of 'nationhood' in New Zealand

On 27 January 2004, the recently elected leader of the opposition National Party in New Zealand delivered a speech titled 'Nationhood' to a Rotary Club in the affluent suburb of Orewa, north of Auckland. Don Brash had been party leader for three months but had received no bounce in the opinion polls and National's party support was low, at 29 per cent, not much more than its disastrous vote of 21 per cent in the 2002 election.[77] The tactic used by Brash to change this situation was to manipulate fears experienced by conservative and older pakeha (white) voters who were disturbed by the growing cultural prominence of Maori in New Zealand society and by the belated recognition of the Indigenous rights affirmed in the *Treaty of Waitangi*.[78] The speech occurred soon after Helen Clark's Labour Government declared it would overrule a decision by the Court of Appeal to recognise that Maori ownership of the foreshore and seabed could potentially remain in areas without freehold title.[79] There was a dramatic response in opinion polls to Brash's speech, with a rise of 18 per cent in National Party support, and higher increases for certain groups, such as 29 per cent for retirees.[80] Tariana Turia, one of the founders of the Maori Party who resigned from Labour to protest against its rejection of the Court of Appeal decision, compared Brash's Orewa speech with the anti-refugee strategy of electoral salvation used by Howard during the Tampa crisis, in which one group of vulnerable people was 'cynically set up to be feared'.[81] The difference was that Howard used the power of incumbency to create uncertainty and division, while Brash achieved a similar result operating from a position of weakness in opposition.

Brash sparked the change in his party's political fortunes by focusing on a very simple idea, and reinforcing it through a very selective representation of history. The simple idea was to proclaim that 'the essential notion of one rule for all in a single nation state' requires 'one standard of citizenship', not different rights for different groups of people.[82] He conflated equality before the law with a uniform New Zealand identity, encapsulated in a particular mistranslation of words spoken in Maori to Maori chiefs by the English emissary William Hobson at Waitangi during the treaty signing in 1840: 'we are one people.' A culturally informed understanding, however, is that a better translation of the words '*he iwi tahi tatou*' is to say 'we two peoples together make a nation'.[83]

Brash relied on a widespread reluctance among pakeha to accept that New Zealand was a bicultural nation, a feeling he manipulated by implying that Maori were getting more than others. As the New Zealand historian Michael King observed, 'Brash actually sent out very carefully constructed coded messages that suggested that National is going to turn back the tide on Maori privileges', without saying what those privileges were.[84] Given that levels of poverty are greater among Maori than among pakeha, Brash's criticism of the Labour Government for creating a society with 'two standards of citizenship...where the minority has a birthright to the upper hand' is absurd.[85] It showed clearly, however, 'how emotion, when stimulated, can swamp reason, especially when saliency about race issues is high'.[86] A particular example was the Maori seats in Parliament, which Brash described as an 'anachronism' that he would abolish.[87] The seats do not give Maori more votes as individuals than other New Zealanders. They are merely a way of organising part of the Maori electorate into distinct seats, which has been important for the development of Maori political influence, although voter turnout in those seats has often been lower than in general electorates. It was accepted in New Zealand politics that the Maori seats would remain as long as Maori wished. By proposing their abolition, Brash made a 'calculated appeal to latent prejudice'.[88]

In creating a false impression of Maori privilege, Brash's distortion of history, and his denigration of the role of the *Treaty of Waitangi*, was central. Revaluing the treaty as a founding document of New Zealand has been crucial for the pakeha recognition that Maori have legitimate historical grievances against the Crown for breaching the terms of the treaty.[89] Brash did not entirely reject the process of settling those grievances, which previous National politicians had contributed to, but he claimed there could be only 'a gesture at recompense' and 'no more than that'.[90] He dismissed the common view that 'this 19th century treaty' contains lessons for contemporary New Zealand, asserting that it 'did not create a partnership' but instead 'was the launching pad for the creation of one sovereign nation', in which the pakeha majority had the same rights as Maori.[91] Brash said the treaty should be seen only as an anachronism, not, as one historian has interpreted it, as a 'modern' and 'tribal' treaty with a substantial 'rationale for Maori autonomy' under Article 2.[92] According to Brash, even Maori had benefited when the treaty was replaced by 'one standard of citizenship'—that is, assimilation—as the framework for government policy until the 1970s.[93] He claimed that social disparities between Maori and pakeha 'are not Treaty issues', just 'social welfare issues' involving individuals rather than groups.[94] The purpose of Brash's rhetoric, spoken to an affluent pakeha audience, was highlighted towards the end of his speech. When discussing the obligations of citizenship, he said 'we ask Maori to take some responsibility themselves for what is happening in their own communities', as if they had not yet done so.[95] That was like the message Howard tried to convey during the NT intervention when, like Brash, he rejected a partnership with Indigenous peoples and implied that their poverty was their fault.

While Brash lost the subsequent election, his 'rhetoric of illusion' had a big impact on New Zealand politics and ideas of citizenship.[96] The Labour Government diluted its support for respecting the principles of the *Treaty of Waitangi* in public policy, in an effort to counter his attack.[97] Brash's replacement, John Key, later admitted that Brash's rhetoric was misleading, when seen in the 'daylight' of hindsight. He said 'there's actually a pretty good reason for most of what goes on' in Maori policy, creating a very different impression from the cultural division that Brash had conveyed.[98] Remarkably, after winning the 2008 election, Key formed a National-led government that was supported by the Maori Party as well as by small right-wing parties. The shift in the National Party's rhetoric was reflected in its formal agreement with the Maori Party. The National Party said it would 'act in accordance with' the *Treaty of Waitangi* and 'not seek to remove the Maori seats without the consent of the Maori people'.[99] It seems that New Zealand has turned significantly away from Brash's divisive rhetoric.

This does not mean that Brash's rhetoric had no lasting impact, because it had already substantially influenced the Labour Government's policies after the Orewa speech. The extent of that influence was seen in the government's response to international criticism of policies that discriminated against Maori, such as over their historic rights to the foreshore and seabed. In 2005, the UN Special

Rapporteur on Indigenous rights and basic freedoms, Rodolfo Stavenhagen, visited New Zealand at the government's invitation. In 2006, he released a report in which he dismissed talk of Maori privilege as nonsense and called for recognition of Maori 'collective citizenship', as expressed in the *Treaty of Waitangi*.[100] Stavenhagen's report was met with what one editorial called 'defensive resentment' from both major parties.[101] Such an attitude contributed to New Zealand's rejection in 2007 of the Declaration on the Rights of Indigenous Peoples, when it was approved by the UN General Assembly. Only three other states joined New Zealand in opposing this declaration, which had been subject to significant dilution in order to get support from most other states. Australia was another recalcitrant state, together with Canada and the United States.[102] All these states share, to varying degrees, an inability to deal adequately with the unfinished business of achieving substantial Indigenous citizenship, understood as a substantive entitlement to real equality of opportunity, not just as a position of formal equality.

Conclusion: the politics of history in comparative perspective

In Australia and New Zealand, it is certainly true that 'productive learning from history does not come easily' for politicians dealing with Indigenous policy.[103] One reason for this has been the use by politicians not of analogical filters to understand problems in a proper historical and comparative perspective, but of history merely to justify existing policy. The idea of a partnership with Indigenous peoples, which was central to the apology delivered by Rudd in February 2008, represented a new approach, in that Rudd used history insightfully in his speech, including a reference to 'the unfulfilled spirit of the 1967 referendum'.[104] He has yet to facilitate such a partnership by creating a formal process of dialogue, as proposed by Pat Dodson.[105]

There are various reasons for this. One is Rudd's style as a 'strong leader', more adept at controlling others than at cooperating with them.[106] That style, however, does not explain the contradiction between his promotion of partnership with Indigenous peoples and his continuation of paternalistic controls in the Northern Territory. As a political exercise in 'crisis exploitation', Howard's intervention was only 'partially successful' because of criticism of his motives and scepticism about the impact of those controls.[107] There was no rise in support for Howard measured by opinion polls, but he got Rudd to follow a set of largely bureaucratic measures that was not linked to any partnership. Rudd still followed most of Howard's program despite surpassing him so clearly with the apology. This was seen in the slowness with which the new government reviewed the NT intervention. When challenged about the intervention on a TV forum after being in office for six months, Rudd twice referred to 'the government' of his predecessor in the present tense, even when saying how his policy differed from Howard's. Significantly, Rudd mentioned the suspension of the *Racial Discrimination Act* as a point of difference, but he was unable to say when that suspension, on which Howard's intervention was based, would end.[108] Almost a year later, in March 2009, Aboriginal people successfully took a complaint against Australia's racial discrimination to the UN Committee for the Elimination of Racial Discrimination. The committee called on the Australian Government to reinstate the act and to reform its policy in direct consultation with Aboriginal communities and individuals affected by the intervention.[109] The impression that this created was of a government that had been 'slow to act' and that was moving to meet Australia's international obligations reluctantly as a result of international pressure.[110]

What conclusions can be drawn about uses of history by politicians in Australia and New Zealand to justify policies in Indigenous affairs? The central similarity between Howard's intervention and Brash's appeal to pakeha prejudice derived from the claim that Indigenous success demanded less from government and more from Indigenous people themselves. The latter expectation is desirable in itself, but the Orewa episode shows it can be used as an excuse for diminished government responsibility for Indigenous citizenship, understood as access to substantive equality. Brash used a simplistic misrepresentation of New Zealand's past to support policies designed to promote not real equality, but nostalgia for an era that had supposedly been marked by cultural homogeneity. He attempted to diminish Maori concerns, by ignoring the *Treaty of Waitangi* and by acting more unilaterally, like governments in Australia have often done on Aboriginal issues. The results of such an approach are evident in the huge backlog of under-funded housing, health and education services in the Northern Territory that the intervention has revealed, including the discriminatory lack of provision of many basic services, such as education, to Aboriginal people.

Howard and Brash ultimately suffered political defeats, but the legacies of their constraining uses of history to justify unilateral policies regarding Indigenous peoples remain. They both used the rhetoric of formal equality to deny the need to deal with the unfinished business of Indigenous citizenship. Although their narrow approach to historical understanding has been put aside, it has not yet been effectively transcended in either country. Comparing Howard's constraining use of history with Brash's reveals two things.

First, if a political use of history succeeds as an exercise in crisis exploitation, its impact should be assessed in terms of its effect on a broader policy agenda, not by the chief political actor's immediate fate. When an old leader departs the scene, his rhetoric might be decisively rejected, as with Rudd's apology to the Stolen Generations and Key's post-election affirmation of National's support for the relevance of the *Treaty of Waitangi*. This does not mean, however, that the new approach to history has already informed relevant policy making in

Indigenous affairs. For that to occur, a critical assessment is needed of the reasons for past policy failures.

Second, the similarities between Australia and New Zealand are arguably as important as the differences, particularly in view of the struggles in New Zealand to turn government declarations of 'partnership' into a real 'association of equals'.[11] One year after Australia's belated apology to Indigenous peoples, the dominant feeling remains one of a potential rather than a real partnership. Australians who want the Rudd Government to honour its commitment to a real partnership with Indigenous peoples by creating a treaty can learn from the recent history of New Zealand. Meanwhile, the lesson for New Zealanders from Australia's apology to the Stolen Generations is that, without an enduring bicultural partnership, great rhetoric alone cannot transcend the legacies of assimilation. While the challenge of biculturalism is more familiar to New Zealanders, the Orewa episode reveals the large political obstacles to creating a genuine partnership with Maori. Australians and New Zealanders face similar challenges of achieving substantive equality by creating partnerships with Indigenous peoples. Resolving this unfinished business of Indigenous citizenship will be assisted by understanding the history of past policy failures in a comparative light.

Endnotes

[1] *New Zealand Lawyer*, 22 January 2007, p. 1.

[2] Kirby, Michael 2002, 'The unfinished trans-Tasman business', *Commonwealth Law Bulletin*, vol. 28, no. 2, pp. 1083–4, 1088, 1090.

[3] For example, Evans, Chris 2006, The Labor approach to Indigenous affairs, Speech by the Shadow Minister for Indigenous Affairs to Progressive Branch Alliance, Perth, 26 September 2006, p. 3, <http://eherald.alp.org.au/download/now/evans_indigenous_affairs.pdf>

[4] For the historical lack of a fair go, see Buckley, Ken and Wheelwright, Ted 1988, *No Paradise for Workers: Capitalism and the common people in Australia 1788–1914*, Oxford University Press, Melbourne.

[5] Annan, Kofi 1997, *Renewing the United Nations: A programme for reform*, Report to the fifty-first session of UN General Assembly, New York, p. 10.

[6] Brändström, Annika, Bynander, Fredrik and 't Hart, Paul 2004, 'Governing by looking back: historical analogies and crisis management', *Public Administration*, vol. 82, no. 1, pp. 194–5.

[7] For a summary of different analogical uses of history, see ibid., p. 207.

[8] Lebow, Richard Ned and Gross Stein, Janice 1994, *We All Lost the Cold War*, Princeton University Press, Princeton, NJ, pp. 120–3; May, Ernest R. and Zelikow, Philip D. (eds) 1997, *The Kennedy Tapes: Inside the White House during the Cuban missile crisis*, Harvard University Press, Cambridge, Mass., pp. 121, 149.

[9] Lebow and Stein, *We All Lost the Cold War*, p. 124, point out: 'The Kennedy inner circle was so worried about the consequences of publicity that they rewrote history.'

[10] Brändström et al., 'Governing by looking back', pp. 195, 207.

[11] Ibid., pp. 195, 207.

[12] MccGwire, Michael 2006, 'Nuclear deterrence', *International Affairs*, vol. 82, no. 4, pp. 773–6.

[13] Gunstone, Andrew 2007, *Unfinished Business: The Australian formal reconciliation process*, Australian Scholarly Publishing, Melbourne, pp. 89, 290.

[14] Dodson, Patrick 2007, 'Whatever happened to reconciliation?', in Jon Altman and Melinda Hinkson (eds), *Coercive Reconciliation*, Arena, Melbourne, pp. 27–8.

[15] Baubock, Rainer 1994, *Transnational Citizenship: Membership and rights in international migration*, Edward Elgar, Aldershot, p. 23.

[16] Pearson, Noel 2000, *Our Right to Take Responsibility*, Noel Pearson and Associates, Cairns, pp. 13–14, 30, 99. Pearson's view is supported by Marcia Langton (2008, 'Trapped in the Aboriginal reality show', *Griffith Review*, no. 19, pp. 158–9). See also Walter, James and Macleod, Margaret 2002, *The Citizens' Bargain: A documentary history of Australian views since 1890*, UNSW Press, Sydney, pp. 10, 12–13.

[17] Megan Davis, 'Arguing over Indigenous rights: Australia and the United Nations', in Altman and Hinkson, *Coercive Reconciliation*, pp. 104–5.

[18] Pearson, David 2004, 'Rethinking citizenship in Aotearoa/New Zealand', in Paul Spoonley, Cluny Macpherson and David Pearson (eds), *Tangata Tangata: The changing ethnic contours of New Zealand*, Dunmore Press, Southbank, pp. 294–5, 311.

[19] Castles, Stephen 2005, 'Nation and empire: hierarchies of citizenship in the new global order', *International Politics*, vol. 42, no. 2, p. 205.

[20] Ibid., pp. 205, 206–7.

[21] McHugh, Paul 2004, *Aboriginal Societies and the Common Law*, Oxford University Press, Oxford, p. 609.

[22] Baubock, *Transnational Citizenship*, pp. 278, 298.

[23] Castles, 'Nation and empire', pp. 205, 219–20.

[24] Quoted in Chesterman, John and Galligan, Brian 1997, *Citizens Without Rights: Aborigines and Australian citizenship*, Cambridge University Press, Melbourne, p. 218.

[25] Moreton-Robinson, Aileen 2007, 'Writing off Indigenous sovereignty: the discourse of security and patriarchal white sovereignty', in Aileen Moreton-Robinson (ed.), *Sovereign Subjects: Indigenous sovereignty matters*, Allen & Unwin, Sydney, pp. 98–9.

[26] Rubenstein, Kim 2000, 'Citizenship and the centenary: inclusion and exclusion in 20th century Australia', *Melbourne University Law Review*, vol. 24, no. 3, pp. 577–8.

[27] Moreton-Robinson, 'Writing off Indigenous sovereignty', p. 99; Darryl Cronin, 'Welfare dependency and mutual obligation: negating Indigenous sovereignty', in Moreton-Robinson, *Sovereign Subjects*, pp. 187–8.

[28] Walter and Macleod, *The Citizens' Bargain*, p. 1.

[29] Wendy Brady, 'That sovereign being: history matters', in Moreton-Robinson, *Sovereign Subjects*, p. 149.

[30] Beckett, Jeremy 1998, 'Aboriginality, citizenship and nation-state', *Social Analysis*, no. 24, p. 10.

[31] In a submission to a case involving Alec Kruger, a member of the Stolen Generations, the Australian section of the International Commission of Jurists noted that the 'total control' that the State had over the lives of Aborigines such as Kruger was 'the hallmark of totalitarianism and is the antithesis of representative government'. See Buti, Tony (ed.) 1996, *After the Removal: A submission by the Aboriginal Legal Service of Western Australia (Inc) to the National Inquiry into Separation of Aboriginal and Torres Strait Islander Children from their Families*, Aboriginal Legal Service, Perth, Appendix A, p. 418. For the impact of such control on one family across generations, see Beresford, Quentin 2006, *Rob Riley: An Aboriginal leader's quest for justice*, Aboriginal Studies Press, Canberra.

[32] For the development of Neville's views, see Beresford, *Rob Riley*, pp. 13–23.

[33] Speech by A. O. Neville to initial conference of Commonwealth and State Aboriginal Authorities, Parliament House, Canberra, April 1937, reprinted in 1995 as Appendix A in *Telling Our Story: A report by the Aboriginal Legal Service of Western Australia (Inc) on the removal of Aboriginal children from their families in Western Australia*, Aboriginal Legal Service, Perth, p. 208.

[34] Haebich, Anna 2000, *Broken Circles: Fragmenting Indigenous families 1800–2000*, Fremantle Arts Centre Press, Fremantle, pp. 162–4.

[35] Moreton-Robinson, Aileen 2001, Treaty talk: past, present, future, Ngunnawal Lecture, University of Canberra, p. 7.

[36] Apology to Australia's Indigenous Peoples, *Commonwealth Parliamentary Debates* [hereafter *CPD*], Representatives, 13 February 2008, p. 167.

[37] Kevin Rudd, *CPD*, Representatives, 13 February 2008, p. 169.

[38] *CPD*, Representatives, 13 February 2008, p. 172.

[39] Sam Watson, interviewed on 'Saying sorry', *Message Stick*, ABC TV, 25 May 2008. He was sceptical because of a concern that there would be no follow up to the apology after the opening of the new parliamentary session.

[40] *CPD*, Representatives, 13 February 2008, p. 167.

[41] Ibid., p. 167.

[42] Nobles, Melissa 2008, *The Politics of Official Apologies*, Cambridge University Press, New York, p. x. Justice Kirby affirmed such a change in the Blue Mud Bay native title case decided in July 2008, when he said the apology was now a crucial 'element of the social context' in which native title must be understood and applied. *Northern Territory vs Arnhem Land Aboriginal Land Trust* [2008], 82 ALJR 1099 at 1115 [71] per Kirby J.

[43] *CPD*, Representatives, 13 February 2008, p. 171.

[44] Ibid., p. 172.

[45] Ibid., p. 169.

[46] For the importance of compensation and the relevance of comparisons with Canada, see National Inquiry into the Separation of Aboriginal and Torres Strait Islander Children from their Families 1997, *Bringing Them Home: Report of the National Inquiry into the Separation of Aboriginal and Torres Strait Islander Children from their Families*, Human Rights and Equal Opportunity Commission, Sydney, pp. 278–9, 302–13, 573–7.

[47] *CPD*, Representatives, 13 February 2008, p. 172.

[48] Ibid., p. 171.

[49] Dodson, Pat 2007, A call for a new national dialogue between Indigenous and non-Indigenous Australians, La Trobe University Centre for Dialogue lecture, Brunswick, 10 October 2007 (excerpted in *Connections: Newsletter of the Centre for Dialogue*, vol. 2, p. 2).

[50] Rudd, *CPD*, Representatives, 13 February 2008, p. 172. The main reason for the failure to establish this commission was the Opposition's insistence on involving the former Minister for Aboriginal Affairs, Mal Brough, who lost his seat at the 2007 election.

[51] Ibid., p. 172.

[52] See Pitty, Roderic 2008, 'Faith Bandler: campaigning for racial equality', in G. Stokes, R. Pitty and G. Smith (eds), *Global Citizens: Australian activists for change*, Cambridge University Press, Melbourne, pp. 35–9.

[53] 'Dodson wants intervention review brought forward', *ABC News*, 2 February 2008, <www.abc.net.au/news/stories/2008/02/02/2152845.htm>; Calma, Tom 2007, *Social Justice Report 2007*, ch. 3, part 4, <www.hreoc.gov.au/social_justice/sj_report/sjreport07/chap3.html>

[54] Calma, Tom 2008, Speech, Sydney, 31 March 2008, p. 4, <www.hreoc.gov.au/pdf/social_justice/speech/protecting_indigenous_children.pdf>

[55] Ibid., p. 4.

[56] Behrendt, Larissa 2008, What follows sorry, Speech, University of Technology, Sydney, 19 March 2008, p. 6, <www.uts.edu.au/new/speaks/2008/March/resources/1903-transcript.htm>

[57] Rudd, *CPD*, Representatives, 13 February 2008, p. 171.

[58] Rudd, Kevin 2007, On the future of reconciliation, Speech at the Fortieth Anniversary of the 1967 Referendum, Canberra, 27 May 2007, p. 2, <www.reconciliation.org.au/downloads/156/Kevin_Rudd_Their_Spirit_Still_Shines.pdf>

[59] Howard, John 2007, Their spirit still shines, Speech at the Fortieth Anniversary of the 1967 Referendum, Canberra, 27 May 2007, p. 1, <www.reconciliation.org.au/downloads/156/John_Howard_Their_Spirit_Still_Shines.pdf>

[60] Ibid., p. 2.

[61] Ibid., p. 3 [emphasis added].

[62] Ibid., p. 1.

[63] Toohey, Paul 2008, 'Last drinks: the impact of the Northern Territory intervention', *Quarterly Essay*, no. 30, p. 48.

[64] The last federal budget brought down by Howard and his Treasurer, Peter Costello, in May 2007, actually had the lowest spending on Indigenous affairs as a percentage of Federal Government revenue (1.18 per cent) of any of the 12 budgets they had delivered since 1996. This percentage was lower than in any year since 1990 (*National Indigenous Times*, 29 May 2008, p. 16).

[65] Statement by Reconciliation Australia in response to the national emergency measures to protect Aboriginal children, 21 June 2007, <www.reconciliation.org.au/downloads/157/Family_Violence.pdf>

[66] Behrendt (What follows sorry, p. 3), referring to Downer's comments on ABC TV's *Insiders* on 25 November 2007.

[67] Rudd, On the future of reconciliation, p. 4.

[68] Ibid., pp. 1, 4.

[69] Ibid., p. 4.

[70] Howard, John 2007, Press conference transcript, 21 June 2007, p. 6, <www.eniar.org/news/JohnHowardPM.html>

[71] On this responsibility, see Dillon, Michael and Westbury, Neil 2007, *Beyond Humbug: Transforming government engagement with Indigenous Australia*, Seaview, Adelaide, pp. 196–7.

[72] Commentary by Ian Anderson comparing those recommendations with the intervention as originally formulated by the Howard Government, *Australian Policy Online*, 29 June 2007, <www.apo.org.au/webboard/results.chtml?filename_num=161613>

[73] Dodson, Mick 2007, Whatever happened to reconciliation?, Public lecture, 20 June 2007, p. 4, <www.reconciliation.org.au/i-cms.isp?page=110>

[74] Altman, J. C. 2007, The Howard Government's Northern Territory intervention: are neo-paternalism and Indigenous development compatible?, Address to Australian Institute of Aboriginal and Torres Strait Islander Studies conference, Canberra, 7 November 2007, pp. 9, 13, <www.anu.edu.au/caepr/Publications/topical/Altman_AIATSIS.pdf>

[75] Howard, Press conference transcript, 21 June 2007, p. 6; Rudd, Interview with Laurie Oakes, *Sunday*, Channel 9, 24 June 2007, p. 2, <http://sunday.ninemsn.com.au/sunday/political_transcripts/article_2236.asp>

[76] Roderic Pitty, 'Michael Kirby: speaking for human rights', in Stokes et al., *Global Citizens*, pp. 168–9. Justice Kirby applied his reasoning to a case concerning the discriminatory nature of the Commonwealth's NT emergency response legislation in *Wurridjal vs The Commonwealth of Australia* [2009], HCA 2 [2 February 2009], paragraphs 214–15, 264–73, <www.austlii.edu.au/au/cases/cth/HCA/2009/2.html>

[77] Johansson, Jon 2004, 'Orewa and the rhetoric of illusion', *Political Science*, vol. 56, no. 2, pp. 115–6.

[78] Ibid., p. 123; James, Colin 2004, The political context of the Treaty of Waitangi and human rights, Speech at Human Rights Commission symposium, Wanganui, 20 July 2004, pp. 2, 3, <www.colinjames.co.nz/speeches_briefings/Hn_Rights_Comm_04Jul20.htm>

[79] Hongston, Ken 2006, 'Foreshore and seabed', in Malcolm Mulholland (ed.), *State of the Maori Nation: Twenty-first century issues in Aotearoa*, Reed, Auckland, p. 111.

[80] Johansson, 'Orewa and the rhetoric of illusion', p. 124. The attitudes typical of many pakeha retirees were expressed by middle-aged and some younger pakeha as well. For examples, see McCreanor, Tim 2005, 'Talking pakeha identities', in James Liu et al. (eds), *New Zealand Identities: Departures and destinations*, Victoria University Press, Wellington, pp. 61–4.

[81] Tariana Turia, *South Taranaki Star*, 29 November 2007, <www.maoriparty.com/index.php?option=com_content&task=view&id=1462&Itemid=82>

[82] Brash, Don 2004, Nationhood, Address to Orewa Rotary Club, 27 January 2004, p. 3, <www.national.org.nz/files/OrewaRotaryClub_27Jan.pdf>

[83] Williams, David 2004, 'Myths, national origins, common law and the Waitangi Tribunal', *Murdoch University Electronic Journal of Law*, vol. 11, no. 4, p. 10, <www.murdoch.edu.au/elaw/issues/v11n4/williams114_text.html>

[84] King, Michael 2004, Interview with Kim Hill, *Face to Face*, NZ TV One, 3 March 2004, p. 2, <http://www.anewnz.org.nz/paper_comments.asp?paperid=30>

[85] Brash, Nationhood, pp. 2–3.

[86] Johansson, 'Orewa and the rhetoric of illusion', pp. 122, 125.

[87] Brash, Nationhood, p. 14.

[88] Durie, Mason 2005, *Nga Tai Matatu: Tides of Maori endurance*, Oxford University Press, Melbourne, p. 223.

[89] Consedine, Robert and Consedine, Joanna 2005, *Healing Our History: The challenge of the Treaty of Waitangi*, Updated edn, Penguin, Auckland; Snedden, Patrick 2005, *Pakeha and the Treaty: Why it's our treaty too*, Random House, Auckland.

[90] Brash, Nationhood, p. 5.

[91] Ibid., pp. 8, 13.

[92] Belgrave, Michael 2005, *Historical Frictions: Maori claims and reinvented histories*, Auckland University Press, Auckland, pp. 84, 85.

[93] Brash, Nationhood, p. 5.

[94] Ibid., p. 14.

[95] Ibid., p. 14.

[96] Johansson, 'Orewa and the rhetoric of illusion', p. 128; David Pearson, 'Citizenship, identity and belonging: addressing the mythologies of the unitary nation state in Aotearoa/New Zealand', in Liu et al., *New Zealand Identities*, pp. 21, 33; O'Sullivan, Dominic 2008, 'The Treaty of Waitangi in New Zealand politics', *Australian Journal of Political Science*, vol. 43, no. 2, p. 324.

[97] Vowles, J. 2005, 'New Zealand', *European Journal of Political Research*, vol. 44, nos 7–8, p. 1137; Durie, *Nga Tai Matatu*, pp. 223–4.

[98] John Key, interviewed by Simon Wilson, *Auckland Metro Live*, 22 January 2008, pp. 3–4, <www.grownups.co.nz/read/lifestyle/people/leaders-interview-john-key>

[99] Relationship and Confidence and Supply Agreement between the National Party and the Maori Party, 16 November 2008, pp. 1, 2, <www.parliament.nz/NR/rdonlyres/22CACF7A-2530-45E6-9569-518E53CF0056/94925/NationalMaori_Party_agreement20092.pdf>

[100] Stavenhagen, Rodolfo 2006, *Mission to New Zealand*, Report of the Special Rapporteur on the Situation of Human Rights and Fundamental Freedoms of Indigenous People, UN Doc E/CN.4/2006/78/Add.3, 10 March 2006, pp. 9, 12, <www.converge.org.nz/pma/srnzmarch06.pdf>

[101] 'UN report worthy of discussion', *New Zealand Herald*, 6 April 2006.

[102] Daes, Erica-Irene 2008, 'An overview of the history of Indigenous peoples: self-determination and the United Nations', *Cambridge Review of International Affairs*, vol. 21, no. 1, p. 22. Australia announced on 3 April 2009 that it now endorsed the Declaration on the Rights of Indigenous Peoples.

[103] Brändström et al., 'Governing by looking back', p. 208.

[104] Rudd, *CPD*, Representatives, 13 February 2008, p. 172.

[105] Dodson, Patrick 2008, 'After the apology', *Arena Magazine*, vol. 94, pp. 20–3; Calma, Tom 2009, 'Laying the foundations', *Koori Mail*, 11 March 2009.

[106] 't Hart, Paul 2008, *The Limits of Crisis Exploitation: The NT intervention as a reform boomerang*, p. 10, <http://polsc.anu.edu.au/staff/hart/pubs/NTinterventionARENAversionMarch08.pdf>, citing Walter, J. and Strangio, p. 2007, *No, Prime Minister: Reclaiming politics from leaders*, UNSW Press, Sydney.

[107] 't Hart, Paul 2007, 'Crisis exploitation: reflections on the "national emergency" in Australia's Northern Territory', *Dialogue*, vol. 26, no. 3, pp. 53–5. Langton ('Trapped', p. 158) accepts that 'there are critics with a genuine concern about the extent and implementation of the intervention'.

[108] Kevin Rudd, interview on *Q & A*, ABC TV, 22 May 2008, approximately 42 minutes into program. In October 2008, the Rudd Government rejected advice from its official Review Board report into the NT intervention, which had recommended an 'immediate change' of policy to conform with the *Racial Discrimination Act* (*Report of the Northern Territory Emergency Response Review Board*, Commonwealth of Australia, October 2008, p. 47, <www.nterreview.gov.au/docs/report_nter_review/default.htm>).

[109] Letter from Fatimata-Binta Victoire Dah, Chairperson, Committee for the Elimination of Racial Discrimination, to Australia's Ambassador in Geneva, 13 March 2009, annexed to a statement on 18 March 2009 by Les Malezer, <www.indigenousportal.com/index.php/News/-Australia-promises-to-end-racial-discrimination.html>

[110] Williams, George 2009, 'Rudd must act if race complaint upheld', *Sydney Morning Herald*, 10 February 2009.

[111] Durie, Mason 1994, *Whaiora: Maori health development*, Oxford University Press, Auckland, p. 87. For struggles in New Zealand, see Belgrave, Michael, Kawharu, Merata and Williams, David (eds) 2005, *Waitangi Revisited: Perspectives on the Treaty of Waitangi*, Oxford University Press, Auckland. For Australia, see Read, Peter, Meyers, Gary and Reece, Bob (eds), *What Good Condition? Reflections on an Australian Aboriginal treaty 1986–2006*, Aboriginal History Monograph 13, ANU E Press, Canberra.

3. Oblivious to the obvious? Australian asylum-seeker policies and the use of the past

Klaus Neumann

References to the past play a crucial role in the development of government policy. Those drafting a new policy often try to heed what they consider to be historical lessons. In order to construct such lessons, they might, for example, analyse the effectiveness of analogous previous policies. Contributors to public debates about government policy, be it within or outside the parliamentary arena, also regularly draw on the past in support or criticism of new initiatives. In discussions about new policies, however, relevant pasts tend to be invoked selectively. Occasionally, policy makers or contributors to public debate ignore historical policies and practices. Often they do so because they assume that the situation prompting the formulation of a new policy is unprecedented.

Two instances of a highly selective remembering of precedents and relevant historical contexts are the subject of this chapter. My first case concerns the development of an Australian Government response to the anticipated arrival of Vietnamese 'boat people' in 1975; here, I am particularly concerned with the selective use of the past by policy makers. In the second case—a debate about a bill designed to prevent asylum-seekers from engaging Australia's protection obligations—I am concerned mainly with the public use of the past by supporters and opponents of the proposed legislation.

In the first case, policy makers ignored what appeared to be highly relevant historical precedents in their deliberations. In the second case, contributors to public debate invoked histories that were blatantly inaccurate. It is tempting simply to identify and highlight such omissions and errors in order to draw attention to inadequacies in the process of policy formulation, and to the shortcomings of particular political debates. As satisfying as such an approach might be, however, it would add little to our understanding of the political process. In the following, I demonstrate that the analysis of apparent failures to draw on the past could contribute to a better understanding of the role of histories in policy making and historical debate.

'Boat people' (I)

On 6 May 1975, a week after the US military had evacuated some 7000 people from Saigon in the course of Operation Frequent Wind, an Australian newspaper ran the following headline on its front page: 'Fleeing Vietnamese ships may risk voyage to Australia.'[1] The article referred to the exodus of refugees from southern Vietnam. It reported that 5700 refugees had already arrived in Singapore, where 32 vessels carrying refugees could be counted in the harbour. The Singaporean authorities, however, while willing to provide food, water and medical aid, were adamant that the refugees had to move on. Other South-East Asian nations were equally reluctant to accommodate Vietnamese refugees, including those rescued in the South China Sea by cargo ships. As Singapore, Hong Kong and Thailand were trying to shut their doors to people fleeing Vietnam, other countries in the region became obvious potential destinations. According to the newspaper article, 'there were unconfirmed reports that a tanker with 200 refugees aboard was heading for Australia'. The story was picked up by the Opposition's foreign affairs spokesperson, Andrew Peacock, who echoed the concerns expressed in the article.[2] That same day, Australia's Foreign Minister, Don Willesee, wrote to Prime Minister, Gough Whitlam:

> I am concerned that the question of the Vietnamese refugees in Singapore and the 'spectre of an armada' sailing for Australia will now become the issue which will most attract public opinion and potentially present the greatest problems.[3]

A paper drafted by a Department of Foreign Affairs officer three days later painted a picture that was even more alarming than that depicted in the newspaper. According to information received by the department, one of the ships in Singapore Harbour, which was carrying 'several hundred Vietnamese', intended to proceed to Sydney, while another, with 287 refugees on board, was also headed for Australia. The officer reported that 'the Singaporean authorities have provided the refugee ships with water and charts for Australia', and concluded that 'it is only sensible to assume that some smaller craft will also make the attempt'.[4]

On 19 May 1975, the Department of Labour and Immigration convened an interdepartmental meeting 'to consider contingency planning in case sea craft carrying South Vietnamese…should arrive in Australian waters or make landfall on the Australian coast without approval'.[5] The meeting was attended by 20 representatives from the Departments of Labour and Immigration, Foreign Affairs, Prime Minister and Cabinet, Health, Police and Customs, Transport, Defence, Northern Territory, Social Security, and Housing and Construction. Its main outcome was the decision that the Departments of Labour and Immigration, Foreign Affairs and Prime Minister and Cabinet jointly draft a paper assessing the situation and exploring options available to the government should the anticipated arrival of Vietnamese refugees eventuate.

The authors of that paper noted Australia's international legal obligations under the UN Convention Relating to the Status of Refugees, the Agreement Relating to Refugee Seamen, the Convention for the Safety of Life at Sea, the Declaration on Territorial Asylum and Article 14 of the Universal Declaration of Human Rights ('Everyone has the right to seek and to enjoy in other countries asylum from persecution'). They also outlined two 'political considerations'—namely, that the arrival of a boat carrying Vietnamese refugees could not be kept a secret, and that

> [i]t must be expected that if the Australian Government allows people arriving in small boats to land and remain in Australia this would create a precedent which would not go unremarked by people in a number of countries to the north of Australia. Even if it did not lead to an influx of South Vietnamese it could have future implications in the event of internal political or economic crises developing in other countries to our north.[6]

The authors discussed two options: the refugees could be either prevented from landing in Australia (by stopping refugee boats entering Australian territorial waters or by preventing their passengers and crew from disembarking) or allowed to land. They counselled against the first option on account of Australia's international legal obligations and of the anticipated 'weight of public opinion' in favour of Vietnamese refugees, and pointed out that the second option entailed several possibilities: the refugees could be allowed to land without granting them entry permits, they could be issued with limited permits or they could be disembarked 'into custody' in order to be able to return them to their boat 'for the purpose of departing them from Australia'.[7] The paper did not explore to what extent any of these options was practicable and did not advocate a particular course of action.

On 2 April 1975, Prime Minister Whitlam had assumed responsibility for all issues concerning Vietnamese refugees. He had already overseen two controversial initiatives: the two so-called 'baby lifts' on 5 and 18 April, which brought 281 Vietnamese children, many of them orphans, to Australia, and the evacuation of the Australian Embassy on 25 April. Whitlam decided that should Vietnamese refugees reach Australia by sea, they would be disembarked 'into custody'. He added that the Australian authorities ought to ensure 'that the boat is not made deliberately unseaworthy so that any Operation Phoenix or like types can be returned to the boat before other passengers are permitted to remain'.[8]

The deliberations on 19 May and the paper prepared for Whitlam and the Ministers for Immigration and Foreign Affairs were informed by the assumption that

> despite Australia's previous involvement and experience in refugee matters it had never been faced with the present kind of situation where

> there existed the possibility, if not the probability, of the unauthorised
> arrival of an unknown number of refugees by surface vessel...

and that

> as the present problem is 'without precedent' it would be necessary for
> the Government in taking any decisions to give close attention to the
> possible consequences in relation to similar refugee situations which
> might arise in the future.[9]

How accurate was the assumption that there was no relevant historical precedent
and that it was not possible to draw any useful historical analogies? By taking
for granted that 'Australia's previous involvement and experience in refugee
matters' had no bearing on the response to refugees arriving by boat, members
of the interdepartmental working party drew a clear line between Australia's
traditional approach to refugees and an approach to be taken in the case of
'unauthorised arrivals'. By drawing this line, they also excluded two
contemporaneous issues from their discussions, which related to Australia's
previous involvement in refugee matters: Australia's response to Vietnamese
refugees in Vietnam and Australia's contribution to the debate about a proposed
UN convention on political asylum.

Australia's previous experience in refugee matters also extended to the
government's policy regarding the selection of refugees in Vietnam for
resettlement in Australia. Under the direction of Whitlam, who was reported to
have said that 'Vietnamese sob stories don't wring my withers',[10] the
government had formulated a miserly response to those who had aligned
themselves with the United States and its allies and who were desperate to leave
South Vietnam before the fall of Saigon and the surrender of the South Vietnamese
forces. By 30 April, only 78 Vietnamese refugees, excluding those who arrived
on the two baby lifts, had been brought to Australia. These included a group
of 34 nuns. Of the remainder, 40 were the spouses, children or fiancées of
Australian citizens or permanent residents. Another 350 people had been
approved for entry, but were unable to leave by the time the last Australian
officials left Vietnam.[11] When referring to public opinion sympathetic to
Vietnamese refugees, the authors of the briefing paper were clearly informed
by the debates of the previous six weeks, but they did not relate possible
responses to boat arrivals to the previous response to refugees seeking admission
to Australia from South Vietnam, Hong Kong or Singapore.

The Labor Government's response to refugees trying to leave Vietnam or being
stranded elsewhere in South-East Asia had been widely criticised; the Opposition
and sections of the media had argued that Australia could accommodate and
should accept more Vietnamese refugees. The Australian approach contrasted
starkly with that of the United States, which was taking in tens of thousands of

people who had fled, or had been evacuated from, South Vietnam. The Whitlam Government's policy was, however, in line with that taken by its counterpart in New Zealand, where the National Party opposition had in fact tried to use the Australian response to shame the government into allowing more Vietnamese into the country, even though the Labor Government in Canberra was hardly more generous than the Labour Government in Wellington.[12]

The second omission concerns the Australian position in negotiations about the wording of relevant international instruments. Since the 1950s, various UN forums had been devoted to the issue of a convention that would give substance to Article 14 of the Universal Declaration of Human Rights. Australia had played a prominent role in those discussions. In 1967, Australia voted with the majority in the UN General Assembly for a Declaration on Territorial Asylum—safe in the knowledge that it did not thereby commit itself to responding to asylum-seekers in any particular way. Discussions about a proposed Convention on Territorial Asylum intensified in the first half of the 1970s. In fact, the government considered its response to the proposed convention at about the same time as it formulated its response to the anticipated arrival of refugees by sea.[13] Representatives of the department centrally involved in the negotiations about the wording of the convention, the Attorney-General's Department, were not, however, invited to the meeting of 19 May.

In the version agreed to by Australia in 1954, the 1951 Refugee Convention applied only to people who had become refugees as a result of events happening in Europe before 1951. These temporal and geographical limitations were abolished by means of the 1967 Protocol to the 1951 Convention. Australia signed that protocol only in December 1973, less than 18 months before the meeting to draw up a contingency plan for the mass arrival of Vietnamese asylum-seekers. If Australia had not signed the protocol, it would have had no international legal obligations under the Refugee Convention to treat any Vietnamese 'unauthorised arrivals' other than as illegal immigrants.

Australia had good reasons not to sign the protocol until December 1973. They relate to the most intriguing absence from the discussions of 19 May 1975: the issue of Australia's previous response to asylum-seekers. Contrary to what those meeting that day assumed, the arrival of Vietnamese 'unauthorised arrivals' would not be unprecedented. Between 1963 and 1973, Australia had dealt with the unauthorised arrival of thousands of West Papuans who crossed into the Australian territory of Papua and New Guinea. Hundreds had been allowed to remain on temporary residence permits, while many others had been returned across the Indonesian border.[14]

In 1968, the Australian Government drew up detailed contingency plans because it feared that a large number of West Papuans would flee to Papua and New Guinea as a result of 'over-reaction by the Indonesian authorities' to nationalist demonstrations in West Papua planned for Indonesian Independence Day on 17 August.[15] Similar contingency plans were developed the next year because it was feared that the so-called Act of Free Choice—when a select few West Papuans were given the opportunity to vote on the incorporation of West Papua into Indonesia (which by then had long been a fait accompli)—would be accompanied by violence and an influx of up to 3000 refugees.[16] (None of these plans was ever activated because the number of refugees did not increase as dramatically as had been feared.)

On at least one occasion, West Papuan refugees had reached Australia itself: in 1969, a small group landed on one of the Torres Strait islands. They were threatened with deportation to Indonesia and persuaded to agree to their transfer to Papua and New Guinea to lodge applications for temporary residence permits in the Australian territory. These applications were later rejected and the applicants returned to Indonesia.[17]

West Papuans aside, Australia had had ample experience with people who sought Australia's protection *after* reaching Australia. They included, for example, diplomats, crew from Eastern European ships and sportspeople. Since 1956, Australia had a policy that guided its response to requests for asylum.[18] Since 1962, it had a similar policy with respect to asylum-seekers from the western half of New Guinea who sought Australia's protection in the Territory of Papua and New Guinea.[19]

Why did those meeting on 19 May refer neither to what appeared—not merely with the benefit of hindsight—to be highly relevant earlier developments nor to any precedents? Vietnamese selected in Saigon in April 1975 were refugees much like Hungarians selected in Austrian refugee camps in 1956 and 1957. They were admitted to Australia as immigrants and had to meet selection criteria that were akin to those in place for other immigrants. For Vietnamese refugees in April 1975, these criteria were particularly restrictive, whereas at the same time, the normal immigration selection criteria had been relaxed for other refugees, such as Chileans who had fled to neighbouring South American countries in the wake of the overthrow of the Allende Government.[20] Irrespective of that difference, however, the admission of both groups of refugees was meant to be the outcome of a selection process, the criteria of which were informed by Australia's broader immigration policy, rather than determined by a distinct refugee policy—one divorced from immigration policy. In fact, the Whitlam Government had been less inclined than its conservative predecessors to make special allowances for refugees wanting to settle in Australia. In July 1974, several voluntary agencies concerned with the resettlement of refugees had made a joint submission to the Minister for Labour and Immigration in which they noted 'with great concern...that during the last eighteen months or so the Government has very largely discarded the application of compassionate and humanitarian considerations to refugee and near-refugee cases'.[21]

Refugees selected for resettlement made up merely one of many categories of applicants selected overseas for immigration to Australia. Those arriving uninvited did not come in response to Australia's needs and would not go through a selection process that resembled that in place for ordinary immigrants; they were therefore not comparable with overseas applicants, including refugees, who wanted to migrate to Australia. The fact that the minutes of the meeting of 19 May refer to those selected offshore for resettlement and those thought to be on their way to Australia by boat as refugees easily obscures the fact that the former were not conceptualised in the same way as the latter.

The absence of references to the discussions about the UN Declaration on Territorial Asylum, and to the precise nature of Australia's international legal obligations, is likely to have been a result of the fact that the Attorney-General's Department was not invited to the interdepartmental meeting. International instruments seemed to matter mainly because, faced with the realistic prospect of scores of asylum-seekers reaching the country by boat, Australia wanted *to be seen* to abide by them—as long as they did not get in the way of Australia's prerogative to decide whether or not a non-citizen was allowed to enter the country.

In May 1975, Papua New Guinea's independence was still almost four months away. Papua New Guinea was, however, being eased towards nationhood. On 1 December 1973, the former Australian colony had become self-governing; few exceptions aside, the government of Michael Somare was in charge of the country's domestic affairs. The Office of the Administrator had been abolished and its previous incumbent had become Australia's first High Commissioner to Papua New Guinea. The government in Port Moresby, rather than that in Canberra, made decisions about the fate of West Papuans entering Papua New Guinea to seek its protection. Australians were now able to regard the issue of West Papuans seeking Australia's protection as a unique problem that belonged to an ostensibly closed chapter in Australia's history. Furthermore, by May 1975, Australian colonial rule in Papua New Guinea was already being treated as if it had been an episode of comparatively minor significance. Not only was the chapter considered closed even before Papua New Guinea became independent, it was already being omitted from the histories Australians remembered and told about their nation.

While the arrival of refugees on Australia's shores was not unprecedented, the manner in which those meeting on 19 May 1975 could deal with such an event certainly was. The government officials exploring various options would have been conscious of certain well-established procedures: since 1945, decisions about the admission to Australia of non-citizens were the prerogative of the

Department of Immigration and its minister; in cases in which prospective residents applied for political asylum, the Immigration Department liaised with the Department of Foreign Affairs. Both departments also sought advice from the Australian Security Intelligence Organisation (ASIO). In some instances, the two ministers would have to take a case to cabinet. Cabinet would usually make a decision on the basis of a submission prepared by the relevant department(s). In relation to Vietnamese refugees, however, such procedures were no longer followed. Nancy Viviani and Joanna Lawe-Davies concluded that 'Australian refugee policy in 1975 was Whitlam policy and his alone'[22] and that Whitlam's 'Cabinet and Caucus colleagues [and] the departments most concerned…played almost no role in policy-making, and there was little sense of continuity with previous policies and practices on refugees'.[23]

In April and May 1975, the Department of Labour and Immigration was involved in revising Australia's refugee policy. At the Labor Party's Terrigal conference in February 1975, the platform concerning immigration policy had been amended: a Labor government was now required to allow for '[s]ympathetic consideration of people who for political and other reasons would face danger to life and liberty upon return to their country of origin'.[24] Those involved in formulating the new policy, however, including the Minister for Immigration, Clyde Cameron, had to exclude from any revised formula Vietnamese and Cambodians, 'where decisions of acceptability have been made by the Prime Minister'.[25]

In 1975, the government officials discussing contingency plans for the arrival of Vietnamese asylum-seekers talked about an unprecedented situation. Their deliberations were, however, also indebted to a particular understanding of Australian history. The reference to the precedent 'which would not go unremarked by people in a number of countries to the north of Australia' was informed by long-held fears about Australia's vulnerability to being invaded by people living in countries to its north. While those attending the meeting of 19 May 1975 did not make any references to specific incidents in the past, their ideas were nevertheless informed by particular memories: in this case, memories of deep-seated anxieties about an Asian invasion. These anxieties had been partly responsible for the development of the White Australia Policy (including the notorious *Immigration Restriction Act 1901*) and for the fact that that policy had remained in place until 1973, and had continued to be a powerful force well beyond 1973. It is not surprising that when sizeable numbers of Vietnamese refugees did arrive from late 1976, the most prominent 'historical' references were to a human tide swamping Australia. Earlier instances in which Australia had to deal with asylum-seekers did not seem to be relevant because they had not been interpreted through the prism of that fear.

Whitlam's decision that any Vietnamese asylum-seekers were to be disembarked into custody was also informed by particular memories. Much like his Labour

Party counterpart in New Zealand, Bill Rowling, who was equally reluctant to commit his government to admitting a sizeable number of refugees from Vietnam,[26] Whitlam had opposed Australia's involvement in the Vietnam War and had been a critic of the American execution of that war. He assumed that at least some of those fleeing Vietnam had been the agents of highly dubious South Vietnamese and US policies (such as the notorious Operation Phoenix) and were now escaping retribution at the hands of the victors.

There was no debate—in Parliament or in the media—about the government's contingency plans of May 1975. The plans, and Whitlam's decision about what to do in the eventuality that a boat with Vietnamese refugees arrived in Australia, were never made public. There was, of course, public speculation about what Australia might do in such an eventuality. Such speculation was particularly rife in May 1975, after reports of the imminent departure of refugees for Australia (see above). Those engaged in such speculation were, however, unaware of the fact that the government carefully considered its options and decided on a policy.

By the time the first boat with Vietnamese refugees arrived, however, the policy that had been developed in May 1975 no longer applied. On 21 April 1976, in the course of the 1975–76 Senate inquiry into Australia's response to refugees from Vietnam, an Immigration Department official commented on the possibility of asylum-seekers arriving: 'We are well aware of the likelihood of future situations in which we may be the country of first asylum and are developing processes that will look after the situation of that kind in the future.' The development of such processes was apparently necessary because 'we do lack a policy for that sort of situation'.[27]

The official did not tell the committee that less than 12 months earlier, his department had been involved in the development of such a policy. Neither did he refer to events that demonstrated that the policy of May 1975 did not apply to asylum-seekers generally. In the second half of 1975, Australia had accommodated a substantial number of refugees arriving from East Timor by boat and using Australia as a country of first asylum without following the policy agreed to with respect to Vietnamese boat arrivals in May 1975. On 8 December 1975, another interdepartmental meeting involving officers from all departments represented at the meeting of 19 May 1975, as well as from Treasury, drew up contingency plans for the arrival of East Timorese refugees by boat. The December meeting considered the guidelines developed in May but found that they

> were not strictly relevant to the present situation, and the precedent which should be followed was that established in September of this year, when some hundreds of persons arrived in Darwin from Portuguese Timor and were permitted to land under temporary entry permits.[28]

55

The minutes of the December meeting do not spell out why the existing policy was no longer relevant. It seems safe to assume that the bureaucrats convening in December were aware that the policy developed in May represented Whitlam's personal views about Vietnamese refugees (rather than refugees generally), that these views were at odds with those held by other members of his government and that they were diametrically opposed to those of Malcolm Fraser, who had succeeded him as Prime Minister on 11 November 1975.

The immigration official appearing before the Senate inquiry in April 1976 was not referring to a specific scenario when he mentioned the likelihood of Australia being a country of first asylum. Given that the government was not aware of any particular group of refugees heading towards Australia at the time, it is unlikely that he had a specific scenario in mind. Only a week after he had given evidence, however, the event that had been anxiously anticipated in May 1975 finally eventuated. On 27 April 1976, the first boat carrying Vietnamese refugees arrived in Darwin. Its arrival came as a surprise, but caused barely a ripple at the time. As Viviani and Lawe-Davies write, '[T]hese first arrivals stirred no recollection of earlier anxieties'[29] —the government, the Immigration Department, journalists and members of the public seemed not to be concerned about the precedent that was set when the first five 'unauthorised arrivals' were allowed to land, were given temporary residence permits a day after their arrival and soon afterwards were granted permanent residence.[30] In fact, when the government identified the need for an extra customs patrol boat in northern Australian waters only a week after the arrival of the first Vietnamese 'boat people', it did so because it was concerned to combat drug smuggling rather than to detect vessels carrying refugees.[31]

'Boat people' (II)

In my second case, I am concerned not so much with the deliberations of policy makers as with the debates taking place after the policy in question has been announced and with what this indicates about the uses of history in political debate. In May 2006, the Liberal-National Coalition Government introduced the Migration Amendment (Designated Unauthorised Arrivals) Bill into Parliament.[32] If passed, it would have excised the Australian coastline from the migration zone and thereby prevented asylum-seekers who had reached the mainland by boat from engaging Australia's protection obligations and having their request for a protection visa heard in Australia. Instead, their applications for a visa would have been processed offshore, in Nauru or Papua New Guinea, in the same way in which the applications of asylum-seekers who had reached Australian islands excised from the migration zone in the wake of the Tampa crisis had been processed offshore. The bill was drafted in response to vociferous Indonesian protests against the granting of protection visas to a small group of West Papuan refugees who had landed on the Queensland coast in January 2006; ostensibly it was to rectify the alleged anomaly that asylum-seekers were treated differently depending on whether or not they had been able to reach the mainland.

When the government introduced the proposed legislation, it assumed that it would be passed much like most other amendments to the *Migration Act* since 1999, the more so as the government commanded a majority in both houses of Parliament. In the end, however, the government withdrew the legislation before it could be debated in the Senate because it looked certain to be defeated with the help of two members of the Coalition and a minor party senator who usually voted with the Coalition.[33] The proposed legislation was, however, debated at length in the House of Representatives. That debate, on 9 and 10 August 2006, ranks as one of the most memorable parliamentary events during John Howard's 11-year reign as prime minister because of the impassioned speeches delivered by four Liberal MPs who condemned the government's bill, and because for once the Labor opposition rejected outright a measure purportedly designed to protect Australia's borders.

In the four-month public debate over the bill,[34] the past loomed large. The *specific* historical contexts, however, for the introduction of legislation designed to extend the reach of the extraterritorial processing regime for asylum-seekers *and* to keep West Papuan asylum-seekers out of Australia barely featured. Australians following the debate and relying on a combination of respectable print and electronic media were likely to assume that the 43 West Papuans who arrived in early 2006 were the first West Papuan asylum-seekers Australia had to deal with, and the first Indonesian nationals who were allowed to remain in Australia because they could convincingly claim that they would be persecuted on their return to Indonesia.

The fact that West Papuan refugees had sought Australia's protection since 1962, the fact that for many years Australia had tried to avoid granting protection visas to East Timorese refugees (while nevertheless permitting them to remain in Australia on temporary visas) in the interest of its relationship with Indonesia[35] and the fact that small numbers of Indonesian nationals had been granted protection or humanitarian visas under Immigration Minister, Philip Ruddock, and his successor, Amanda Vanstone, were all but omitted from the debate.

The fact that Australia had not signed the 1967 protocol, which made the provisions of the 1951 Convention universal, until after Papua New Guinea became self-governing in December 1973, was also not mentioned. The informed public could have been forgiven for assuming that Australia had been constrained by its international legal obligations with regard to asylum-seekers since the establishment of the Office of the UN High Commissioner for Refugees and the drafting of the 1951 Refugee Convention.

My intention here is not to comprehensively analyse the controversy over the 2006 migration amendment bill. Rather, I focus on the debate in Parliament, which in many ways was both the apex and the conclusion of the larger public debate. References to the past featured prominently in the nine-and-a-half hour exchange in the House of Representatives, during which 31 members made a contribution. Not surprisingly, most historical references were to the application of laws introduced since 2001 to underpin the government's 'Pacific Solution', as the proposed legislation would have extended the application of that policy. There were, however, only two references to the widely held fear (if not to say hysteria) that had allowed the government to introduce the Pacific Solution in the first place, and then to benefit from its introduction at the 2001 federal election.[36] Another obvious history that was frequently invoked was that of legislation introduced—with bipartisan support and on the instigation of several Liberal backbenchers—in 2005 to exempt children from Australia's policy of mandatory detention for unauthorised boat arrivals.[37] One other relevant piece of legislation was explicitly referred to: the introduction of mandatory detention by the Labor Government in 1992.[38]

Only two mentions were made of previous instances when refugees arrived by boat in Australia. Renegade Liberal backbencher Petro Georgiou began his speech with such a reference: 'Thirty years ago, after a long and hazardous journey, a small group of Vietnamese refugees landed on a remote beach in Northern Australia.'[39] Labor's Jill Hall recounted a potted history of Australian responses to refugees, starting with the convicts ('The first people of English descent who came to Australia were refugees from the prison system in the UK'), and also mentioning '95,000 Vietnamese refugees' accommodated between 1975 and 1985 at 'a time when people came in boats to Australia and Australia recognised their needs, embraced them and took them into our society'.[40] Hall did not clarify that of those 95 000, only about 2 per cent actually came to Australia by boat. In 1996, Viviani commented on this issue:

> Even though this historic period of upheaval in Southeast Asia and its effects are within living memory of most Australians, it is extraordinary how the interpretations of this experience have diverged from the clear facts…[T]he fact that just over 2000 boat people arrived on the northern shores of Australia from 1976 to 1989 has been wildly distorted in the media on every occasion that a boat arrives.[41]

Only Labor's Duncan Kerr drew attention to the fact that West Papuans had been fleeing their country since Indonesia assumed control of it (although he did not say when that had happened).[42] He also mentioned that many fled to Papua New Guinea (but he did not mention that this also occurred when Papua New Guinea was under Australian control, that the Australian Government's response was informed by its desire to appease Indonesia and that Australian officials routinely sent refugees back to Indonesia). Kerr's discussion of the historical context took up no more than 10 minutes (or about 2.5 per cent of the parliamentary debate).

Other members briefly referred to the 1951 Refugee Convention. None mentioned that until 1973 that convention had been, strictly speaking, irrelevant for Australia's response to West Papuan asylum-seekers. Labor's Chris Bowen said:

> In 1951 the United Nations convention for the protection of refugees came into force. The world realised the mistakes of the 1930s, when many Western nations turned their backs on Jews fleeing persecution in Germany. Collectively, we said, 'Never again.'[43]

Bowen was wrong about the date. He was also mistaken about why and how the convention had been drafted. And who was included in his first-person plural? Those who said 'never again' in 1949 or 1951 were a minority—in the context of global politics and in the context of Australian politics.[44]

While the speeches by Hall, Kerr and Bowen are easy targets for historically informed criticism, they nevertheless stand out on account of the interest the three Labor MPs showed in the broader historical context of the proposed legislation. In public debates about asylum-seeker policy, statements that make comparatively specific reference to historical detail have been the exception. Besides, the speeches were marginal: they were not quoted in major newspapers or on the evening news.

Unspecific references to traditional Australian generosity and hospitality were far more central to the debate itself and to how it was reported than references to relevant historical contexts and precedents. 'Can I say that Australia's generosity towards refugees is outstanding,' the Liberal Party's Don Randall said, adding elsewhere the hyperbolic statement, 'Australia is incredibly overgenerous.'[45] Other Coalition members repeatedly referred to Australia's record on resettling refugees, of which 'we' could be proud.[46] In the debate's closing speech, Andrew Robb, the Parliamentary Secretary to the Minister for Immigration and Multicultural Affairs, noted Australia's 'very proud record over 55 years'.[47]

Those opposed to the legislation also talked about Australia's traditional generosity, only to claim that this 'proud record' would be undermined by the proposed legislation. Labor's Ann Corcoran said: 'I am embarrassed and ashamed to see our once proud reputation for upholding principles of human rights further sullied by this amoral government.'[48] Jill Hall also thought that 'Australia's history in relation to refugees has been somewhat sullied over the last few years'.[49] Their party colleague Carmen Lawrence accused the Prime Minister of 'having trashed Australian standards of compassion and decency'.[50] Georgiou made a similar point:

> The ancient and universal tradition of providing sanctuary to those in danger is part of our refugee regime in Australia today, and it is demonstrated by the community at large when Australians respond generously to the suffering of others, both at home and abroad. The [bill] does not reflect this tradition. It does not uphold the deeply held Australian values of giving people a fair go, and of decency and compassion.[51]

Bruce Baird, another Liberal dissident, claimed that an Australia preventing West Papuan refugees from applying for a protection visa 'is not the Australia that we know and respect. Australia is a generous nation. It is one that has shown enormous compassion to people in need and on an ongoing basis.'[52]

Australia's current Prime Minister, Kevin Rudd, considers compassion to be one of five values 'which might underpin a vision for the nation's future'.[53] His rhetoric about compassion as an essential value in Australia's past and for Australia's future is similar to that of two of his most recent predecessors, former Labor leader Mark Latham and former Prime Minister John Howard.[54] The latter employed references to Australia's and Australians' compassion also to reject criticism of his government's policies—in particular, its asylum-seeker policies. In late August 2001, while the *Tampa* was drifting in waters near Christmas Island, Howard told Fran Kelly of ABC TV's *7.30 Report*: 'We are a decent generous, compassionate humanitarian country, but we also have an absolute right to decide who comes to this country.'[55]

Howard used the attributes 'decent', 'generous' and 'compassionate' to describe an Australia past and present. He and other members of his government were always ready to provide evidence of Australia's generosity, such as the fact that, in relation to its population, Australia had resettled more refugees since the end of World War II than any other nation except Israel.

The assertion that Australia and Australians have *traditionally* been generous and compassionate has become something of a background chorus accompanying debates about public policy, particularly in the area of immigration and refugee policy. The level of that noise increases if Australia is condemned in international forums, be it in relation to the government's Aboriginal policies or in relation to its asylum-seeker policies, almost as if repeated appeals to Australia's and Australians' intrinsic generosity can drown out such criticism. The noise itself, however, is not triggered by external criticism. This chorus needs to be seen in the context of the rhetoric about aspiration, about the desirability of living in a shareholder society and about citizens' responsibility to help themselves before society comes to their assistance. Australians want to be reassured that, after all (and contrary to much available evidence), they are *by nature* a decent, generous, compassionate and hospitable people. The chorus is also related to the notion that compassion is accorded to people who deserve it, rather than that human beings are entitled to respect and assistance.

Conclusion

It is important to draw attention to relevant histories that are ignored. That is particularly true for narratives about specific historical responsibilities—towards South Vietnamese refugees or towards West Papuans, for example. It would be a mistake, however, to leave it at that, because any triumphant finger-pointing could easily get in the way of an exploration of why certain narratives do not have sufficient currency and how policy makers and others contributing to public debate really use the past; to claim that the debate about asylum-seeker policies has been marked by the absence of informed references to the past is not to say that it has been devoid of any historical connotations.

It is tempting to think of the past as a repository open for inspection. According to such an understanding, those failing to draw on the past simply do not inspect the repository available to them. It is not so much the past that policy makers draw on, however, as histories and memories. It is not the past itself that is available to them, but a limited number of accounts of that past. The question to ask is not only why did the officials pondering the imminent arrival of Vietnamese 'boat people' ignore relevant historical precedents and other relevant previous instances of policy making, but why don't Australian social memories of Australia's response to refugees feature the arrivals of West Papuan asylum-seekers in the Australian territory of Papua and New Guinea, and why do Australian refugee policies tend to be remembered as continuations of or deviations from a long-established tradition of compassionate and generous approaches to refugees?

References to relevant historical precedents did not inform the discussions in 1975 about what to do if Vietnamese refugees were to seek asylum in Australia, or the debate in 2006 about the merits of the government's response to the arrival of 43 West Papuan asylum-seekers. Those formulating policy in 1975, however, and those debating policy in 2006 relied on their particular understanding of Australia's past. In 1975, policy makers were concerned not to set a precedent that would realise historical fears of an invasion by 'people in a number of countries to the north of Australia'. They did not attempt to draw on the past to identify the best policy solution; rather, the past 'encroached' on them.[56] In 2006, many of those debating the proposed legislation invoked the image of a traditionally compassionate Australia—again, not in order to identify the best possible policy solution but as a spontaneous response to anxieties about Australians' apparent tendency to be self-interested.

Leaving aside the threat of a Japanese attack during World War II, fears of an Asian invasion have been as unjustified as the idea that Australia has a better humanitarian record and is more compassionate than other comparable nations. That does not make those fears, and ideas about compassion as a quintessentially Australian value, less real; it demonstrates that those formulating and debating public policy do not look back at the past, but draw on histories and memories of that past.

Acknowledgments

This chapter was written in response to an invitation to present at the Governing by Looking Back conference in December 2007 at The Australian National University. I thank Tim Rowse and Paul 't Hart for inviting me to the conference, and Gwenda Tavan for her helpful comments on an earlier version of the paper.

Endnotes

[1] Terry, Peter 1975, 'Fleeing South Vietnamese ships may risk voyage to Australia: federal govt takes tough stand on uninvited refugees', *Australian*, 6 May 1975.

[2] Viviani, Nancy 1980, *Australian Government Policy on the Entry of Vietnamese Refugees in 1975*, Centre for the Study of Australian–Asian Relations, Griffith University, Brisbane, pp. 14, 21 n. 71.

[3] Willesee to Prime Minister, 6 May 1975, National Archives of Australia [hereafter NAA], A1209, 1975/1156.

[4] Vietnamese refugees in Singapore, Draft, n.d., attachment to K. H. Rogers to Gilchrist and others, 9 May 1975, NAA, A1838, 1634/70/2 part 1.

[5] D. McElligott and R. Tynan to Prime Minister, 20 May 1975, NAA, A1209, 1975/1333.

[6] Contingency planning: unauthorised arrival of Vietnamese, n.d. [20 May 1975], NAA, A1209, 1975/1333.

[7] Ibid.

[8] Quoted in K. H. Rogers to Feakes, 3 July 1975, NAA, A1838, 1634/70/2 part 3.

[9] Department of Labour and Immigration, Summary of discussions at interdepartmental working party meeting, Canberra, 19 May 1975, n.d. [ca 26 May 1975], NAA, A1209, 1975/1157, p. 4.

[10] Quoted in Viviani, *Australian Government Policy on the Entry of Vietnamese Refugees in 1975*, p. 11.

[11] Foreign Affairs to all posts, 6 May 1975, NAA, A1209, 1975/1144. See also Community Affairs Branch, Vietnamese refugees, 13 August 1975, NAA, A1209, 1976/242 part 1. Some of those approved for immigration to Australia were subsequently evacuated by the US military.

[12] *New Zealand Parliamentary Debates* [hereafter *NZPD*], vol. 396, 3 April 1974, p. 170; *NZPD*, vol. 396, 11 April 1975, p. 411. By 3 September 1975, New Zealand had admitted a mere 99 Vietnamese (*NZPD*, vol. 401, 3 September 1975, p. 4091).

[13] See correspondence in NAA, A1838, 938/43 part 2.

[14] Neumann, Klaus 2004, *Refuge Australia: Australia's humanitarian record*, UNSW Press, Sydney, ch. 5.

[15] D. O. Hay to Secretary, Department of External Territories, 28 June 1968, NAA, A452, 1968/2812. The part of Indonesia commonly known as West Papua was then called West Irian.

[16] Department of the Administrator, Border contingency plan, 3 June 1969, NAA, A1838, TS689/2/1.

[17] Neumann, Klaus 2007, 'Been there, done that?', in Dean Lusher and Nick Haslam (eds), *Yearning to Breathe Free: Seeking asylum in Australia*, Federation Press, Annandale, pp. 21–34.

[18] Cabinet decision no. 487, 16 October 1956, NAA, A4926, 398. See also Neumann, *Refuge Australia*, ch. 4.

[19] Cabinet decision no. 375, 6 August 1962, NAA, A5819, vol. 8/agendum 330.

[20] Peter Wilenski, Draft submission to Minister, May 1975, NAA, A446, 1974/77554.

[21] Australian Council of Churches (Resettlement Department) and others to C. R. Cameron, 31 July 1974, NAA, A446, 1974/95371.

[22] Viviani, Nancy and Lawe-Davies, Joanna 1980, *Australian Government Policy on the Entry of Vietnamese Refugees 1976 to 1978*, Centre for the Study of Australian–Asian Relations, Griffith University, Brisbane, p. 1.

[23] Viviani, *Australian Government Policy on the Entry of Vietnamese Refugees in 1975*, p. 15.

[24] Quoted in Dempsey to Minister, 2 April 1975, NAA, A446, 1974/77554.

[25] R. U. Metcalfe to Minister, 4 July 1975, NAA, A446, 1974/77554.

[26] Rabel, Roberto 2005, *New Zealand and the Vietnam War: Politics and diplomacy*, Auckland University Press, Auckland, ch. 13; Gallienne, Robin 1991, *The Whole Thing Was Orchestrated: New Zealand's response to the Indo-Chinese refugees exodus 1975–1985*, Centre for Asian Studies, University of Auckland, Auckland, ch. 3.

[27] John Selwyn Dempsey in Commonwealth of Australia 1976, *Standing Committee on Foreign Affairs and Defence (Reference: South Vietnamese Refugees)*, Senate, Government Printer, Canberra, vol. 2, pp. 858, 881.

[28] K. H. Rogers to Minister, 10 December 1975, NAA, A1838, 1634/69/2 part 2.

[29] Viviani and Lawe-Davies, *Australian Government Policy on the Entry of Vietnamese Refugees 1976 to 1978*, p. 4.

[30] In the most prominent press report, in Darwin's *Northern Territory News* ('Vietnamese refugees can stay', 28 April 1976), no mention was made of concerns about further boat arrivals; Australia's major newspapers either did not report the arrival or mentioned it in only a brief note.

[31] 'Extra patrol boat in north to combat drug smuggling', *Northern Territory News*, 4 May 1976.

[32] Harris Rimmer, Sue 2006, 'Migration Amendment (Designated Unauthorised Arrivals) Bill', *Bills Digest*, Parliamentary Library, 138 (22 May 2006), <http://parlinfo.aph.gov.au/parlInfo/search/display/display.w3p;query=BillId_Phrase%3Ar2559%20Dataset%3Abillsdgs;rec=0>

[33] National Party Senator Barnaby Joyce, Liberal Party Senator Judith Troeth and Family First Senator Steve Fielding.

[34] The debate lasted from when the bill was first foreshadowed by Immigration Minister Vanstone on 13 April 2006 until its withdrawal by the Prime Minister on 14 August 2006. Vanstone, Amanda 2006, Strengthen border control measures for unauthorised boat arrivals, Media release, 13 April 2006, <http://pandora.nla.gov.au/pan/32192/20060606-0000/sievx.com/articles/westpapua/20060413AmandaVanstone.html>; Howard, John 2006, Transcript of press conference, Parliament House, Canberra, 14 August 2006, <http://pandora.nla.gov.au/pan/10052/20060921-0000/www.pm.gov.au/news/interviews/Interview2073.html>

[35] Piotrowicz, Ryszard 1996, 'Refugee status and multiple nationality in the Indonesian archipelago: is there a Timor gap?', *International Journal of Refugee Law*, vol. 8, no. 3, pp. 319–46; Mathew, Penelope 1999, 'Lest we forget: Australia's policy on East Timorese asylum seekers', *International Journal of Refugee Law*, vol. 11, no. 1, pp. 7–59.

[36] Sharon Grierson from the Labor Party claimed that 'this legislation is just a continuation of that same inflammatory hysteria' (witnessed during the Tampa affair) (*CPD*, Representatives, vol. 283, 9 August 2006, p. 137). Labor's Bob McMullan also suggested that the legislation was 'part of a long history in Australia of the easy appeal to fear' (*CPD*, Representatives, vol. 283, 10 August 2006, p. 8).

[37] *Migration Amendment (Detention Arrangements) Act 2005*.

[38] Don Randall, *CPD*, Representatives, vol. 283, 9 August 2006, p. 25.

[39] *CPD*, Representatives, vol. 283, 9 August 2006, p. 40.

[40] *CPD*, Representatives, vol. 283, 10 August 2006, p. 39.

[41] Viviani, Nancy 1996, *The Indochinese in Australia, 1975–1995: From burnt boats to barbecues*, Oxford University Press, Melbourne, pp. 10–11.

[42] *CPD*, Representatives, vol. 283, 9 August 2006, pp. 119–20. Kerr's office had produced a substantial background paper on the issue of West Papuan asylum-seekers (Sophia Rihani, Human rights abuse in Papua: implications for Australian foreign policy [15 May 2006]).

[43] *CPD*, Representatives, vol. 283, 10 August 2006, p. 15.

[44] Labor's Shadow Minister for Immigration, Tony Burke, made a similar statement when he claimed that the 1951 convention 'was put in place because Jewish people fled Germany and no country would take them. The rest of the world swore they would never let this happen again.' *CPD*, Representatives, vol. 283, 9 August 2006, p. 20. Labor's Anthony Albanese argued in a similar vein: 'Why was the refugee convention developed by the United Nations in the post-World War II period? It was because

of the experience of Jewish citizens fleeing Nazi Germany and the other fascist persecutors in Europe. These Jewish refugees were *pushed back offshore in their boats*, in many cases sent back to their deaths. The world said: "Never again."' *CPD*, Representatives, vol. 283, 10 August 2006, p. 35; emphasis added.

[45] *CPD*, Representatives, vol. 283, 9 August 2006, pp. 27, 29. Similarly, Andrew Robb claimed: 'As a country, we are strong and fair on these matters and generous to a fault.' *CPD*, Representatives, vol. 283, 10 August 2006, p. 44.

[46] For example, the Liberal Party's Peter Slipper (*CPD*, Representatives, vol. 283, 9 August 2006, p. 117) and the Liberal Party's Alan Cadman (*CPD*, Representatives, vol. 283, 10 August 2006, p. 11).

[47] *CPD*, Representatives, vol. 283, 10 August 2006, p. 39.

[48] Ann Corcoran, *CPD*, Representatives, vol. 283, 9 August 2006, p. 40. Similarly, Labor's Maria Vamvakinou expressed her fear that Australia's reputation would be compromised (*CPD*, Representatives, vol. 283, 9 August 2006, p. 114). Labor's Sharon Grierson said that the Australian nation 'is capable of generosity, compassion, integrity and international leadership' (*CPD*, Representatives, vol. 283, 9 August 2006, p. 140).

[49] *CPD*, Representatives, vol. 283, 10 August 2006, p. 39.

[50] *CPD*, Representatives, vol. 283, 9 August 2006, p. 129.

[51] Ibid., p. 44.

[52] Ibid., p. 126.

[53] *CPD*, Representatives, vol. 271, 30 May 2005, p. 86. Rudd's other values are security, competition, fairness and sustainability. In his first speech as Leader of the Opposition, he nominated six values: liberty, security, opportunity, equity, sustainability and compassion (*CPD*, Representatives, vol. 287, 5 December 2006, p. 41).

[54] Mark Latham cited four Australian values: work, reward for effort, aspiration and compassion (*CPD*, Representatives, vol. 259, 4 December 2003, p. 23857). 'This is a free, stable, prosperous and compassionate nation,' Howard said—for example, in his New Year message at the end of 2002 (Howard, John 2002, Media release, 31 December 2002, <http://pandora.nla.gov.au/pan/10052/20080108-1314/livetest.pm.gov.au/media/Release/2002/media_release2055.html>).

[55] Howard, John 2001, Transcript of television interview with Fran Kelly, *7:30 Report*, ABC TV, 27 August 2001, <http://pandora.nla.gov.au/pan/10052/20080108-1314/livetest.pm.gov.au/media/Interview/2001/interview1188.html>

[56] Brändström, Annika, Bynander, Fredrik and 't Hart, Paul 2004, 'Governing by looking back: historical analogies and crisis management', *Public Administration*, vol. 82, no. 1, p. 194.

4. 'A modern-day concentration camp': using history to make sense of Australian immigration detention centres

Amy Nethery

In a letter to the *Illawarra Mercury* published on 15 July 2003, the Federal Member for Cunningham, Michael Organ (Greens), wrote of his visit to the Villawood detention centre: 'The overall impression was one of a modern day concentration camp—razor wire, mud, sad faces, and shame.'[1] Our understanding of contemporary events is shaped, in part, by how we position them within history. Particularly in times of crisis, the connections we make between the present and the past can help us to make sense of contemporary events. Such a process reveals a hidden logic in events that otherwise seem inexplicable, unfair or unjust. By retrospectively judging the historical actors, we create a template for how we should act in the current circumstance. By focusing on some aspects and not others to make the historical precedent 'fit', we can, however, arrive at a limited understanding of the present.

The policy and practice of immigration detention have been among the most controversial aspects of Australia's immigration policies and border protection strategies. Between 2000 and 2005, public concern about detention centres was at its height. During this time, the number of detainees, the length of their detention and the harsh conditions they endured peaked. Resistance from detainees against their continued confinement raised public awareness of their situation and initiated public debate about Australia's treatment of asylum-seekers.

Many of those contributing to the public discussion about detention centres established a connection between this contemporary Australian policy and German concentration camps. Organ saw parallels between the conditions of detention centres and concentration camps, and the destitution of those incarcerated within both institutions. For him, this particular historical precedent provided a means to make sense of immigration detention policy.

The comparison of concentration camps with detention centres allowed contributors to public debate to articulate their opposition to government policy by tapping into a body of shared knowledge. The focus on this comparison, however, effectively prevented recognition of the many institutional predecessors to detention centres in Australia. Ultimately, positioning immigration detention centres in an Australian historical context can facilitate a far more comprehensive understanding of administrative detention in Australia and its contemporary form.

In this chapter, I examine the discourse that links detention centres with concentration camps. Specifically, I analyse letters that appeared in the mainstream print media to demonstrate the different ways in which this discursive shortcut facilitated public discussion. I then argue for an understanding of detention centres that positions them firmly within Australia's history. Aboriginal reserves, quarantine stations and enemy-alien internment camps were institutional predecessors. While they were implemented at different times and targeted different categories of people, there were striking similarities between these carceral practices. An analysis of these practices—who was incarcerated, for what purpose and to what effect—reveals a continuity between the different forms of incarceration and facilitates a more informed understanding of the function of immigration detention in contemporary Australia.

The policy and practice of immigration detention

Between November 1989 and 1995, about 2000 Cambodian and Chinese asylum-seekers arrived in Australia by boat. The arrival of the Cambodians, in particular, embarrassed the Hawke Labor Government, which had recently played a leading role in negotiating a UN peace agreement for Cambodia, because it undermined the government's claims that the peace process had been successful.[2] In 1989, the government requisitioned disused single-men's quarters from a mining company in Port Hedland (Western Australia) and turned them into the first of a new generation of immigration detention centres—ostensibly to prevent asylum-seekers from absconding, but also to limit their access to lawyers and the media. Three years later, the Keating Labor Government introduced the policy of mandatory detention into the *Migration Act 1958*. It provides that every asylum-seeker who arrives in Australia without a valid entry visa is detained until their application for a protection visa has been processed.

Although, after 1989, immigration detention centres were initially intended for asylum-seekers, they are presently used for two categories of non-citizens. Those who arrive in Australia without a valid entry visa make up the first category. They include asylum-seekers who are detained while the Department of Immigration processes their application for refugee status. If that application is successful, they are released into the community. If their application (and any subsequent appeal) is unsuccessful, they are removed from Australia (see Chapter 1). Generally, only asylum-seekers who reach Australia by boat arrive without a valid entry visa and are therefore subject to the policy of mandatory detention. Checks at international and Australian airports mean that asylum-seekers travelling to Australia by plane usually come with a valid visa, such as a tourist, business or student visa, and seek asylum once they have entered the country. People who arrive in this way are able to live in the community for the duration of their application process. This first category of detainees also includes foreign fishermen arrested in Australian territorial waters. These people, usually young men from Indonesia or other South-East Asian countries, are held in immigration detention until they are removed from Australia or charged with an offence and transferred to the judicial prison system.

The second category of detainees comprises non-citizens who initially entered the country on a valid visa. They include, first, people who have stayed beyond the length of their visa or have been found to be working without the necessary visa, and second, people to be removed on 'character grounds'. This latter category includes permanent residents who have been convicted of a crime and sentenced to prison for more than one year, thus breaching the conditions of their visa. These people are detained until they can be deported (see also Chapter 1).

Five immigration detention centres are currently in operation. Maribyrnong (Melbourne), Villawood (Sydney), Perth and Northern (Darwin) are on the mainland and are used to accommodate Indonesian fishermen and people awaiting deportation. The fifth centre, on Christmas Island, opened in December 2008. Used to accommodate onshore asylum-seekers, it is the largest and most secure centre, with the capacity to hold 800 people. In addition, there are three immigration transit accommodation centres at airports in Sydney, Melbourne and Brisbane. Other centres, including Port Hedland, Curtin, Baxter, Woomera and the original facility at Christmas Island, have been either closed or mothballed. In 2005, the *Migration Act* was amended to ensure that children were not accommodated in detention centres,[3] and a number of immigration residential housing and community detention options were established to accommodate children and their parents. In addition, some non-immigration facilities are used for immigration detention, including prisons, hospitals and psychiatric institutions.

Three key aspects of immigration detention have been subject to public criticism: the potential for unlimited incarceration, the detention of children and the harmful effects of detention. In 1994, the reference to a time limit of 273 days, or nine months, was removed from the *Migration Act*, so that there were now no legal impediments to indefinite detention. In fact, in August 2004, the High Court found that detainees could be confined indefinitely if they could not be removed from the country and could not be granted an entry visa. Since 2005, the Commonwealth Ombudsman has had the power to review all cases in which individuals have been detained for two years or more, but not the power to order their release. So far, the longest period that someone has been detained is seven years. The Human Rights and Equal Opportunities Commission report

A Last Resort? found that, as at December 2003, the average length of detention for a child was one year, eight months and 11 days.[4] The longest-serving child detainee was released in 2004 after five years, five months and 20 days in detention.

There is no space here to comprehensively discuss the conditions in the camps.[5] It appears to be conclusive, however, that conditions in detention centres and the often undetermined length of confinement can cause psychological and physical damage to detainees.[6] These problems stem from confinement within razor wire or electric fences; the remote location of some of the centres; constant surveillance, including roll calls at night; insufficient showering, toileting and cooking facilities; lack of adequate access to mental and physical health care, education and legal services; and insufficient communications technology. In addition, there are many examples of inhumane treatment of detainees by staff, and the lack of protection of detainees from abuse by staff and other detainees. Staff also have the power to punish detainees. Such punishments can include the removal of basic rights and the imposition of solitary confinement. Until 2005, no distinction was made between the treatment of adults and children. Psychiatrist Fiona Hawker, who treated a number of detainees from the Baxter detention centre, argued that the symptoms of mental illness were so similar in each patient that they must have been caused by the environment, and she called these symptoms 'Baxter Syndrome'.[7]

In the late 1990s, protests, riots and acts of self-harm within the centres brought the issue of detention to the attention of the media and the Australian public. Public concern heightened in the early 2000s as increasing numbers of asylum-seekers, including children, from the Middle East pushed the number of people in detention above the capacity of the centres, further compromising the conditions. At the same time, the Howard Coalition Government's increasingly punitive policies and language towards asylum-seekers gained a lot of support within the community. Within this climate, public discourse about detention centres reflected the heightened emotion aroused by Australia's asylum-seeker policies.

Using history to make sense of immigration detention centres

According to Brändström et al., in times of crisis, decision makers have to act quickly, often with little information about the current event and without informed projections of the consequences of their decision. They argue that, to overcome these limitations, decision makers rely on 'shortcuts' drawn from references to the past:

> Among these shortcuts are a resort to personal experience, educated guesses by key associates and advisors, readily available precedents

embedded in institutional memory and official contingency planning…and storylines developed in mass media accounts of the events. All of these mechanisms make reference to the past, whether the personal or the shared, the recent or the distant, the community's own or some other people's past.[8]

While their analysis focuses on decision makers, Brändström et al.'s insights are equally useful in analysing the use of the past to make sense of current events in wider community discourse. The shortcuts used in public debate facilitate the creation of a sense of meaning about a sometimes inexplicable issue. They are, according to the authors, often emotional rather than cognitive connections. In addition, the shortcuts provide a guide for how, or how not, to respond to the crisis at hand.

This chapter argues that, in the early 2000s, concentration camps became a shortcut within the public discourse about detention centres. In an analysis of newspaper and magazine articles and letters to the editor in mainstream print media between 2000 and 2007, I identified 168 articles and letters in which immigration detention centres were compared with concentration camps. In some news articles, the authors made the connection directly, either by drawing parallels or by simply referring to detention centres as concentration camps. Other news articles reported on individuals making the connection, including Members of Parliament, a former Federal Court judge, the head of the Australian Council of Trade Unions, lawyers, church leaders, local councillors and former detention centre staff.[9] In addition, the comparison often appeared in other forms of mainstream and alternative media.

Here I focus on the comparison between the two forms of incarceration in letters to the editor. These are interesting because they are often emotive and illustrate the energy of the public discussion at the time. They also reveal how this particular shortcut was used in different ways to support a number of arguments and viewpoints.

In some letters, the link is straightforward. Alan Donald wrote to the *Northern Territory News* that '[a] detention centre by any other euphemism still smells like a concentration camp'.[10] The shortcut was also used to describe the conditions within detention. Otto DeVries wrote to the *Hobart Mercury*:

> For the first time in my life I am ashamed to be an Australian. I became ashamed after I was made aware that the Woomera detention centre was actually a concentration camp, complete with three layers of security; razor wire, barbed wire and steel palisade fencing, with Australian protective services officers patrolling the perimeter. The conditions of the camp are atrocious. The illegal immigrants who are detained there are treated as criminals or worse; they are detained under stricter rules

than most prisoners, while the only wrong-doing they have been accused of is arriving in Australia without a visa. In a place which can become intolerably hot in summer, inmates have no air-conditioning or fans. As soon as detainees arrive there, they lose there [sic] identity and are given a number. They are required to wear this identification number at all times. There are allegations of child sexual abuse as well as under-age prostitution. Australia is probably the only country in the Western world which uses concentration camps, something which the Australian government strenuously denies.[11]

Brändström et al. observe that one of the functions of historical shortcuts is to provide a guide for how people should respond. This was evident in a number of letters. In the *Sydney Morning Herald*, Don Palmer used the example of the Germans' professed ignorance of concentration camps to call for more information about detention centres:

> My father, an army veteran, recently returned from Europe where he visited one of the World War II Nazi concentration camps. He spoke to people who had lived nearby when the camps operated. Many said they had no idea at the time about what was happening just up the road. Now Australians are being kept in the dark about the detention/concentration facilities run in our name. If there is nothing to hide, then the Prime Minister and the Minister for Immigration must allow us to know everything. Decency requires it. Justice demands it.[12]

Similarly, Abraham Cykiert, a survivor of the concentration camps, used the shortcut to support protests outside the detention centres. He wrote to the *Age*:

> The arrested demonstrators outside the detention camp in [South Australia] should not be prosecuted but saluted. They have done for Australia what the Germans failed to do for themselves and the world in 1933 when the first concentration camp in Germany, Dachau, was legally established...From the final edge of my old life I, a survivor of Buchenwald, fear the way the Government handles the asylum seeker issue. Those who have not experienced its similarity to the past may not begin to understand it, but I salute the demonstrators for their healthy instinct of doing everything possible to stop this shameless and dangerous development.[13]

The comparison of the two forms of incarceration was controversial. Indeed, nearly half of the letters to the editor protested against the comparison. The protests were mostly along two lines. First, writers were upset on the basis of the purpose of concentration camps, which, they argued, was not comparable with the purpose of detention centres. Henk Verhoeven wrote to the *Manly Daily*:

Some humanitarians have referred to the Woomera detention centre as a concentration camp. How silly and how preposterous! Anyone with even a rudimentary knowledge of Nazi concentration camps, and of the atrocities committed both within and outside the precincts of those camps, would never dare to use that word in a Woomera context. Using the misnomer is also a horrible insult to those who did suffer shockingly and survived, and to the many millions more who perished after having been taken to the death camps. Woomera detainees were never forced into Australia against their will.[14]

Others protested on the grounds that the shortcut gave an incorrect picture of conditions in detention centres. Barbara Horkan wrote to the *Newcastle Herald*:

I find it infuriating when correspondents…describe Woomera detention centre as a concentration camp. Are the inmates branded like cattle, starved to death, given no access to medical attention, little shelter and allowed to freeze to death in winter? I was in Europe when the concentration camps were liberated and heard first hand from a nursing colleague who entered Belsen what the conditions were like. Surely your correspondents have seen the films? It must be very hurtful for the few remaining survivors.[15]

Finally, some writers compared the behaviour and actions of the inmates of concentration camps with those in detention centres to support the argument that asylum-seekers deserved detention. In the *Mornington Peninsula Leader*, a correspondent argued:

To compare the Woomera Detention Centre to a concentration camp, shows an unbelievable ignorance and it is an insult to all the people that were transported to such places against their will. Talk to some of the survivors. I have lived with refugees in Germany. I can assure you, they did not burn their papers in there, nor did they riot. It would be helpful for you to brush up on your geography. Firstly, refugees cannot go to a travel agent and buy a ticket. Afghanis could have asked for asylum in Russia, India, Iran, Irak [sic], Thailand and of course, Indonesia. All these countries would have Australian, American, or British consular services. Why did they not go there for protection.[16]

The comparison of detention centres with concentration camps is a potent and emotive shortcut which taps into a body of assumed knowledge about the lowest human treatment of others. The analogy evokes images of shocking inhumanity, of extreme power and powerlessness, of injustice and of frustration at the inaction of people with the ability to speak out. Without having to make a comprehensive argument, using the shortcut was a way of articulating one's objection to the Howard Government's asylum-seeker policies. In the same way, rejection of the shortcut articulated support for these policies. As evident in the letters to the editor, whether in support of the analogy or against it, all correspondents understood its use.

Some politicians also appreciated the subtext of the comparison and similarly employed the shortcut to express their support for, or objection to, the policy and practice of immigration detention. In Parliament, Shadow Immigration Minister, Con Sciacca, used the shortcut when speaking against proposed legislation that would give guards more power to sedate detainees: 'What are you going to do, make [the detention centres] into stalags? Are you going to invoke the ghost of Dr Mengele and go around injecting them with chemicals?'[17]

When former Federal Court judge Marcus Einfeld compared the behaviour of detention centre staff with that of SS guards in concentration camps,[18] Prime Minister Howard demonstrated the potency of this shortcut; that, when the comparison was made, every Australian knew how to read it. Howard referred to Einfeld's speech as 'outrageous and offensive':

> I don't mind people attacking the policy but to endeavour in any way to liken what is occurring in detention centres to Nazi gas camps; it is just outrageous that kind of comparison...The SS were the evil of the evil, the most evil of the lot. They were the people who carried out the dirtiest deeds.[19]

The power of this discursive shortcut, therefore, lies in the widespread understanding within the community of what concentration camps 'mean'. There are also some important structural similarities between the two forms of incarceration. Both are forms of administrative detention, to which people are subjected not because of what they have done, but because of who they are. Being outside the judicial system, it is the State, not the courts, that determines who will be incarcerated. Furthermore, inmates of detention centres are not sentenced for a defined period and their incarceration may be indefinite.

Discussing the lack of basic human rights of those subject to administrative detention, Giorgio Agamben highlights the continuity between detention centres, concentration camps and other such forms of incarceration.[20] These forms of administrative detention constitute 'zones of exception' in which people have no access to rights granted by nation-states. He argues that these zones of exception, which were once historical anomalies, are now a permanent part of the landscape of the modern nation-state. In fact, nation-states depend on them to facilitate the exclusion of certain groups of people; nation-states are defined by those they exclude. Agamben's theory of incarceration has been applied to the Australian context by a number of scholars, who have emphasised the lack of basic human rights that detainees in immigration detention enjoy.[21] The absence of rights makes detention centres, in Suvendrini Perera's terms, simultaneously part of Australian territory but at the same time 'not-Australia'.[22]

It is here that we find a problem with this discursive shortcut. The comparison of immigration detention in Australia with concentration camps in Europe has the effect of making detention seem exceptional in the Australian context. As Brändström et al. explain, when particular historical analogies monopolise the discourse, other possible analogies become 'blind spots' or 'silences'.[23] The comparison reveals a blind spot in public memory towards Australia's own history of administrative detention.

As a form of administrative detention, immigration detention is not anomalous in Australian history. To the contrary, Australia has a long history of administrative detention that spans most of European settlement. Other examples include Aboriginal reserves, quarantine stations, civilian internment camps, psychiatric institutions, reformatory schools and homes for the disabled and blind. The first three forms in particular share with immigration detention the specific function of managing social and geographical boundaries. Inmates are incarcerated not because of what they have done, but because of who they are. In addition, all three share the particular social function of regulating the entry of people into Australia and regulating membership to the community for those who already reside here. As such, these forms of incarceration, like immigration detention centres, are intimately connected with the nation-state. Recognising that these other forms of incarceration are institutional predecessors to immigration detention, with shared aims and methods, ultimately contributes to a more informed understanding of immigration detention in contemporary Australia.

Aboriginal reserves

From the last decades of the nineteenth century to the 1960s, a system of reserves, missions and other institutions isolated, confined and controlled Aboriginal people. While the aims of these institutions and the purposes of confinement changed over time, incarceration was always the solution to perceived social problems. Of particular concern to administrators was the perceived need to keep Aboriginal people separate from the white population.

By the late nineteenth century, disease and violence had devastated the Aboriginal population throughout Australia. It is estimated that in Queensland, for example, the Aboriginal population decreased from 100,000 in 1788 to 26,670 in 1901.[24] Precise figures of the drop in population after 1788 are difficult to establish as original numbers can only be estimated, and the numbers of deaths by disease and massacre were obscured. Social Darwinist notions of racial hierarchy and of the survival of the fittest helped rationalise the decline in the

Aboriginal population. It was widely believed that Aboriginal people were a primitive race doomed to extinction.

To quell the violence on the frontiers, to reduce devastation by disease and to provide Aborigines with a 'humane' environment while their race died out, colonial governments introduced systems of 'protective' legislation. The first was in 1860 in South Australia, where a Chief Protector was appointed to watch over the interests of Aboriginal people and to 'smooth the dying pillow'.[25] Similar legislation was passed in Victoria (1869), Queensland (1897), Western Australia (1905) and New South Wales (1909). These laws were a way of 'protecting' Aborigines from violence on the frontier. By designating territory for Aborigines, it was hoped that the conflict between settlers and Aborigines over land would stop and that Aborigines would use the settlement land to farm and become self-sufficient, thus improving their 'destitute' state and reducing their reliance on the government for rations.

The reserve laws gave governments a great degree of regulatory powers over all aspects of Aborigines' lives. They lost basic human rights such as freedom of movement and labour, custody of children and control over personal property.[26] In some states and the Northern Territory, the Chief Protector had legal guardianship over all Aboriginal children, usurping the power of the parents.[27] These restrictive policies reached their peak in the 1930s.[28] 'In the name of protection,' suggest the authors of *Bringing Them Home*, 'Indigenous people were subject to near-total control.'[29]

The reserve system was designed primarily to separate Aborigines from white society. This was complicated, however, by the growing population of people of mixed descent. By the 1920s, it became clear that while the 'full-blood' Aboriginal population was still declining in number, the population of people of mixed descent was increasing. A problem of classification therefore emerged: were 'half-castes', 'quadroons' (people with one-quarter Aboriginal blood) and 'octoroons' (people with one-eighth Aboriginal blood) white or were they Aboriginal? Should people containing some 'European blood' be allowed to continue to live with Aborigines or should they be integrated into settler society? Should they be encouraged to marry whites, further 'diluting' the degree of Aboriginal blood, or should their choices be restricted to Aborigines or others of mixed descent? Where could the boundary between white and Aboriginal society be positioned?

The policy of assimilation provided one solution to this problem. Conveniently, this required the continued incarceration of Aborigines of all degrees of descent. Reserves were intended to be sites for training Aborigines, particularly those of mixed descent, in the ways of white society. Children were removed from their parents and taught the values and behaviours that would make them acceptable to white society. With the reserve system, governments created and maintained social and territorial boundaries between Aboriginal people and the white community. At a time when Australia, as a young nation, was defining itself, the reserve system helped to delineate who was included in the nation and who was not.

Quarantine stations

From the 1830s to the 1950s (when air travel to Australia largely replaced sea travel), all vessels, cargo, crew and passengers entering Australia were subject to quarantine. Like other forms of administrative incarceration, this involved spatial segregation and confinement from the rest of the Australian community. Originally determined by each colony, the policy was brought under federal jurisdiction with the *Quarantine Act 1908*. One important aspect was how notions of hygiene, pollution and public health functioned to classify certain categories of people as a threat to the Australian community. In the era of the White Australia Policy, ideas of cleanliness corresponded with ideas of whiteness.

Like Aboriginal reserves, quarantine stations are an example of administrative detention used for many decades and throughout Australia. While Aboriginal reserves were a method of maintaining boundaries between groups already living in Australia, quarantine was primarily about controlling and regulating the entry of people from the outside. As such, quarantine stations functioned as the threshold to the newly federated nation. By far the majority of people in quarantine were eventually allowed to enter, but only after they had demonstrably met the requirements for entry. Quarantine was therefore one means by which the government could regulate entry into the country and ensure exclusion when it was deemed necessary.

Just as the healthy and sick received different treatment, so too were people treated differently because of their race or class. These often shaped one's experience of quarantine, determining different levels of medical treatment, access to facilities and, ultimately, the possibility of entering Australia.[30] People of particular racial backgrounds were considered more likely to carry contagious diseases and were subsequently treated differently in quarantine. Krista Maglen explains that before the smallpox pandemic of 1881, Asian ports were not regarded as a potentially dangerous source of disease. In contrast, vessels from England, where smallpox was always present, were checked thoroughly. In 1881, Australian health authorities determined that the smallpox pandemic affecting hundreds of people in Sydney had originated in China. From this time, ships, cargo and people of Asian origin became the key targets of quarantine, and ideas of race and of Asia as a source of disease began to inform medical theory and policy.[31] Such ideas also supported more widespread derogatory stereotypes about the Chinese in Australia.[32]

Quarantine, like Aboriginal reserves, played an important role in the formation of Australia as a new, federated nation. In particular, it contributed to the symbolic 'imagining' of the new nation.[33] Geographically, the quarantine boundaries outlined the boundaries of the nation. With regard to population, quarantine identified particular races as a threat to the nation and provided a mechanism for their exclusion.

Enemy-alien internment camps

In both world wars, individuals regarded as a threat to Australia's war effort were incarcerated in internment camps. Ostensibly, an individual could be interned because of their birth or familial connections with enemy nations or because of their allegiance. In practice, however, internment was used much more broadly. Many people were interned with very little evidence of their threat to either the war effort or Australian society. Some ethnic groups, such as Japanese in World War II, were interned en masse. Internment, then, became a tool for social control and provided a mechanism for the removal of certain categories of people from Australian society.[34]

In World War I, 6890 people were interned.[35] At the peak of World War II, the number of civilian internees was closer to 12 000.[36] In World War I, the policy stipulated that local authorities could intern 'enemy subjects with whose conduct they were not satisfied'.[37] Originally, the policy was concerned with people who had recently migrated to Australia. In 1915, however, it was broadened so that naturalised British subjects who were born in Germany or Austria could be interned, as well as people of 'enemy descent'—that is, those who were born in Australia but whose father or grandfather was a subject of an enemy nation. Also interned were Australians of British descent who were thought to be 'disaffected and disloyal'.[38] They were singled out on account of their anti-war and anti-patriotic political persuasions and included radical pacifists, socialists, unionists and political and church leaders who campaigned against conscription.

In a time of war, when national security took priority over civil liberties, the people in the community who were not of British heritage became the objects of suspicion, surveillance, internment and, in many cases, more permanent exclusion. Australians of British descent who had worked for years alongside naturalised Europeans went on strike until the latter were sacked, and people reported on their neighbours. In some cases, even naturalisation was viewed with suspicion. Prime Minister, Billy Hughes, and other politicians in World War I argued that for the Germans naturalisation was only a ruse, 'a cunningly and ruthlessly exploited cover' that allowed them to continue their quest to undermine Australian society.[39] Despite good relations in times of peace, the ethnic other remained an outsider in the Australian community. The internment experience, therefore, raised the question of whether people of non-British heritage could ever become Australians, and at what point they did belong to the Australian community.

Like Aboriginal reserves and quarantine stations, internment camps provided a mechanism for regulating the social boundaries of the Australian nation. While quarantine stations regulated the entry of people into the nation, Aboriginal reserves and enemy-alien internment camps regulated the membership of people who already resided in Australia. In much the same way, immigration detention centres regulate the entry of people into Australia and the membership of people who already live here. As a contemporary form of administrative detention, immigration detention centres raise the same questions of race, citizenship and belonging in the Australian nation-state as their institutional predecessors.

Conclusion

I have shown how references to German concentration camps were used to object to the policy and practice of immigration detention in Australia. This discursive shortcut reflected the high emotion surrounding the issue in the first years of the twenty-first century. By connecting the two forms of incarceration, members of the public were able to articulate, in shorthand, their objections to the Howard Government's immigration policies. The comparison also made detention centres seem exceptional to the normal workings of the Australian nation-state when, in fact, many forms of administrative detention in Australian history have performed similar social and political functions.

In his social history of incarceration in the United States, David Rothman stresses the importance of positioning it in a historical context.[40] To do so, he explains, reveals a continuity between carceral practices that might be forgotten when examining specific instances. Since the 'invention' of the penitentiary, the insane asylum and the almshouse in the early nineteenth century, incarceration has been an 'enduring' feature of the modern nation-state. Rothman explains how incarceration, as a political solution to a social problem, is reinvented to fit each social circumstance.

Concentration camps in Germany, like immigration detention centres in Australia, were a government solution to the 'problem' of certain categories of people. As in the case of the other forms of administrative detention explored in this chapter, people were incarcerated not because of what they had done, but because of who they were. By controlling who had membership to the community, all these forms of administrative detention were intimately connected with the nation-state.

Ultimately, though, the study of administrative detention in the Australian context can facilitate a far more comprehensive understanding of the contemporary policy and practice of immigration detention than can be achieved by making the comparison with German concentration camps. Throughout Australia's history, administrative detention has been used to manage social and geographical boundaries. This has involved the classification of people into social groups, the identification of some of these groups as outsiders to Australian society and the attempt to regulate these groups.

Immigration detention is not a new solution invented to solve a particular social problem. Neither is the social problem unique to our times. Rather, immigration detention is best understood as a reinvention, a recycling, of an old solution to a perennial issue. Recognition of this continuity, however, does not mean that incarceration is an inevitable part of our social and political landscape. For Rothman, the knowledge that carceral systems have been recycled and reused to respond to particular social situations encourages us to experiment with new solutions: 'We need not remain trapped in inherited answers.'[41]

Acknowledgments

I conducted the research for this chapter while I was a visiting fellow at the Institute for Social Research, Swinburne University of Technology.

Endnotes

[1] Organ, Michael 2003, 'Villawood centre disgrace', *Illawarra Mercury*, 15 July 2003.

[2] McMaster, Don 2001, *Asylum Seekers: Australia's response to refugees*, Melbourne University Press, Melbourne, pp. 75–6.

[3] *Migration Amendment (Detention Arrangements) Act 2005*.

[4] Human Rights and Equal Opportunity Commission 2004, *A Last Resort? Report of the inspections of Baxter Immigration Detention Facility and Port Augusta Residential Housing Project*, Commonwealth of Australia, Canberra.

[5] Numerous studies have outlined the problems in depth. See Mares, Peter 2002, *Borderline: Australia's response to refugees and asylum seekers in the wake of the Tampa*, UNSW Press, Sydney; Human Rights and Equal Opportunity Commission, *A Last Resort?*; Briskman, Linda, Latham, Suzie and Goddard, Chris 2008, *Human Rights Overboard: Seeking asylum in Australia*, Scribe, Melbourne.

[6] Mares, *Borderline*; Leach, Michael and Mansouri, Fethi 2004, *Lives in Limbo: Refugees under temporary protection in Australia*, UNSW Press, Sydney; Sultan, Aamer and O'Sullivan, Kevin 2001, 'Psychological disturbances in asylum seekers held in long term detention: a participant–observer account', *Medical Journal of Australia*, vol. 175, pp. 593–6; Steel, Zachary et al. 2004, 'Psychiatric status of asylum seeker families held for a protracted period in a remote detention centre in Australia', *Australian and New Zealand Journal of Public Health*, vol. 28, no. 6, pp. 527–36; Joint Standing Committee on Migration 2005, *Report of the Inspections of Baxter Immigration Detention Facility and Port Augusta Residential Housing Project*, Commonwealth of Australia, Canberra; Debelle, Penelope 2005, 'Suicidal and without hope', *Sunday Age*, 12 June 2005.

[7] Miller, Nick 2008, 'New mental illness hits refugees', *Age*, 28 May 2008.

[8] Brändström, Annika, Bynander, Fredrik and 't Hart, Paul 2004, 'Governing by looking back: historical analogies and crisis management', *Public Administration*, vol. 82, no. 1, p. 193.

[9] Crabb, Annabel 2001, 'Bill to seek more power for guards', *Age*, 24 January 2001; Hart, Cath and Lewis, Steve 2006, 'Rebels to force PM's hand: asylum bill faces defeat in Senate', *Australian*, 10 August 2006; Banham, Cynthia 2002, 'Woomera conditions likened to Nazi days', *Sydney Morning Herald*, 20 September 2002; Clennell, Andrew 2002, 'Howard on spot over UN check', *Sydney Morning Herald*, 6 February 2002; Pippos, Chris 2001, 'Woomera "worse than a prison": lawyer', *Eastern Courier*, 12 December 2001; Vainoras, Tim 2004, 'Councillor slams refugee jail "hellhole"', *Whittlesea Leader*, 22 September 2004; Kissane, Karen 2000, 'Neglect and abuse in detention: refugee furore', *Age*, 2 December 2000.

[10] Donald, Allan 2002, 'Smell of detention', *Northern Territory News*, 4 February 2002.

[11] DeVries, Otto 2000, 'Letter to the editor', *Hobart Mercury*, 2 December 2000.

[12] Palmer, Don 2005, 'Nation kept in the dark about our concentration camps', *Sydney Morning Herald*, 10 February 2005.

[13] Cykiert, Abraham 2005, 'Letter to the editor', *Age*, 30 March 2005.

[14] Verhoeven, Hank 2002, 'Concentration camps claims are insults to Nazi victims', *Manly Daily*, 29 January 2002.

[15] Horkan, Barbara 2002, 'Short takes', *Newcastle Herald*, 11 February 2002.

[16] Arndt, I. 2002, 'No comparison', *Mornington Peninsula Leader*, 12 February 2002.

[17] Quoted in Crabb, 'Bill to seek more power for guards'.

[18] Merritt, Chris 2006, 'Lapses in judgement', *Australian*, 15 August 2006.

[19] 'The nation detention centres Nazi gibe riles PM', *Gold Coast Bulletin*, 21 September 2002.

[20] Agamben, Giorgio 1998, *Homo Sacer: Sovereign power and bare life*, Translated by Daniel Heller-Roazen, Stanford University Press, Stanford.

[21] Pugliese, Joseph 2002, 'Penal asylum: refugees, ethics, hospitality', *Borderlands*, vol. 1, no. 1; Perera, Suvendrini 2002, 'What is a camp...?', *Borderlands*, vol. 1, no. 1; Holt, Matthew 2003, 'Biopolitics and the "problem of the refugee"', in Michael Leach and Fethi Mansouri (eds), *Critical Perspectives on Refugee Policy in Australia*, Deakin University, Melbourne; Kumar Rajaram, Prem and Grundy-Warr, Carl 2004, 'The irregular migrant as homo sacer: migration and detention in Australia, Malaysia and Thailand', *International Migration*, vol. 42, no. 1, pp. 33–63.

[22] Perera, 'What is a camp ...?'.

[23] Brändström et al., 'Governing by looking back', pp. 205–6.

[24] Chesterman, John and Galligan, Brian 1997, *Citizens Without Rights: Aborigines and Australian citizenship*, Cambridge University Press, Melbourne, p. 31.

[25] Bolton, G. C. 1982, 'Aborigines in social history: an overview', in Ronald M. Berndt (ed.), *Aboriginal Sites, Rights and Resource Development*, University of Western Australia Press, Perth, p. 59.

[26] Attwood, Bain and Markus, Andrew 1999, *The Struggle for Aboriginal Rights: A documentary history*, Allen & Unwin, St Leonards.

[27] National Inquiry into the Separation of Aboriginal and Torres Strait Islander Children from their Families 1997, *Bringing Them Home: Report of the National Inquiry into the Separation of Aboriginal and Torres Strait Islander Children from their Families*, Human Rights and Equal Opportunity Commission, Sydney.

[28] Attwood and Markus, *The Struggle for Aboriginal Rights*, p. 8.

[29] National Inquiry into the Separation of Aboriginal and Torres Strait Islander Children from their Families, *Bringing Them Home*, p. 22.

[30] Foley, Jean Duncan 1995, *In Quarantine: A history of Sydney's quarantine station 1828–1984*, Kangaroo Press, Kenthurst.

[31] Maglen, Krista 2005, 'A world apart: geography, Australian quarantine, and the mother country', *Journal of the History of Medicine and Allied Sciences*, vol. 60, no. 2, pp. 196–217.

[32] Irving, Helen 1999, *To Constitute a Nation: A cultural history of Australia's Constitution*, Cambridge University Press, Cambridge.

[33] Bashford, Alison 2004, *Imperial Hygiene: A critical history of colonialism, nationalism and public health*, Palgrave Macmillan, New York.

[34] Evans, Raymond 2000, '"Tempest tossed": political deportations from Australia and World War I', in Kay Saunders and Roger Daniel (eds), *Alien Justice: Wartime internment in Australia and North America*, University of Queensland Press, St Lucia, pp. 28–46.

[35] Fischer, Gerhard 1989, *Enemy Aliens: Internment and the homefront experience in Australia 1914–1920*, University of Queensland Press, St Lucia.

[36] Neumann, Klaus 2006, *In the Interest of National Security: Civilian internment in Australia during World War II*, National Archives of Australia, Canberra, p. 7.

[37] Fischer, *Enemy Aliens*, p. 65.

[38] Ibid., p. 65.

[39] Ibid., p. 101.

[40] Rothman, David J. 1971, *The Discovery of the Asylum: Social order and disorder in the new republic*, Little, Brown and Company, Boston.

[41] Ibid., p. 295.

5. Refugees between pasts and politics: sovereignty and memory in the Tampa crisis

J. Olaf Kleist

Were a conflicting event, the initiative of one or several members, or, finally, external circumstances to introduce into the life of the group a new element incompatible with its past, then another group, with its own memory, would arise, and only an incomplete and vague remembrance of what had preceded this crisis would remain.

— Maurice Halbwachs[1]

The citizen voice can be controlled by the control of migrants.

— Alastair Davidson[2]

On the morning of 25 August 2001, few Australians had heard of the merchant vessel *Tampa*. The Norwegian ship had left the port of Fremantle three days earlier and was on its way to Singapore. The next day, the *Tampa* rescued 439 people from a sinking boat, prompting a major shift in Australian refugee policies, sparking a major political controversy and turning around the ailing fortunes of the governing Liberal-National Coalition ahead of a federal election later that year. On the morning of 25 August, Melbourne's *Age* carried an article on its opinion page that would become far more relevant than its author, Hugh Mackay, could ever have anticipated. He warned:

> When there is a lack of inspirational leadership, two things always happen. The community's focus narrows and turns inwards as people disengage from the national agenda and become almost exclusively concerned with local issues, and the vacuum created by the lack of social vision sucks a flood of vicious prejudice to fill the space.[3]

With much derogatory language already used against refugees, Mackay predicted that the Coalition would draw on racist prejudices against asylum-seekers during the forthcoming election campaign. Such rhetoric did indeed become a constitutive part of the Tampa debate.[4] Still, this was by no means a new attribute of Australian discourse and could not fully explain the specific character of the debate.[5] Although the event sent shockwaves through Australian society, it seems difficult to determine the distinct qualities that characterised the political changes of this event. I suggest that the response to the *Tampa*'s rescue efforts modified the conception of sovereignty in a far-reaching manner, causing a new perception of citizenship, memory and the situation of asylum-seekers.

Sovereignty is not a fixed but a politically contested concept. Internally, it relates citizens to the State as the self-determination of people within a contained territory. Internationally, it circumscribes the territorial borders of a polity defined by its self-determination. The relationship of this inner and outer conception of sovereignty creates, as Giorgio Agamben argues, a paradox: they are the factual foundation of each other's potential to sovereign power.[6] In other words, sovereignty is an existing *contradictio per se*: its limits define belonging and vice versa. Stateless people fall in between the sovereigns that make up the world of nation-states. For asylum-seekers, this is not only important with regard to the detention centres that Agamben writes about. To them, the sovereign is on the one hand the potential guarantor of rights and on the other an obstacle—as protective power over its subjects and its territory.

In the politics of the Tampa crisis, sovereignty's contradiction allowed a political shift that reconfigured its relationship to refugees: from excluding asylum-seekers from civil rights to excluding them from the claim to sovereign protection under human rights. This shift established a qualitative change in political action and debate. The implications of the policies implemented due to the crisis for refugees and the specificity of their exclusion can be illuminated by looking at the use of the past in parliamentary debates before and after the Tampa incident. The use of memories signifies shifting perceptions of belonging, sovereignty and refugees.

The relevance of the past for social belonging and political action was an important issue not only after, but immediately before the Tampa crisis. Right next to Mackay's op-ed article, the historian Janet McCalman reminded readers that '[t]eaching history safeguards the truth':

> There are many reasons why history matters in a healthy and democratic society. Our understanding of the past—both in our own lives and in society—shapes our sense of identity and provides an accumulation of human experience to guide us in the present and for the future.[7]

Public life needed, she wrote, a trustworthy engagement with history. The past, however, is a very uncertain category that relies much on the circumstances in which it is remembered. Theories of social memory agree on the constructivist character of memories.[8] This means, for one, that people remember the past selectively to find answers to current problems and, for another, that the act of remembering imagines a social group to connect the present with the past.[9] If, however, the present determines the perception of the past, it determines how the social group is imagined too. Theories of memory have analysed the various roles of social memories, including the role of memory in political processes.[10]

I suggest that looking at how social memories are used can help us to understand the political shift that occurred in the debate about the *Tampa* in regard to Australian self-perception and its relation to refugees. In analysing parliamentary debates about refugee issues, I show that before Tampa the use of memories suggested a communal belonging and, in its political context, an unmediated understanding of sovereign action. As the response to refugees changed, the past, as it was employed in political debates, played a decisive new role. Now memories referred merely to isolated elements of sovereignty, leaving not only refugees in a position devoid of sovereignty, but citizens and the State. I argue that the distinct forms of memory and their application of sovereignty, as they emerge in this analysis, are related 'ideal types'. The qualitative change in the actions and attitudes towards refugees can be understood as the result of the government's use of sovereignty in the Tampa crisis and the resulting shift in the public significance of the described forms of memory. Ultimately, this confrontation of different forms of political memory before and after the crisis questions the legitimacy of sovereign state power over refugees.

The old and the new of the Tampa crisis

The unauthorised arrival of asylum-seekers was highly controversial long before the Tampa crisis occurred. Between 1992 and 2001, successive Australian governments responded to these arrivals by detaining all onshore asylum-seekers until their applications for a protection visa had been accepted or until they were deported. With arrivals increasing in the late 1990s, the number of detainees grew while the situation in detention centres deteriorated rapidly. On the one hand, riots, escapes and incidents of self-harm were causes of concern for the Howard Coalition Government; on the other hand, the ordeal of the detainees functioned as a barely concealed method of deterrence, with its implicit warning that suffering awaited those who attempted to subvert Australia's sovereign integrity.

Although the government failed in its attempt to reduce the number of unauthorised boat arrivals, it stuck to its tactic of deterrence through detention of 'illegal' immigrants. In April 2001, it introduced the Migration Legislation Amendment (Immigration Detainees) Bill 2001, the so-called 'strip-search bill', to give staff at immigration detention centres more powers. The bill was modified during that year and discussed in Parliament just as the Tampa crisis was unfolding. As more and more refugee boats arrived in Australian territory, the main response by Immigration Minister, Philip Ruddock, was to declare, as late as 23 August 2001, that more detention centres would be built.[11] 'The Tampa changed those circumstances,' David Marr and Marian Wilkinson assert. 'Suddenly here was an opportunity for Howard to show Canberra was in control.'[12] Now, navy, police and security services became the preferred weapons to deter refugees from arriving by strengthening border protection.

What was behind the sudden change from what Peter Mares calls a strategy of *'deterrence by example'*—that is, the show of harshness and potential force—to *'deterrence by force'*, the use of the Navy and real force to prevent boats from entering the Australian migration zone?[13] The answer, I propose, was flying at the stern of the *Tampa*.

As the *Tampa* sailed towards Australia under the flag of a sovereign state (Norway), the Australian Government finally had an appropriate counterpart to deal with 'boat people'.[14] Until then, refugee boats could not be ordered (or expected) to respect Australian borders because they had no obligations to any sovereign state. Conversely, the *Tampa*, flying a sovereign flag, under international law, had to defer to Australia's legal jurisdiction in its territory. The Norwegian vessel did so, at least partially, and did not land its passengers at Christmas Island. With the *Tampa* following orders, Australian authorities assumed they were in a position to direct boats carrying refugees. According to Marr and Wilkinson, the government's initial response to the *Tampa* and the subsequent interception of refugee boats developed spontaneously rather than according to a detailed plan.[15] Only after the *Tampa*'s rescue effort did border security become the front line of refugee deterrence, sparking a major political controversy. Suddenly, by neglecting the special circumstances under which the refugees travelled on board the *Tampa*, it seemed possible to keep all refugees outside the migration zone through the use of real force.

In the beginning, the government, despite its intuition for popular moods, was possibly not fully aware of the implications regarding sovereignty, refugees and belonging. The swing in the pre-election polls towards the Coalition justified its actions. The delicate relationship between sovereign power and refugees, however, and its domestic implications with regard to citizens, should not be underestimated in comprehending the impact of the Tampa incident on Australian public debate and politics.

Sovereignty and refugees (I)

The Tampa affair precipitated a change in refugee policy and political discourse, but also in perceptions of the sovereign body politic. In the first days of the crisis, Ruddock, in statements to the media and to Parliament, was still committed to a policy of deterrence by example. To him, the introduction of new refugee legislation was 'crucial to ensuring that we reduce Australia's relative attractiveness',[16] while the deportation of unsuccessful asylum-seekers was regarded as 'a strong message to the world that Australia intends to fight people trafficking'.[17] Australian refugee policies were not directed at subjects under Australian jurisdiction but at potential refugees who could neither be engaged nor specifically located. With the emphasis shifting from dealing with asylum-seekers on shore to protecting the borders against their arrival, the tone of the political debate also changed. When Howard first announced to the House of Representatives that the merchant vessel *Tampa* had picked up refugees who were on their way from Indonesia to Australia, he reiterated his mantra that it was Australia's right as a sovereign nation to determine who came into the country and under what circumstances.[18] Within days, sovereignty changed from being the foundation of the polity that needed protection against stateless asylum-seekers to being the reason for policies to exclude refugees.

The new policy of deterrence by force seemed appropriate for the new situation. It was, however, founded on the basic contradiction of sovereign power. The *Tampa*'s breach of Australia's territorial sea border off Christmas Island on the morning of 29 August prompted several responses. On the practical side, Special Air Service (SAS) elite troops intercepted the *Tampa* in inflatable Zodiac boats. In order to prevent the refugees from engaging Australia's protection obligations as a sovereign nation under the 1951 Refugee Convention, the boats did not fly Australian flags.[19] At a first glance, this action appeared to invert the relation between refugees and border control. The refugees were on a huge ship under Norwegian jurisdiction while the Australian soldiers approached them in tiny vessels that did not display any sign of sovereignty. It seems the Australian troops were attempting to take advantage of the precarious position of stateless 'boat people' not affiliated to a sovereign. They were, however, Australian military forces, displaying the Australian flag on their uniforms and they acted on behalf of the sovereign in Australian territorial waters. Besides, the power relations were made obvious when armed Australian soldiers boarded the Norwegian ship. The captain had no choice but to let the SAS proceed with its operation. In the same instance, however, the refugees could not claim their rights to apply for asylum. The Australian soldiers were at once representatives of Australian sovereignty and not. Being subject to the power of sovereignty but having no rights to asylum posed a pertinent contradiction and a dilemma for the refugees.

This contradiction of sovereignty was also true in relation to the Norwegian ship and had been highlighted under different circumstances 20 years earlier. The UN High Commissioner for Refugees (UNHCR) argued in response to Indochinese 'boat people' who had been rescued in 1981 by cargo ships on the high seas:

> While…there is a clear duty for ships' masters, their owners and their Governments to rescue asylum-seekers at sea, there is no obligation under international law for the flag State of a rescuing vessel to grant durable asylum to rescued refugees. It is, of course, correct that by boarding a vessel, the refugee comes under the jurisdiction of the flag State which is considered to exercise jurisdiction over the ship on the high seas.[20]

The responsibility for asylum-seekers rescued at sea has since been disputed and remains unresolved.[21] Due to the ambiguities surrounding the issue of sovereign power on the high seas, having powers of jurisdiction on the one hand and the absence of obligations to asylum-seekers on the other, rescued refugees are caught in a legal limbo.

Refugees aboard the *Tampa* were thus 'caught', not only physically but legally between two sovereign powers, Australia and Norway. The situation reflected the potential for both conflict and cooperation between two overlapping sovereign entities: a Norwegian boat within Australian territory. More importantly, the engagement allowed Australian executive powers to position refugees as legal objects, in between the two powers, and to deal with them accordingly.

As a legal reaction to the border breach by the *Tampa* and the refugees aboard, and in response to the apparently delicate contradiction of sovereignty, the government introduced the Border Protection Bill 2001 into Parliament. This proposed to legalise the removal of unwanted ships from the territorial sea (Sections 4–6), to render any actions of Australian officers in regard to those ships not reviewable in any Australian court (Section 7) and to invalidate any application for a protection visa from aboard such a ship (Section 9).[22] It was to apply retrospectively from the morning of 29 August, just before the SAS boarded the *Tampa* (Section 11). When Prime Minister Howard informed the Opposition of the bill, 40 minutes before it was to be debated in the House of Representatives, he asked for it to be approved in both chambers that same night. After a lengthy debate, however, the Senate, in which the government parties did not have a majority, rejected the bill.

In Parliament, the dispute centred on the issue of where sovereignty lay within the body politic. Howard underlined the importance of the bill by saying that '[i]t is essential to the maintenance of Australian sovereignty, including our sovereign right to determine who will enter and reside in Australia'.[23] Every breach of the Australian border seemed to question the authority of the government and therefore undermine Australia's sovereignty. Senator Robert Hill (Liberal) declared: 'Surely, a reasonable person would say that the Australian government should have all necessary powers to do what is necessary to protect the integrity of Australia's borders.'[24] It seemed unreasonable not to use all force available to the government in order to re-establish the sovereignty that seemed to be violated by the *Tampa*'s border breach. The government's interpretation, however, reduced sovereignty to only the executive power within Australian territory, represented of course by the government itself.

The opposition parties rejected the bill for several reasons—one being that the government had not consulted them about the legislation ahead of its introduction. Apart from such formal objections, the Labor Party doubted the severity of the situation. The Leader of the Opposition, Kim Beazley, rejected the government's alarmism, saying that 'we do not face in these circumstances a national catastrophe; we face a serious problem'.[25] While the Opposition agreed with the government on Australia's sovereign right to determine questions of immigration, it did not equate sovereignty merely with the executive power of the government but with the institutions of the State. For the Opposition, it was not so much the refugees who were a threat to sovereignty; rather, it considered the bill a danger to Australian sovereignty because it undermined the balance of power. That actions committed under the law proposed by this bill would not fall under Australian jurisdiction was considered a threat to the balance of power and therefore, as one parliamentarian suggested, the bill might even undermine the constitution.[26] Overall, the debate about a bill designed to prevent refugees from entering Australian territorial waters turned into a debate about the legal parameters of the State's sovereign power.

The problem of sovereignty in relation to refugees is not new. Hannah Arendt describes this problematic relationship in her 1948 book *The Origins of Totalitarianism*.[27] The nation-state, she argues, is based on two doctrines: the universal rights of man—or human rights—and the sovereignty of people as citizens. Refugees, who lose the protection of their state, are not citizens anymore but can still claim human rights—in principle at least. With regard to refugees, the doctrines of the nation-state are therefore separated. This has grave consequences for the idea of sovereignty, as Agamben explains:

> If in the system of the nation-state the refugee represents such a disquieting element, it is above all because by breaking up the identity between man and citizen, between nativity and nationality, the refugee throws into crisis the original fiction of sovereignty.[28]

Sovereignty presupposes a solid concept of self-determination with a clear distinction between those who belong and those who do not. It has, however, both a civic foundation, originating from people's self-rule as citizens, and a universal foundation, the universal recognition of people's right to sovereignty. In respect to refugees, however, these two concepts collide because stateless people reveal, *qua* their existence, the fiction of the right to sovereignty. For a state, this means, on the one hand, that it has an obligation to recognise the refugees' universal right to sovereignty, because the State itself is based on this recognition; on the other, it can do so only under its sovereign powers, which by definition are limited to citizens. With regard to refugees, a state has to be a sovereign and a non-sovereign power at the same time, thereby undermining its legitimacy.

The challenge of refugees to the government was (and always is) to translate this 'fiction of sovereignty' into politics. In 1992, the Labor Government under Paul Keating confronted this dilemma by enforcing the distinction between citizens possessing and non-citizens not possessing civil rights under a sovereign power by introducing administrative immigration detention for non-citizens who did not hold a valid visa. That same year, the High Court ruling on immigration detention in *Chu Kheng Lim vs Minister for Immigration, Local Government and Ethnic Affairs* asserted the distinction of this policy, according to which those who were not Australian citizens had no claims against administrative incarceration.[29] The policy and the ruling affirmed in principle, however, that refugees in detention retained the human right to claim asylum within a sovereign territory.

What was new after Tampa was that refugees were denied civil rights and their human right to asylum. Australian authorities now completely separated sovereignty from universal rights. For one, they acted as a sovereign power against the Norwegian vessel, practically detaining the stateless refugees at sea. With the Border Protection Bill 2001, the government attempted to legalise this approach. Furthermore, the authorities prevented the refugees from reaching the migration zone or from applying for asylum by other means.[30] They confronted refugees with sovereign power without conceding that the new arrivals had any rights under this power, especially the right to claim asylum. The *Migration Amendment (Excision from Migration Zone) Act 2001* would later establish exactly this separation in the distinction between territory and migration zone. In order to deal with stateless people, the government separated human rights not just from citizenship but from sovereignty altogether.

Conversely, this meant disaggregating sovereignty from the expression of pure power directed at stateless people when preventing them from claiming asylum. This had implicit repercussions for Australian sovereignty, rearranging the relationship between Australian citizens and the State. In the parliamentary debate about the Border Protection Bill 2001, this new situation was interpreted as denoting a shift in sovereign power. The Opposition pointed to the danger of separating sovereign powers from rights, not just in relation to refugees but to all citizens. Some parliamentarians noted that sidelining the judiciary and giving unlimited powers to the executive with regard to unwanted vessels in the territorial sea would undermine the rule of law and the balance of power within state institutions.[31] Since the balance of power is to safeguard democratic self-rule, an executive power without institutional checks and balances would not only be uncontrollable with regard to refugees, it would separate the power of the State from the broader principle of sovereignty.

Sovereignty, the Opposition's remarks implied, was a question not just of executive power but of all state institutions; yet, neither was it a privilege of state institutions as a means in itself. The sovereignty of the nation-state is, as Arendt observes, intrinsically bound to citizenship. The Opposition was concerned, as Labor MP Robert McClelland outlined in a later debate, that the implications of cutting off the control mechanism between the citizenry and the sovereign power would extend beyond stateless people. Contemplating the

Opposition's rejection of the border protection legislation, during the parliamentary debate on the so-called 'Pacific Solution', he pointed out:

> Clause 6 [of the Border Protection Bill 2001] gave power for a Commonwealth officer, or a person assisting an officer, to return to a ship 'a person' who was on board the ship. Of course 'person' could mean an Australian citizen, a citizen of the United States, Canada, Great Britain or from anywhere in the world—'a person'; a human being.[32]

The goal of deterrence by force, which, in the Opposition's view, the Border Protection Bill 2001 failed to deliver, was of course intended to target unprotected humans without endangering citizens. Indirectly, the Opposition wanted to retain the old model based on the fiction of sovereignty without human rights.

The imaginary distinction between a migration zone and a territory, established during the Tampa crisis, created two seemingly distinct powers in regard to refugees: one within the migration zone being checked and approachable as a sovereign, and another outside being apparently pure power. This division, employed as a policy of deterrence by force, placed the executive power of the State in a new and unchecked situation outside the sphere of sovereignty. As a result of neglecting the sovereign source of its power, the government was able to use force outside the migration zone without exposing itself as a sovereign on which refugees could have called for protection. This meant excluding refugees' access to sovereignty and splitting governmental power from citizenship. If sovereignty demarcates not only the reach of power but the confines of responsibility then Australian territorial integrity is defined by 'pure' governmental power and no longer by the principle of sovereignty. In the government's policies—and legally since the *Migration Amendment (Excision from Migration Zone) Act 2001*—sovereignty extended to the migration zone only but not to Australia's territorial seas and some excluded islands. This new understanding of sovereignty, which was created to exclude refugees, in turn had an immense impact on Australian self-conceptions, as expressed through social memories in the debates on refugee policies.

Sovereignty and memories (I)

Whenever Members of Parliament debated issues concerning refugees they also negotiated Australian inclusion in general. The question of sovereignty is just one way of relating these two issues; it is the legal perception of the refugee issue and of the issue of belonging. Belonging to a sovereign society has also been expressed through memories in terms of tradition, especially before the Tampa crisis unfolded. This implied a very different perception of the Australian sovereign, including the relationship between politics and citizens.

In the Tampa-related debate about the Border Protection Bill 2001, both sides of Parliament accused the other of adopting their standpoint for electoral gain, yet the electorate didn't figure significantly in the debate.[33] Citizens were neither the object nor the reason for the bill. It was directed at non-citizens and international actors, and arguments focused on domestic legal issues. Clear distinctions were made between citizens' and non-citizens' legal status. This was quite different from earlier discussions about refugee policies. To understand the novelty, I want to revisit the debate on the 'strip-search bill' (the Migration Legislation Amendment [Immigration Detainees] Bill [No. 2] 2001). This was adopted in the Senate on the same day as the Border Protection Bill 2001 was introduced, and had been discussed in the House of Representatives just days before the Tampa debate began. While the bill was adopted after *Tampa*'s arrival, its conception, debate and policy, concerned with issues of immigration detention, belonged to the pre-Tampa doctrine of deterrence by example.

During the debate on the strip-search bill, the situation of non-citizens in detention was discussed indirectly in relation to Australian citizens. At the same time, the question of state power played a significant role in the debate. After all, the bill was introduced to guarantee the authority of the State over refugees within detention centres. Danna Vale (Liberal Party) went so far as to warn the House of Representatives about the dangers that rioting inmates at immigration detention centres posed to Australian sovereignty:

> We either uphold the rule of law in Australia—and that is the rule of law for everyone—or we do not. We should all be very much aware that the alternative to an orderly immigration process is immigration that is out of control—and that would be the triumph of chaos over order.[34]

Chaos meant that not everyone, no matter what legal status, was treated the same—an assumption that was shared by those who criticised the incarceration of non-citizens.

An immigration process that was considered 'in order' was the offshore processing of refugee resettlement through the UNHCR and Australia's Immigration Department. In 2001, as in previous years, Australia granted approximately 12 000 residence visas on humanitarian grounds. This refugee program was, however, always closely connected to Australia's immigration policy and candidates were selected mostly for their suitability to contribute to Australian society.[35] Even when the government accepted refugees because of needs identified by the UNHCR, it did so on its own free terms, based on its judgment of social benefit. In this regard, onshore refugees were, on the one hand, condemned for avoiding procedures that were considered Australia's sovereign right—namely, to decide who comes and under what circumstances—while on the other hand, they were evaluated as migrants in their relation to Australian society. In other words, refugee issues were considered a matter of the Australian sovereign, which did not stand solely for the State, citizens or non-citizens but appeared to encompass all elements. Vale made this point clear by emphasising 'the rule of law for everyone'.[36]

The central unspoken question was how to define Australian sovereignty if State and citizens were not distinguished from refugees and migrants by their legal status. In comparison with the debate about the Border Protection Bill 2001, the parliamentary debate on the strip-search legislation did not focus so much on sovereignty as on Australia's alleged social character as a whole. This was done with references to collective pasts. Social memories were evoked in arguments, combining elements of sovereignty, power and belonging. As McCalman wrote in her op-ed article, 'understanding of the past...shapes our sense of identity'.[37] Indeed, proponents of memory studies agree that memories contribute to the impression of belonging. Benedict Anderson famously suggested that people remembering a common past imagined a shared communality.[38]

In the debate about the strip-search bill, such communalities were imagined in relation to refugees. Senator Bob Brown (Greens) claimed that immigration detention was 'very similar to the Port Arthur asylum treatment of over 150 years ago'.[39] While making a point about the current treatment of asylum-seekers, the reference to Australia's convict history invited listeners to imagine a common past. The condemnation of the historical practice created a form of social belonging based on empathy for those suffering from current 'asylum treatment'. To imagine belonging, however, the considered past must be constitutive to the person remembering instead of just being a historical fact like any other. The individual act of imagining communality, shared by a small number of people, is, contrary to what Anderson suggests, not congruent with the implied community of the memory—all Australians in this case.[40] The legitimacy of Brown's argument rested on the assumption that the Port Arthur penal station represented a past that was personally important to all Australians. This memory is not, however, relevant to all Australians to whom this memory is supposed to apply, even if it is understood as a historical reference. Belonging is thus created on two levels of memories: the level of those remembering and the level of those imagined in the act of remembering.

The group remembering and the community imagined are not identical. Communal memories are not necessarily shared by all who are considered part of the community. An example of that was given by Senator Jim McKiernan (Labor) in the debate about the strip-search bill. To demonstrate the prejudices existing in the electorate, he read a letter he had received from a member of the public, who argued:

> Being a fourth generation Australian it was my ancestors who fought to keep Australia a free country and Christian country for our families. All the deaths of our ancestors in war, I feel now is [sic] in vain and our

rights as citizens of Australia are being compromised by the influx of refugees.[41]

The imagined Australian community through which the author perceived the contemporary relation to refugees was taken from Australian history. Like McKiernan, however, many Australians would not agree that this imagined community was a legitimate representation of Australia. In other words: communal memories are directed at the whole of the community but they are understood as an expression thereof by the remembering group only.

A multitude of communal memories contest Australia's character in relation to refugees. While many such memories exist simultaneously, they are exclusive in a political context, each claiming to represent the imagined community Australia. Beyond the symbolism of representation, the exclusivity is based on another widely accepted function of memories, which is described by McCalman: they 'guide us in the present and for the future'.[42] The memories and their imagined communities contest each other not just for the specific ideas of Australia they contain, but because the way they relate this idea to the present situation has explicit political implications. Whether the plight of refugees is equated with Australian experiences or refugees are presented as being opposed to an imagined Christian community has a desired effect on policies towards refugees.

Different memories suggest different interpretations of the present situation and thus different solutions for which they compete. It was in fact the contemporary political situation, the question of how 'Australia' should treat refugees, which evoked memories as expressions of political interests in the first place. Different solutions presented by communal memories compete because they depend on a collective ability to act. In regard to migration and refugee policies, the government, representing the executive power of the sovereign, thus serves as the focus of communal memories. Different versions of the past presented by memories stood for different policies competing in order to be adopted by the executive power for an apparently common good.

Communal memories are justifications of competing political interests within the same political body and claim to represent the current solution for the whole of the political body presented as a community. Communality is imagined as a traditional relationship of its members, veiling the power of the State to which they are commonly subjected. From this viewpoint, belonging is not a question of legal status or of the rights-based relation to the State, but of seemingly shared homogenous values expressed in memories and traditions. Communal memories have the function of bridging the partiality of interest groups by remembering the communality of the government's political action. In fact, it is the power of the State under which members of the imagined community are united and through which partial interests can become common policies.

In terms of sovereignty, communal memories veil the democratic legal institutions, the legislature and the judiciary, which mediate between citizens and the government as central authority, with a homogenous perception of belonging. Consequently, political interests are discussed in apparently hyper-political and non-partisan terms of communal belonging. The government seems to reflect shared values and to work for an apparently common interest of 'all', representing homogenous sovereignty. The State is therefore confronted in refugee policies with the dilemma of having to act in the name and for the benefit of a disputed community while having to act according to legal distinctions that define and separate refugees. During the Tampa crisis, the past acquired a different function and the way refugees related to the sovereign changed.

Sovereignty and memories (II)

Before the Tampa crisis refugees were treated like any immigrant, potentially belonging to or being excluded from politically imagined versions of Australia. During the Tampa crisis, this perception changed. Refugees came to be discussed in terms of border protection and of their legal relation to the Australian State.[43] They were perceived as a threat to Australian sovereignty and were thus confronted at the border with powers apparently unrelated to sovereignty. The government denied that refugees were humans seeking protection.[44] Cutting asylum-seekers off from any relation to sovereignty, debates now referred to the past in three new and distinct ways: as *governmental memories*, as *citizenship memories* and as *universal memories*.

The government, making a distinction between sovereignty and its power in dealing with refugees during the Tampa crisis, removed the civic foundation of political action by dividing the imagined community. It still relied, however, on the past or particular versions of it to deal with the problem at hand. It has been overlooked by commentators that Howard often introduced his line about Australia's prerogative to determine who enters the country with references to the past. When he first spoke about the *Tampa* in the House of Representatives in the early afternoon of 27 August, he said:

> Australia has a record in relation to caring for refugees of which every member of this House should be proud. No nation in the last 50 years has been more generous or more decent in relation to refugees than has Australia…But that does not mean that we are abandoning in any way our right to decide who comes here.[45]

Similarly, two days later, he asserted, hours before the Border Protection Bill 2001 was introduced:

> Nobody pretends for a moment that the circumstances from which many people flee are not very distressing. But equally, it has to be said that,

in the last 20 years, no country has been more generous to refugees than Australia. After the Indochinese events of the 1970s, this country took, on a per capita basis, more Indochinese refugees than any other country on earth. We have continued to be a warm, generous recipient of refugees, but we have become increasingly concerned about the increasing flow of people into this country. Every nation has the right to effectively control its borders and to decide who comes here and under what circumstances, and Australia has no intention of surrendering or compromising that right.[46]

These memories of successful immigration policies of the past served to provide a backdrop to evaluate the situation that was unfolding. They are 'governmental memories' because they refer to the previous actions of the government in order to evaluate the current situation.

Such interpretations of past Australian immigration policies were not exclusive to the governing Coalition. In response to the above statement by the Prime Minister, Labor leader, Kim Beazley, reminded the House:

Over the last 10 years something like 13,000 people have come into Australia this way [from Indonesia by boat]: 2,000 up until about 1996 and 11,000 since then. Quite clearly, there is a job of work to be done in terms of our relationship with Indonesia to in some way check or halt this process.[47]

The Leader of the Opposition in the Senate, John Faulkner, introduced his speech about the Border Protection Bill 2001 by saying:

Over the past 10 years, there have been 13,000 unauthorised entries into this country. Eleven thousand of those have occurred since 1996. Labor has consistently supported measures put up by the Howard government to stem this flow of illegal entries.[48]

Much in the same vein as the Coalition, the Labor Party used governmental memories to legitimise its present position.

The past figured in these arguments in order to 'guide us in the present and for the future', just like communal memories described above. The implications of the use of the past are, however, different here. Communal memories are based on a social level while governmental memories are situated exclusively at the level of state politics—in terms of what is remembered and in their political objectives. Instead of imagining a community in a shared past, the latter uses the past to legitimise the assertion of Australia's sovereign right and power to enforce policies.

References to the past functioned as incentives for political action in lieu of the sovereign community: Howard recalled Australia's generosity but said that this did not change Australia's 'right to decide who comes here'. Beazley counted recent arrivals of refugees by boat, on which he based his call to 'halt this process'. Faulkner referred to the same past in order to claim that Labor had already assisted the government to 'stem this flow of illegal entries'. The most important words in those arguments are Howard's 'but', Beazley's 'halt' and Faulkner's 'stem'. It is not a traditional past of an imagined community that shapes the policy according to governmental memories; rather, the past is intended to show that it lies within the government's power to determine the action taken in regard to refugees. The past of governmental memories is a showcase for state power making history.

When the government initiated its new refugee policy of deterrence by force, it separated state power not only from universal rights but from citizenship. This prompted a new perception of sovereignty that redefined its relationship to refugees and the role of the past in political arguments. Governmental memories figured as justification for state power being autonomous from legal checks and balances and from traditions imagined as communal sovereignty. The new perception of sovereignty and of the past was not, however, limited to governmental memories. Others responded to the new policy situation with the same new perception of sovereignty; but instead of focusing on the government's power, they highlighted the other separated elements of sovereignty: citizenship and universality.

Since Australian society was not perceived as an all-encompassing community anymore, citizenship memories offered a different possibility to relate refugees to Australians. Senator Nick Bolkus (Labor) suggested:

> In that context, you really have an obligation to help those who want to come here as refugees and in humanitarian circumstances—if for no other reason than, in looking back at our history, it can be seen that those who have come here over the years as refugees have made enormous contributions to this country. They have not stagnated and have not been stillborn in their citizenship of Australia. They moved on one after the other and contributed enormously. We have met social responsibilities but, as a nation, we have benefited from those whom we brought in in these circumstances.[49]

Instead of relating refugees to an imagined Australian community, they are evaluated by past actions considered useful to the citizenry. Based on citizenship memories, refugees are judged as equal parts of Australian society rather than as traditionally different or similar. With citizenship being distinguished from state power, however, these memories are not able to relate refugees to the protective power of the sovereign. Refugees remain removed from the State's civil protection and from asylum under international obligations. Society is viewed retrospectively by citizenship memories as being bound neither by communal belonging nor by legal status but by civil action and social usefulness.

Finally, universal memories relate policies to global events and human rights.[50] In the debate about the Border Protection Bill 2001, Senator Andrew Bartlett (Australian Democrats) recalled stories of refugee boats during the twentieth century: he reminded his audience that the passengers of the *St Louis*, the *Strumer* and the *Petchko* all died or were deported to concentration camps because their vessels were turned away. He also recalled that hundreds of thousands of people fleeing Vietnam 'died during their doomed journey to freedom'.[51] He concluded:

> That was an inevitable outcome of the situation that developed when countries sent out the message that they would not be willing to accept people that they knew would be asylum seekers and sent them on and said: 'You have to go somewhere else. It is someone else's problem. It is someone else's responsibility.'[52]

These memories were directed at the Australian State to act according to a set of humanitarian principles. They reminded the audience of universal historical events: of the Holocaust and of the Vietnam War. These memories were not supposed to represent sections of Australian citizenry; instead, their implications were universal and applied to every sovereign, not just to the Australian State and people.

Universal memories point out the rights of man according to which refugees are supposed to be treated as 'humans', and call for humanitarian action. The Democrats therefore protested by calling on the past against the government's strategy of stripping asylum-seekers of their human right to claim asylum under a sovereign power. They appealed, however, not to the sovereign's responsibility but to universal morality. By referring to refugees through events historically unrelated to Australia, the Democrats accepted the separation of universal rights from sovereignty that was evoked by the government's policy with regard to the *Tampa*.

With the change of memories in the Tampa crisis, the relationship of sovereignty and refugees changed dramatically. Before Tampa, the sovereign seemed to act as one traditional community that was marked off clearly from the universal status of refugees. During the Tampa debate, the imagined community that represented Australian sovereignty was split into separate elements: state power, citizenship and universal rights. These elements of sovereignty were represented by different references to the past, which all failed to represent sovereignty in themselves: in governmental memories, state power seemed to exist isolated from sovereignty just like citizens in citizenship memories and human rights in universal memories. Consequently, these memories fail to relate refugees to sovereignty. Instead, they connect refugees to Australia and to political action in different ways: as objects of government action, of civil action or of humanitarian action. While, however, the different uses of the past allowed different approaches to refugees, the dilemma of sovereign political action in respect to asylum-seekers—the obligation of universal sovereignty—was not solved but only shifted.

Before Tampa, the government did not act on the obligation of asylum because the communal perception of sovereignty ignored the distinction of legal status on which refugees might have been able to claim asylum. After Tampa, refugees were related merely to elements of sovereignty, which prevented the full recognition of their legal status in Australia as asylum-seekers and subjected them to arbitrary forms of political power and action. After analysing the shift during the Tampa crisis in regard to memory, sovereignty and refugees, a closer look needs to be taken at what the change entailed and how the before and after relate in order to understand the impact of this event on Australian politics.

Sovereignty and refugees (II)

In Australian politics, the arrival of the *Tampa* was a key event that led to the modification of deterrence by example to deterrence by force, altering the significance of different forms of memory in parliamentary debates and, simultaneously, the relation of sovereignty to the issue of refugees. Shifting the debate of refugee issues from their treatment in immigration detention to border protection, the government's focus moved from the Australian community to state power. This enabled the Howard Government to move forward with the refugee issue in terms of governing.

The past became a reference for change enforced by state action, instead of legitimising social traditions to deter change. The failed policy of deterrence by example, having argued for refugee policies based on perceptions of communal traditions, seemed to be stuck in the past—virtually and literally. Memories, which imagine a community by looking back, derive solutions to political challenges from the logic of an imagined tradition. The strength of such memories is to create the impression of communal belonging, which apparently encompasses all citizens who seem to act jointly through the State. Post-Tampa memories, instead, isolated citizens from each other and from the State. The government now appeared to have powers in regard to the present situation that were autonomous of citizens, of the international sphere and of traditions. It looks back to create a future different from the past. Taking a new stance on refugees in the Tampa crisis, the government adjusted its memories and therefore its understanding of the present situation—namely, sovereignty and refugees.

So far, I have differentiated between concepts of memory and sovereignty before and after the *Tampa*'s arrival. Despite the clear changes, communal and governmental memories always coexist and only their respective significance changes.[53] The debates pre- and post-Tampa were distinct but all forms of memory can be found at any stage of the Australian debate about refugees. Governmental memories were used in the debate about the strip-search bill and much earlier. Conversely, memories uniting citizens and power in an imagined community played a role after Tampa, albeit a much less important one than before. Having differentiated the two phases before and after Tampa allowed me, however, to set apart ideal-type categories of memory and concepts of sovereignty. The forms of memories need to be recognised in order to understand the change precipitated by the Tampa crisis.

Memories pre- and post-Tampa are not simply opposed and unrelated. Both forms of memory have in common that they veil the mediation between citizens and the State. In the case of communal memories, citizens and the State are unmediated in a traditionally and homogenously defined sovereignty. In governmental memories, citizens and the State are separated as non-mediated elements of sovereignty. In both cases, human rights seem separated from the concepts of sovereignty. The politics of sovereign countries, however, rest on universal rights, sovereign citizens and sovereign power. The government derives its power from the universally accepted concept of a sovereign population within a territory while citizens are only citizens as humans and as subjects of the sovereign power. The significance of both forms of memory within the polity, however, focused on community or on the State, changes along with the relevance of the elements of sovereignty in relation to current politics. Not only politicians' perception, but the population's perception of the past and of society changed rapidly with the new politics in regard to the *Tampa*.

When the Howard Government attempted to distinguish between governmental force and sovereign citizenship by separating sovereign territory from the migration zone and introducing Operation Relex—the removal of unwanted ships from territorial waters—it revealed the brutality of a power unchecked by civil and human rights.[54] This approach was initiated by the SAS assault on the *Tampa*. With the government tackling the refugees aboard the Norwegian ship, the standing of the Liberal Party in the polls improved almost instantly. The electorate immediately grasped the new political situation proposed by the government in relation to the *Tampa* and many voters changed their perception of politics accordingly. In relation to border control, Australians no longer saw themselves as members of a community, potentially open to those who were willing to share certain Australian memories and values. Instead, their view 'turned inwards', as Mackay had predicted, to focus on citizenry and civil society. Letters to newspapers, such as this one from Joan Bidio to the *Herald Sun*, can be taken as evidence of the new perspective: 'Perhaps the humanitarian civil liberties groups and others of like mind could now turn their indignant attention to helping ordinary Australians such as the homeless, the struggling poor, basic pensioners and those in nursing homes.'[55] Refugees and asylum-seekers were not connected to Australia anymore, either as part of a multicultural society or as 'others', but were excluded as non-citizens.

Conversely, Australians, in the new perception of a divided sovereignty, were isolated as citizens, isolated from the international sphere and separated from their sovereign power. In the former perception of Australia, the State was an indistinguishable part of the homogenous imagined community. After Tampa, the State and citizens emerged as distinct and separate elements. This change seemed to empower the State, which was no longer hindered either by civil sovereignty or by international obligations. Citizens now perceived themselves, however, as disempowered, isolated and insecure. The government's decision to change its approach to refugees simultaneously created its appeal as a protective power to citizens. Refugees, as objects of the government's action, were blamed for the insecurity stemming from that same change of politics. They appeared as a threat, and the government was applauded for tackling them with force.

That the support for the new policy often took on racist undertones was a sign that traditions of White Australia persisted in society as communal memories.[56] They influenced people's perception despite a change-oriented and state-centred use of the past, which dominated the debate. Governmental memories structured the new public perception of politics while communal categories of cultural inclusion and exclusion underlaid the political interests. Politics transformed not memories altogether but the relationship of governmental and communal memories. Only through the interplay of different forms of memory, and their specific perceptions of sovereignty, can the changes that occurred during the Tampa crisis be understood: governmental memories gained greater public relevance over communal memories in the formulation of policies, and the political significance of the perception of sovereignty shifted, associating Australia in a new relation to refugees.

The political crisis embodied in the Tampa incident, for which refugees were blamed, was not the fault of refugees, but was inherent in the contradiction and fiction of sovereignty. While citizens appeal to the State for protection from external threats, fundamental rights vis-a-vis the State are based on their equality as humans. Sovereignty as a political foundation is challenged not only in relation to asylum-seekers. It is, as a contradiction of the sovereign citizenry, the sovereign state and universal human rights, a fiction to begin with. Refugees demonstrate, no more and no less, this critical state of a world organised by sovereignties. Their existence undermines the illusion of harmonious power relations imagined in communal memories. They become the disturbing representation of the inherent crisis of any state system. They are therefore either futilely repelled with force by proponents of state power or supported as a seemingly positive challenge to power by critics of the State.

Conclusion

Refugees coming by boat, even in their thousands, were and are no threat to Australia's security. Lacking the protection of their own nation-state and possessing nothing more than their humanity, they are perceived as a challenge to the political sovereign. The response to their arrival is dependent on the perception of sovereignty, of the past and the present.

In this chapter, I have outlined how the Tampa crisis changed popular perceptions of refugees, citizens and the State. Before Tampa, sovereignty, which binds citizenship, the State and universal rights, was united in society by references to the past—a past to which refugees could be related as migrants. Those memories allowed social belonging to be imagined as community, which had to be sustained. With the arrival of the *Tampa*, the expectation that the State could deter refugees by force led the government to disaggregate the sovereign polity into state power, citizenship and universal rights. Memories no longer bound society but were related instead to refugees, the State or citizenship. The alteration of sovereignty and memory allowed the government to move beyond the failed policy of deterrence by example. The perception of the past shifted in a way that excluded refugees by their very definition as non-citizens from a newly perceived Australian society.[57] All the while, Australia found itself caught up in an impossible policy of pure force.

Focusing on the interplay of different concepts of memory, this chapter challenges static conceptions of sovereignty. It has shown how policies based on this idea affect images of belonging, which in turn influence refugee policies. Policies based on sovereignty, however, are not compatible with the needs of stateless asylum-seekers. That refugees are the object of sovereign power is a reminder that sovereignty based on any form of the past is always an exclusive concept of power. Refugees could be accommodated only if sovereignty was built on the memory of statelessness.

Acknowledgments

I would like to thank Klaus Neumann, Gwenda Tavan and Tai Sayarath for important comments, criticism and advice on several draft versions of this chapter. Of course, none of them should be held accountable for any deficiencies of the text, which are wholly my responsibility. I wrote this chapter while a visiting scholar at the Institute for Social Research at Swinburne University of Technology. The Friedrich Ebert Foundation supported my work with a postgraduate scholarship.

Endnotes

1 Halbwachs, Maurice 1980 [1950], *The Collective Memory*, Translated by Francis J. Ditter, Jr, and Vidar Yazdi Ditter, Harper & Row, New York, p. 86.

2 Davidson, Alastair 1997, *From Subject to Citizen: Australian citizenship in the twentieth century*, Cambridge University Press, Cambridge, p. 150.

3 Mackay, Hugh 2001, 'Politics fans the flames of ugly prejudice', *Age*, 25 August 2001.

4 Subsequently, that rhetoric became the focus of several studies; see, for example, Corlett, Dave 2002, 'Asylum seekers and the new racism', *Dissent*, vol. 8; Every, Danielle and Augoustinos, Martha 2007, 'Constructions of racism in the Australian parliamentary debates on asylum seekers', *Discourse Society*, vol. 18, no. 4.

5 Hage, Ghassan 1998, *White Nation: Fantasies of white supremacy in a multicultural society*, Pluto, Sydney; Markus, Andrew 2002, 'Racism and refugees: an Australian tradition', *Australian Rationalist*, vols 60–1. Numerous works from different perspectives have dealt with the Tampa crisis as a pivotal point in Australian politics—most importantly, Marr, David and Wilkinson, Marian 2003, *Dark Victory*, Allen & Unwin, Crows Nest; and Mares, Peter 2002, *Borderline: Australia's response to refugees and asylum seekers in the wake of the Tampa*, UNSW Press, Sydney, ch. 5.

6 Agamben, Giorgio 1998, *Homo Sacer: Sovereign power and bare life*, Stanford University Press, Stanford, pp. 15–70.

7 McCalman, Janet 2001, 'Teaching history safeguards the truth', *Age*, 25 August 2001.

8 Olick, Jeffrey K. and Robbins, Joyce 1998, 'Social memory studies: from "collective memory" to the historical sociology of mnemonic practices', *Annual Review of Sociology*, vol. 24.

9 The classic and still one of the most concise concepts of social memory is Halbwachs, Maurice 1992, *On Collective Memory*, Translated by Lewis A. Coser, University of Chicago Press, Chicago. See also Halbwachs, *The Collective Memory*.

10 Brändström, Annika, Bynander, Fredrik and 't Hart, Paul 2004, 'Governing by looking back: historical analogies and crisis management', *Public Administration*, vol. 82, no. 1, pp. 191–210.

11 Ruddock, Philip 2001, 'Detention contingency planning announced', *MPS 123/2001*, 23 August 2001.

12 Marr and Wilkinson, *Dark Victory*, p. 61.

13 Mares, Peter 2007, 'Reassessing the Tampa', in Dan Lusher and Nick Haslam (eds), *Yearning to Breathe Free: Seeking asylum in Australia*, Federation Press, Annandale, pp. 58–9.

14 Australia's cooperation with Indonesia in matters of policing the borders, and later, the government's hope to cooperate with Norway on the Pacific Solution were other attempts of using the recognition of sovereignty to contain border breaches (Marr and Wilkinson, *Dark Victory*, pp. 38–61 and 160–2).

15 Ibid., pp. 88–9.

16 Philip Ruddock, *Commonwealth Parliamentary Debates* [hereafter *CPD*], Representatives, 28 August 2001, p. 30362.

17 Ruddock, Philip 2001, 'Successful removal of 31 People from Australia', *MPS 128/2001*, 28 August 2001.

18 John Howard, *CPD*, Representatives, 27 August 2001, p. 30235.

19 Marr and Wilkinson, *Dark Victory*, pp. 108–9.

20 UNHCR 1981, *Problems related to the rescue of asylum-seekers in distress at sea*, EC/SCP/18.

21 Pallis, Mark 2002, 'Obligations of states towards asylum seekers at sea: interactions and conflicts between legal regimes', *International Journal of Refugee Law*, vol. 14, nos 2–3.

22 The last point was especially odd as the migration zone did not extend to the territorial sea like the sovereign power did; see Hancock, Nathan 2001–02, 'Border Protection Bill 2001', *Bills Digest*, vol. 41, Department of the Parliamentary Library, p. 13.

23 John Howard, *CPD*, Representatives, 29 August 2001, p. 30570.

24 Robert Hill, *CPD*, Senate, 29 August 2001, p. 26976.

25 Kim Beazley, *CPD*, Representatives, 29 August 2001, p. 30571.

26 Bob Brown, *CPD*, Senate, 29 August 2001, p. 26996.

27 Arendt, Hannah 1994 [1948], *The Origins of Totalitarianism*, Harcourt, San Diego, pp. 269–302.

28 Agamben, Giorgio 1995, 'We refugees', *Symposium*, vol. 49, no. 2, p. 117.

[29] High Court, *Chu Kheng Lim vs MILGA* [1992], 110 ALR 97. Mary Crock highlights the critical distinction between civic and international law made by the court in its ruling. Crock, Mary 1993, 'Climbing Jacob's ladder: the High Court and the administrative detention of asylum seekers in Australia', *Sydney Law Review*, vol. 15.

[30] The refugees had to reach the migration zone, which did not include the territorial sea, in order to claim asylum. Alternatively, they could have claimed asylum through an Australian official. Refugees aboard the *Tampa* were prevented from lodging asylum claims with relevant Australian authorities and from receiving legal representation (Marr and Wilkinson, *Dark Victory*, pp. 145–68).

[31] John Faulkner, *CPD*, Senate, 29 August 2001, p. 26973; Natasha Stott Despoja, *CPD*, Senate, 29 August 2001, pp. 26979, 26980, 26982; Andrew Bartlett, *CPD*, Senate, 29 August 2001, p. 26995; Nick Bolkus, *CPD*, Senate, 29 August 2001, p. 26998.

[32] Robert McClelland, *CPD*, Representatives, 19 September 2001, p. 30965. The Pacific Solution was the result of legislation that was debated in Parliament between 18 and 26 September 2001: the Migration Amendment (Excision from Migration Zone) Bill 2001, the Migration Amendment (Excision from Migration Zone) (Consequential Provision) Bill 2001 and the Border Protection (Validation and Enforcement Powers) Bill 2001. The bills included the extended distinction between migration zone and territory, detention in foreign countries and removal of boats from territorial waters, of which the last provision had been rejected in its previous form on 29 August 2001.

[33] Examples of those accusations are statements by Robert Hill: 'The opposition in these circumstances apparently believes that it can get some benefit through not supporting the government today in this difficult time, so be it' (*CPD*, Senate, 29 September 2001, p. 26968); and by Labor's Nick Bolkus: 'My fear is that the Prime Minister is playing politics with the national interest. It diminishes his reputation, although he does not seem to care about that when votes and his hide are at risk' (*CPD*, Senate, 29 August 2001, p. 26999).

[34] Danna Vale, *CPD*, Representatives, 23 August 2001, p. 30112.

[35] Neumann, Klaus 2007, 'Been there, done that?', in Dean Lusher and Nick Haslam (eds), *Yearning to Breathe Free: Seeking asylum in Australia*, Federation Press, Annandale, p. 27; Neumann, Klaus 2004, *Refuge Australia: Australia's humanitarian record*, UNSW Press, Sydney.

[36] Danna Vale, *CPD*, Representatives, 23 August 2001, p. 30112.

[37] McCalman, 'Teaching history safeguards the truth'.

[38] Anderson, Benedict 1991, *Imagined Communities*, 2nd edn, Verso, London, pp. 199–203.

[39] Bob Brown, *CPD*, Senate, 28 August 2001, p. 26822.

[40] Anderson (*Imagined Communities*, pp. 200–1) notes about the nineteenth-century French community, imagined in memories of 'la Saint-Barthélemy', that not every French person would have remembered this past. Anderson fails, however, to distinguish between those who remembered and the much larger group of those who were included in the imagination. Instead, he suggests—not quite coincidentally, as I argue—that 'the state' reminded every French person of the shared history, presenting the notion of 'French' as the beginning and the end point of memories.

[41] Quoted by Jim McKiernan, *CPD*, Senate, 28 August 2001, p. 26820.

[42] McCalman, 'Teaching history safeguards the truth'.

[43] Jeremy Hein, who takes this legal perspective, argues accordingly that the relation to the State is what distinguishes the refugee from other migrants. Hein, Jeremy 1993, 'Refugees, immigrants, and the state', *Annual Review of Sociology*, vol. 19, no. 1.

[44] In order to prevent Australians from recognising refugees as fellow humans, the government tried to restrict the circulation of any humanising photographs of refugees aboard the *Tampa* (Marr and Wilkinson, *Dark Victory*, p. 108).

[45] John Howard, *CPD*, Representatives, 27 August 2001, p. 30235.

[46] John Howard, *CPD*, Representatives, 29 August 2001, pp. 30517–8.

[47] Kim Beazley, *CPD*, Representatives, 29 August 2001, p. 30519. For a very similar statement in the debate about the Border Protection Bill 2001 debate, see *CPD*, Representatives, 29 August 2001, p. 30572.

[48] John Faulkner, *CPD*, Senate, 29 August 2001, p. 26971.

[49] Nick Bolkus, *CPD*, Senate, 29 August 2001, p. 26998.

[50] Daniel Levy and Nathan Sznaider have also used the term 'universal memory' to describe trends in Holocaust memory and in regard to the 'cosmopolitan morality' of human rights. The authors argue

that universal Holocaust memories stand at the beginning of institutional human rights. Today, universal memories are part of what they call 'cosmopolitan memory', which includes the partiality of its application in the genocide discourse. Levy, Daniel and Sznaider, Nathan 2004, 'The institutionalization of cosmopolitan morality: the Holocaust and human rights', *Journal of Human Rights*, vol. 3, no. 2. The use of memory to call on human rights is, however, not exclusive to Holocaust memories—see, for example, the reference to Vietnam below. Furthermore, the term 'cosmopolitan memory' merges the universal with what is considered partial memory without mediation. I argue instead that it is the distinction of different forms of references to the past—universal, governmental and citizenship memories—that helps to explain the current relevance of what seems to be cosmopolitan memory and which also shows the limitations of memories in regard to human rights.

[51] Andrew Bartlett, *CPD*, Senate, 29 August 2001, pp. 26994–5.

[52] Ibid., p. 26995.

[53] This relationship is based on the dialectics of 'abstract time' and 'historical time', suggested by Moishe Postone as an explanation for the 1970s transformation of Holocaust memories. Postone, Moishe 2003, 'The Holocaust and the trajectory of the twentieth century', in Moishe Postone and Eric L. Santner (eds), *Catastrophe and Meaning: The Holocaust and the twentieth century*, University of Chicago Press, Chicago, pp. 102–6.

[54] The danger of separating power—in Operation Relex, it was naval power—from notions of sovereignty was incidentally seen by the Navy itself, which warned of the brutal consequences of such an approach (Marr and Wilkinson, *Dark Victory*, pp. 172–6).

[55] Bidio, Joan 2001, 'Letter to the editor', *Herald Sun*, 7 September 2001.

[56] Jayasuriya, Laksiri, Walker, David and Gothard, Jan (eds) 2003, *Legacies of White Australia: Race, culture and nation*, University of Western Australia Press, Crawley, especially chapters by Ien Ang, Robert Manne and Andrew Markus. The legacies of White Australia are also debated in Tavan, Gwenda 2005, *The Long, Slow Death of White Australia*, Scribe, Melbourne, pp. 221–33.

[57] This is different from assuming a shift in the Tampa crisis from an inclusive to an exclusionary model of citizenship as suggested by Kim Rubinstein. Rubinstein, Kim 2002, 'Citizenship, sovereignty and migration: Australia's exclusionary approach to membership of the community', *Public Law Review*, vol. 13, pp. 102–9.

6. Looking back and glancing sideways: refugee policy and multicultural nation-building in New Zealand

Ann Beaglehole

Bose: 'Aren't' we friends?'

'Time passes, things change,' said the Judge, feeling claustrophobia and embarrassment.

'But what is in the past remains unchanged, doesn't it?'

'I think it does change. The present changes the past. Looking back you do not find what you left behind, Bose.'

— Kiran Desai, *The Inheritance of Loss*[1]

This chapter examines, first, how New Zealand governments have used the past to represent refugee settlement and multicultural nation-building policies. Second, it examines New Zealand's longstanding humanitarian record of refugee settlement, highlighting how politicians have consistently relied on an idealised version of this record for political purposes, and it discusses aspects of the representation of New Zealand's immigration history after the 1986 review of immigration policy, especially in relation to multicultural policies.

The popular myth of New Zealand as an ideal society has contributed to commonplace representations of its response to refugees as outstandingly humanitarian. The myth has also contributed to the development of multicultural policies and discourses, which are partly to counter and disguise the reality of racial discrimination in the country's immigration history.

A number of commentators have observed that images of New Zealand—by New Zealanders and by those on the outside looking in—have been informed by dreams about finding and building a better new world. According to Miles Fairburn's *The Ideal Society and Its Enemies*, for example, colonists saw New Zealand as an ideal society free from the evils of the Old World.[2] Several of the essayists in David Novitz and Bill Willmott's *Culture and Identity in New Zealand* explore aspects of the ideal society, including its egalitarian myths.[3] More recently, Dominic Alessio has argued that utopia has been 'central to the nation's culture and resulted in the paradise myth emerging as one of its dominant tropes'.[4] New Zealand's island status, topography, climate, supposed social mobility, reputation for radical political experimentation and expressed commitment to racial equality for Europeans and Maori have all at different times contributed to the myth of an ideal society.

New Zealand has often been imagined as embodying a vast array of 'heavens on earth'.[5] New Zealand ('Godzone') has at various times been depicted as 'the happy colony', 'islands of the blest', 'the labourer's paradise', 'the poor man's paradise', 'the middle-class paradise', a rural paradise and numerous other variations, such as 'the half-gallon quarter-acre pavlova paradise'.[6] The country—'the farthest promised land'—removed from Old World problems such as industrialisation and class conflict, has been depicted as an ideal place to raise children, a laboratory for advanced social legislation, an egalitarian society without poverty in which 'Jack is as good as his master' and, more recently, as one of the few 'clean and green' oases left on the planet. In international politics, New Zealand's 'sense of national identity' has been 'underpinned' by the country's 'contribution as an independent and principled player on the world stage'[7] —a position that has been significant in recent representations of its response to refugee situations.

The signing of the *Treaty of Waitangi* in 1840 facilitated British colonisation and settlement of the country. The treaty—a compact between New Zealand's Indigenous Maori and the British Crown—aimed to ensure that Maori rights would be protected in exchange for cessation of Maori sovereignty. Although by the end of the nineteenth century, due to large-scale land loss to British settlers, Maori found themselves marginalised in their own country and excluded from reaping the supposed benefits of European settlement, representations of New Zealand as an ideal society have extended to race relations, with New Zealand supposedly having a better record of contact between colonised and coloniser than other countries. The myth of an ideal society has encompassed views of New Zealand as a racial paradise, with terms such as 'brown Britons' and 'better blacks' featuring strongly in paradise discourses.[8]

Since the 1970s, governments have increasingly recognised that the State is liable for wrongs committed in the past in relation to Maori (such as confiscation of land). In 1975, the Waitangi Tribunal was set up to decide 'whether or not the Crown had done what it should have done to and for Maori in the light of Treaty promises and to propose redress when the Crown through its agents is found to have defaulted in its duty'.[9] In 1985, the *Treaty of Waitangi Act 1975* was amended to allow for the scope of inquiries into historical grievances to extend back to 1840. In a series of treaty settlements between Maori and the Crown, Maori have sought and received redress for past injustices.

There is a relationship between the colonial legacy and the themes that are the focus of this chapter. I argue that a connection might exist between the rhetoric of New Zealand's generosity and compassion towards refugees (increasingly prevalent since the mid-1980s) and the growing recognition of the harsh and unjust treatment many Maori were accorded in the nineteenth and early twentieth centuries. Guilt about the latter has in part been addressed through hyperbolic claims in relation to the former. There has also been an uneasy relationship between the growing emphasis, from the mid-1980s, on addressing Maori grievances under the *Treaty of Waitangi* and the recognition that, in view of the acceptance of increasing numbers of refugees and immigrants from Asia and other non-British countries, effort needs to be put into multicultural nation-building. That exercise, however, was at odds with the government's bicultural agenda,[10] according to which Maori grievances had to be resolved before multicultural issues could be addressed. As a way of easing the conflict, moves towards multiculturalism were accompanied by a recasting of New Zealand history to emphasise the immigrant origin of all New Zealanders, including Maori.

New Zealand's 'fine record of humanitarian assistance'

According to the New Zealand Immigration Service, the acceptance of refugees as settlers has been an 'ongoing important humanitarian priority' since the late 1980s, with refugees and asylum-seekers admitted in accordance with the 1951 UN Convention Relating to the Status of Refugees and the associated 1967 Protocol.[11] In fact, this record of international 'good citizenship' goes back much further. Since 1840, thousands of people escaping persecution in Europe, South America, Asia, the Middle East and Africa have found refuge in New Zealand. More than 30 000 refugees have arrived since 1944, when refugees were first distinguished from other immigrants in official statistics.

Until the late 1970s, refugees admitted to New Zealand were predominantly from Europe. Since then, they have come from a variety of ethnic and national backgrounds. In addition to the country's annual refugee quota of 750 people, refugees have entered under humanitarian and family reunion immigration categories. Relatively small numbers of asylum-seekers have entered New Zealand since the early 1980s, seeking to establish their UN High Commissioner for Refugees (UNHCR) mandated refugee status at the border or after their arrival on a temporary visa.[12]

New Zealand's reputation as an 'independent and principled player on the world stage'[13] is undoubtedly justified in parts. The decision in 1959 to accept refugee families with 'handicapped' members showed it leading the world in humanitarian refugee policy. Over the years, the country has consistently resettled refugees rejected by other countries. In accepting Asian refugees from Uganda in 1973, Labour Prime Minister, Norman Kirk, insisted that New Zealand's intake include a significant proportion of 'handicapped' cases.[14] Reporting

Kirk's announcement, the Wellington *Evening Post* wrote: 'New Zealand should not say it wanted only "the best apples in the barrel." He [Kirk] was sure that most New Zealanders would agree that these were the people who needed help most.'[15]

New Zealand continued to accept refugees considered hard to settle on health and other grounds in the 1980s, 1990s and in the twenty-first century. Over the years, the terminology changed from 'handicapped' or 'hard core' to 'medically disabled' in the 1990s. Refugees with special needs, who are considered harder to settle for whatever reason, including medical conditions, have continued to be accepted as part of New Zealand's annual refugee quota. They have come under such categories as 'medical', 'emergency', 'women at risk' and 'protection'.[16] New Zealand has been one of the few countries in the world to accept refugees with HIV/AIDS, who have come in under the 'medical' category.[17]

New Zealand's compassionate and generous response over time is embodied in the operations of the Mangere Refugee Reception Centre in West Auckland, where thousands of newly arrived refugees have for decades received their first introduction to New Zealand. Mangere is in some ways the country's equivalent to the Ellis Island immigrant processing centre in New York (though Ellis Island is for processing only, while Mangere's focus is on providing resettlement assistance as well as on processing a small number of asylum-seekers). It symbolises the capacity and willingness of a small country to shelter the huddled masses of the world before sending them on their way to make new lives.

The country's response to refugees has, however, not been even-handed, with governments adopting diverse approaches to refugee crises around the world. Economic and political considerations, not just humanitarian ones, have played a part in the admission and the selection of refugees. Intakes were much larger when there were clear economic benefits for the country and when the refugee group was considered particularly suitable for settlement on cultural, ethnic and racial grounds.

The government made stringent efforts to keep out all but a very small number of Chinese and Jewish refugees in the 1930s and 1940s, and placed severe restrictions on the immigration of close relatives.[18] The entry of Jewish Holocaust survivors was severely restricted in the immediate postwar years. There were attempts to limit the number of displaced persons accepted after World War II to racially and culturally similar northern European 'Balts' and to exclude 'Slavs' and Jews.[19] The apparently generous acceptance of Hungarian and other Cold War refugees between the 1950s and the 1980s was a case of compassion and other more self-serving motives working together. As Alistair McIntosh, Secretary of External Affairs, observed in November 1956, regarding the Hungarian situation: 'Fortunately this is a case in which political and humanitarian considerations go hand in hand.'[20] The fact that these refugees were white and generally regarded as an economic asset—they were mainly young and had skills needed by New Zealand—contributed to the government's positive response.[21]

In the late 1970s and early 1980s, in the aftermath of the Vietnam War, New Zealand was reluctant to accept Indochinese refugees in significant numbers. When it eventually admitted hundreds of such refugees, it did so only in response to considerable pressure from countries in the region and from the United States.

New Zealand's humanitarian record was considerably boosted in 2001 when the Clark Labour Government admitted some of the asylum-seekers rescued by the Norwegian freighter *Tampa* in the Indian Ocean. The *Tampa* refugees were, however, accepted as part of the country's annual refugee quota, not in addition to it—evidence that pragmatic and political principles were still at work. These are just some examples that show that humanitarianism and compassion have been two aspects of New Zealand's refugee history, but they do not tell the whole story.

New Zealand's 'fine' record of humanitarian assistance has frequently functioned to legitimise contemporary immigration policy and to justify the acceptance of specific groups. Between the 1950s and the 1980s, when welcoming new intakes of refugees, political leaders would typically refer in their public statements to New Zealand's humanitarian tradition and compassionate record of accepting refugees. Aspects of the past, such as discrimination against some refugees on the basis of their ethnicity (typical in the 1930s and 1940s), which did not fit with this humanitarian legacy, were conveniently forgotten.

Prime Minister, Sidney Holland (National Party), for example, when agreeing to accept up to 1000 Hungarian refugees in 1956, after the uprising against the Soviet Union, said:

> The plight of the Hungarian refugees has aroused widespread sympathy and I hope that New Zealand, which has proved so generous in past appeals of this nature, will once again demonstrate to the nations the practical nature of her sympathies in this present European tragedy.[22]

In making the offer in 1972 to accept up to 200 Asian refugees from among the tens of thousands who were being expelled by Idi Amin from Uganda, Prime Minister, Keith Holyoake (National Party), drew a connection between the acceptance of the refugees from Uganda and New Zealand's humanitarian record:

> We in New Zealand have a fine record of humanitarian assistance in situations of this sort and our decision to accept up to 200 people from Uganda is consistent with the policy followed most recently in the cases of refugees from Hungary and Czechoslovakia.[23]

In 1979, at a conference on Indochinese refugees held in Geneva, soon to become Minister of Immigration, Aussie Malcolm (National Party), spoke with some pride about New Zealand's response to 'an unfolding tragedy':

> The contribution of a small country like New Zealand will not, on its own, reduce the dimensions of the problem to a major extent. But we are doing our part, out of humanitarian concern, and in support of our friends of the ASEAN [Association of South-East Asian Nations] region.
>
> Over the past four years New Zealand has played its part in the international effort to resettle the refugees from Indochina. We are three million people but we have been among the first five countries in refugees settled per head of population. Up until the beginning of this year New Zealand had settled 535 Indochinese refugees. For the 1979 calendar year we committed ourselves to settle a further 900. I am pleased to be able to announce that we have now decided to make a further commitment to accept an additional 1800 by June 1981.
>
> By then one in every thousand New Zealanders will have been an Indochinese refugee.[24]

In a 1987 interview, Malcolm focused on the uniqueness of New Zealand's humanitarian contribution. In relation to the government's Indochinese family reunion program, he said:

> The speed of New Zealand bringing them together symbolizes the humanitarianism of the New Zealand programme...and finally the fact that they walked out of that airport and I have never heard anything about them again...that to me is the final seal of a refugee programme, because that's what should happen...nobody should hear of them again...New Zealand becomes the present and the future.[25]

In another interview in 2007, Malcolm again claimed that New Zealand was leading the world in humanitarianism. On the topic of South-East Asian refugees with special needs, he emphasised that the New Zealand policy was in stark contrast with that of countries such as Australia, which 'picked the eyes out of the refugee market'. According to Malcolm, Australia and Canada saw the refugee program in labour-market terms and selected the most intelligent and best trained. Unlike New Zealand, Australia and Canada were not concerned about the needs of refugees. He noted that Australia 'ran extensive medical testing in the camps' and rejected refugees with health problems. New Zealand, on the other hand, had decided not to do such testing. The illness of a refugee was not considered relevant:

> We preferred to put the refugees on a plane and bring them to New Zealand so that their health problems could be taken care of. New Zealand

took pride in selecting refugees who were ill and not chosen by other countries.[26]

Similarly, Don McKinnon (Foreign Minister 1990–99 in the National Government) commented that New Zealand 'had a more generous spirit [than Australia], though we could never compete with Australia on numbers'. In relation to the Canadians, he observed that they 'were the best in going into an area post-conflict (meaning almost the day after) with a C-130 aircraft and offering citizenship to any qualified person'.[27] These views reveal an important aspect of government thinking: that New Zealand has a reputation and a track record of behaving in a more compassionate way to refugees than other countries and that successive governments have an obligation to maintain this image—at least on occasions when it suits them.

Similar thinking was evident in the Tampa episode. The decision to bring approximately 130 of the asylum-seekers to New Zealand to have their refugee status determined there was made by Prime Minister, Helen Clark. 'We came to the conclusion that people couldn't sit on the deck of the ship forever,' she told Australian journalist David Marr in 2006.[28] New Zealand was contributing to solving a regional refugee issue and helping Australia. The fact that the country was maintaining its international reputation *and* showing itself to be more humanitarian than Australia was, however, a matter of some pride. Looking back at the events, former Minister of Immigration, Lianne Dalziel, said she felt 'particularly proud to be a New Zealander'.[29]

The Tampa incident was, in Dalziel's view, 'a symbol of the role a small country can play when called upon to do so'.[30] The country's small size has at various times been used to enhance the magnanimity of the humanitarian gesture being made—as in relation to the acceptance of refugee families with 'handicapped' members in 1959. As Anton Binzegger observes in his history of refugee immigration:

> Once again this shows how a small country like New Zealand can occasionally influence international action...while New Zealand has little impact on wars and military dispositions, its potential in the humanitarian field is considerably greater.[31]

On other occasions in the past, New Zealand's size has provided a convenient excuse for declining to accept a specific group of refugees, further groups or significant numbers of refugees. For example, '[a]s a small country, we are not in a position to make a substantial contribution to the resettlement of large groups of Chinese refugees,' said Prime Minister Holyoake in 1962 when announcing that New Zealand would accept only 50 Chinese orphans.[32]

Since the Tampa episode, New Zealand has retained the high moral ground despite measures introduced to prevent asylum-seekers reaching the country in significant numbers, to allow for their detention and to hasten the deportation of unsuccessful asylum-seekers. At the end of 2006, Minister of Immigration, David Cunliffe (Labour Party), responding to a question on the government's proposals for a major overhaul of immigration legislation, said that the nation had an outstanding reputation for compassionate policy towards refugees and asylum-seekers and that 'the humanitarian strand in New Zealand policy' was 'much stronger than in Australia'.[33]

In September 2007, in another interview, Cunliffe again spoke of New Zealand leading the world in the business of being humanitarian. In relation to the release from custody after a 53-day hunger strike of Iranian asylum-seeker Ali Panah, who had hoped that his conversion to Christianity would give him grounds to be granted refugee status, Cunliffe said: 'We have preserved the integrity of the immigration system and lived up to the highest standards of humanity in New Zealand, for which we are internationally famous.'[34] Cunliffe's rosy view implied that the Labour Government's compassionate policy, if it could be termed as such—after all, Panah had to almost die before he was released and was likely to be deported—was very much in keeping with New Zealand's track record. His view was certainly in keeping with representations of New Zealand as an ideal society—a true haven for genuine refugees.

'We are all immigrants'

As already noted, the period between the 1950s and 1970s was characterised by amnesia about inconvenient aspects of the problematic past of racial bias, with history used to create a myth of New Zealand's tradition of humanitarian responses to refugees and to make further refugee intakes more acceptable to the public. In relation to multicultural nation-building, the problematic past included statements on immigration policy such as the following:

> An implicit element is the desire that people whose stock originated in Great Britain shall always have an overwhelming preponderance in the total population of New Zealand. We believe in the selective and, when required, assisted immigration to ensure that end.[35]

After a major review in 1986, the past began to be used in a new way in relation to immigration policy. In contrast with the previous silence about ethnic bias (which coexisted with the frequent references to the country's fine record of humanitarian assistance), references to the discriminatory immigration policies of past governments started to become acceptable in public discourse. The new openness coincided with a major shift in public policy. It was reflected in the *Immigration Act 1987*, which had followed the 1986 review. The act introduced by the Lange Labour Government ushered in the selection of immigrants on the basis of their skills and qualifications, rather than their ethnicity. The policy shift meant that it was not only possible to publicly acknowledge the problematic past of ethnic discrimination but useful to do so. Revealing the past served the purpose of showing how far New Zealand had moved from earlier discriminatory policies.

Furthermore, public acknowledgment that the days of discrimination on the basis of ethnicity had been an unfortunate mistake became important in order to persuade members of the public of the benefits of the government's post-1987 immigration policies, which were allowing the entry of thousands of migrants from countries other than Great Britain or Ireland. The government needed to build support for ethnic diversity—that is, the presence in the community of increasing numbers of non-British and non-white immigrants. Both acknowledging the past and distancing itself from it became a means of convincing the public that the influx of culturally diverse migrants (including members of groups once despised) was now a matter for celebration.

In 1993, Minister of Immigration, Roger Maxwell, touched on key aspects of this policy shift in a speech to the Federation of Ethnic Councils:

> Our new immigration and refugee policies are leading to a greater diversity in the ethnic groups which are settling in New Zealand…Unlike some of our past immigration policies, national origin is no longer a consideration…This change in direction reflects a new public opinion that discrimination related to accident of birth is no longer acceptable and an acknowledgement that diversity can enrich rather than weaken New Zealand society…Over the years ethnic communities have made immeasurable contributions to economic, social, professional and cultural life in New Zealand. The diversity they have brought to our society has served to enrich and strengthen our country.[36]

From the mid-1980s, official rhetoric and official publications, including material used in schools, depicted New Zealand as a multicultural country of immigrants, with Maori identified as the first wave of immigrants to settle in New Zealand and establish themselves as *tangata whenua* (Indigenous people of the land). Malcolm McKinnon observed that a great deal of attention was paid in the official rhetoric and publications to immigration history at that time as a way of emphasising the legitimate place of non-Anglo-Celtic groups in the wider community, be they continental Europeans, Pacific Islanders or Asians. In the recast version of history, all New Zealanders were portrayed as immigrants, or of immigrant stock, and the population was portrayed as very diverse.[37]

A passage in the introduction to the 1986 Review of Immigration Policy, which treated immigrants from all parts of the world as a whole, illustrates this point:

> New Zealand is a country of immigration. The Maori people established themselves as the tangata whenua after historic voyages of migration from countries in the Pacific. Large scale immigration from European

countries, particularly the United Kingdom, over the last 200 years, changed the ethnic balance and altered the cultural base of New Zealand. This in turn has been modified by more recent migration movements from the South Pacific and from countries on the Pacific rim. Immigration has moulded our national characteristics as a Pacific country and given our community richness and cultural diversity. It has contributed to economic growth and prosperity, presented new challenges for New Zealand society and created pressures for social change. Immigration has been and remains an essential element in this nation's development.[38]

A 1990 study for use in schools—*An Immigrant Nation*—provides another illustration. The publication stated that '[p]erhaps the most important thing about Maori immigration to New Zealand is that it took place so long ago'.[39] McKinnon commented: 'Thus an implicit contradiction between "immigrant" and "indigenous" is solved by a time line (the contradiction was not addressed directly).' He also noted that the study did not canvass British immigration after 1880, or the post-1880 population of British descent, but did discuss the twentieth-century history of Maori, not an immigrant population.[40]

The emphasis given to the immigrant origins of all New Zealanders and to the multicultural character of New Zealand distorts aspects of the country's history. Maori were portrayed as simply one of many immigrant groups. The recasting of New Zealand as a multicultural society obscured the fact that British immigrants were strongly favoured throughout much of its history, with a variety of regulations restricting the settlement of non-British migrants. In the false presentation of history, New Zealanders of Anglo-Celtic heritage were rendered almost invisible because they did not fit the rhetoric about multiculturalism. To draw attention to such a large group would have weakened the case for New Zealand's population being a varied one.[41]

I have presented McKinnon's analysis in some detail as it sheds light on how governments and politicians have used the problematic past for their present purposes. The analysis is particularly useful in highlighting the gap between representation and reality in relation to multiculturalism. It is noteworthy that these changing representations of the past were taking place just as the Waitangi Tribunal acquired a new brief to address historic grievances going back to 1840, and biculturalism was gaining a new and intense focus at government level. According to the bicultural agenda, outstanding issues between the Crown and Maori needed to be resolved before multicultural issues arising from non-British immigration were addressed.

The recasting of history in the way suggested by McKinnon is evident in a speech made by Dalziel at the 2002 launch of a book on women and migration in New Zealand history. The minister began by saying that the book was important and timely because it was 'important that we know our history as a country'. It was 'the essence of identity' for 'each of us to know who we are and where we have come from'. She highlighted her own immigrant roots, revealing that she had a distant non-British ancestor. She noted that all New Zealanders were immigrants and referred to the value of multiculturalism:

> I often make the point that there is not one New Zealander that does not have a migrant story in their past. Each of us, or one of our forebears, including those who are part of the waka traditions, made a journey to make New Zealand home…Reflecting on our own stories and sharing them with each other is a great way to break down the barriers that stand in the way of celebrating the diversity New Zealand represents today…I often hear people saying that migrants should assimilate. I use the word integrate. It is not about swallowing up people's culture and tradition. Moving to another country doesn't mean we stop being who we are.[42]

In concluding, the minister elaborated on the 'waka traditions'[43] and placed Indigenous Maori, descendants of British settlers who came in the 1840s and new migrants from Asia all in the same 'waka traditions'. She noted that those traditions 'not only explain origins but are also expressions of mana and identity'.[44]

Apologising for the past

Dalziel also referred to the pitiable plight of Chinese settlers in New Zealand. Their situation, she said, 'is made more poignant in the knowledge that the New Zealand government has now formally apologized for the discriminatory policies and practices that applied to our early Chinese migrants back then'.[45] The minister was referring to the 2002 apology for the poll tax and other discriminatory legislation. The *Chinese Immigrants Act 1881* had imposed a poll tax of £10 on every Chinese immigrant and restricted the numbers able to enter the country to one person per 10 tonnes of a ship's cargo. These provisions were increased to £100 pounds and the tonnage restrictions to one Chinese person per 100 tonnes of cargo, and consolidated in legislation during the next few years.

A number of other legislative initiatives also singled out the Chinese. In 1907, they had to put a thumbprint on their Certificates of Registration before leaving the country; no members of other ethnic groups had to do so. Chinese were deprived of their right to naturalisation in 1908 and the regulation was not rescinded until 1951.[46] No other ethnic group was deprived of this right. A reading test in English was introduced; other immigrants had only a writing test in their own language. Even in 1935, when entry permits were introduced after a suspension of 15 years for reunification of family and partners of Chinese people, they were severely restricted.[47] The poll tax was abolished in 1944. In doing so, the first Labour Government's Minister of Finance, Walter Nash, said:

'I do not know of anything more pleasing from the Government's point of view…than the removing of the blot on our legislation.'[48]

Apologies and restitution to past victims have become increasingly important strategies in national and international politics since the mid-1990s. In addition to the apology to the Chinese in February 2002, the Clark administration also apologised to Samoa in June 2002 (on the fortieth anniversary of Samoan independence) for 'past mistakes during its occupation of Samoa from 1914 to 1962'—an apology which, unlike the one to the Chinese, was not sought by the people being apologised to.[49]

What are governments really doing when they apologise for wrongs committed by previous governments? Are they saying that they are accountable for the past but not responsible? Or that they are responsible but not guilty? Or simply that by remembering the past they hope not to repeat it? Clues to the motivation of the New Zealand Government in apologising to the Chinese community can be found in the wording of the apology itself. The text emphasised multicultural nation-building, with Clark noting that '[m]odern New Zealand has a bicultural foundation, and today is home to many peoples. It is important that we value, honour, and respect all our communities and see our diversity as a great strength.'[50]

The wording indicated the value placed by the government on contrition and reconciliation as a means of nation-building:

> While the governments which passed these discriminatory laws acted in a manner which was lawful at the time, their actions are seen by us today as unacceptable. We believe an act of reconciliation is required to ensure that full closure can be reached on this chapter in our nation's history.[51]

Clark believed that the apology was comparable with the Treaty settlement process, with 'saying sorry' helping to 'trigger a healing process for those still touched by the injustices'.[52]

New Zealand's changing ethnic composition was a significant factor behind the apology. The 2001 census had shown that the number of people of Asian ethnicity had more than doubled between 1991 and 2001, with 240 000, or one in 15 New Zealanders, of Asian ethnicity. The greatest increase in counts of overseas birthplace between 1996 and 2001 was for people who gave China as their country of birth.[53] In making the apology, Clark noted that the Chinese community was making 'a huge economic and social contribution' to the country. The many new Chinese migrants were 'bringing new ideas, a strong work ethic, and valuable contacts with their countries of origin'.[54] Furthermore, New Zealand was expected to benefit on the international stage (in terms of strengthened relationships) from taking a leading role in reconciliation.[55] As

Minister of Foreign Affairs and Trade, Phil Goff, subsequently observed in a speech to the Otago Foreign Policy School: 'The character of our foreign policy will increasingly reflect its changing domestic roots.'[56]

The apology to the Chinese for the historical grievances they experienced potentially opened the door for other ethnic communities to seek apologies, but the government assessed the 'risk' of their doing so as low. To date, there have been no further apologies.[57] The comparatively small size of other ethnic communities that experienced discrimination (such as the Jewish community) could rule out future apologies.

The apology to the Chinese community is an example of the use of history by the New Zealand Government to distance itself from past policies of discrimination. It was also a way of handling negative reactions in the wider community to Asian immigration and signalling to Asian countries that New Zeland seriously intended to strengthen ties with them. Most importantly, perhaps, in terms of the themes of this chapter, just like representations about the country's compassionate refugee policies, the apology contributed to and fitted with New Zealand's self-image and international reputation as an exemplary global citizen committed to the highest standards of ethical behaviour.

The apology for the poll tax was initiated by the New Zealand Chinese community, influenced in turn by the example of Canadian Chinese organisations, which had pursued redress for a similar poll tax since the late 1980s.[58] New Zealand's apology faced some dissent within the government, particularly from the Ministry of Maori Affairs and the Office of Treaty Settlements. These agencies considered that an expression of regret was more appropriate than an apology on the grounds that apologising to the Chinese might devalue the Crown apology as a form of redress in *Treaty of Waitangi* settlements. Eventually, the government disregarded such reservations and took 'a small political risk in return for a fine gesture'.[59]

The formal apology to Chinese New Zealanders took place on 12 February 2002, a few days after Waitangi Day. It was made by Prime Minister Clark at a function marking Chinese New Year at Parliament House, hosted by Clark and George Hawkins, Minister for Ethnic Affairs, for members of the Chinese community and non-Chinese dignitaries and community leaders. Clark stated that Chinese people were subjected to discrimination from the late nineteenth century through to the mid-twentieth century. The poll tax, in particular, had imposed considerable hardship: 'No other ethnic group was subjected to such restrictions, or a poll tax.' She expressed 'sorrow and regret that such practices were once considered appropriate…Today we recognize the considerable hardship it imposed and that the cost of it and the impact of other discriminatory immigration practices split families apart'.

The apology was meant to mark the beginning of a formal process of 'reconciliation' with the Chinese community. According to Clark: 'We believe this act of reconciliation is required to ensure that full closure can be reached on this chapter in our nation's history.' After suggestions from the New Zealand Chinese Association, the government subsequently entered into discussions with the descendants of those who had paid the poll tax on an appropriate form of reconciliation. One suggestion was for 'a government contribution to the restoration and maintenance of the Chinese heritage, culture, and language in New Zealand, which was severely eroded as a result of the injustice of the poll tax and other discriminatory policies'. A project to foster reconciliation was set up, with a high school history essay competition sponsored by the government focusing on the history of the Chinese in New Zealand. The aim of the competition was to ensure that 'this aspect of our history is better understood by present generations'.[60]

Public reaction to the apology was mainly positive. An editorial in the *New Zealand Herald* observed:

> Encouragingly, the initial response of many Chinese seems spot on. They see Helen Clark's apology as a step towards understanding and reconciliation, a step that, above all, allows the Chinese community to take its rightful place in our society.[61]

The *Herald*'s positive reaction was, however, qualified by the observation that the reconciliation process would be undermined if the Chinese 'chose to board the compensation bandwagon' (the implication being: 'as Maori groups have done'). Reservations were also expressed in letters to newspapers. One correspondent to the Manawatu *Evening Standard* wrote:

> The people of today are not responsible for what happened at that time. Nor are the fair-skinned race responsible for what might have happened with the Maoris over a hundred years ago...So let's forget about apologizing, just let it be known what happened and make sure it doesn't happen again.[62]

Revealingly, in terms of the major themes of this chapter—the idealisation of New Zealand's humanitarian record, immigration history and race relations—an editorial in the Wellington *Evening Post* noted that '[t]he treatment of these early Chinese immigrants remains a dark stain on the history of an otherwise tolerant society'.[63] It also queried 'whether a formal apology nearly a century later serves any purpose other than to assuage liberal guilt over our white colonialist history'.[64] These views support the notion that there might be a link between amnesia over aspects of the colonial legacy and hyperbolic claims about New Zealand's humanitarian record. I have, however, tried not to overstate the case. The politics of memory, especially in relation to the country's colonial legacy, is a complex matter, with 'liberal guilt' a glib oversimplification of the range of emotions engendered in the afterlife of the sometimes harsh treatment of Maori.[65]

Conclusion

History clearly matters to politicians and governments. Unlike historians, however, who usually look back at the past in order to try to understand it better, politicians' main interest in adopting a historical perspective tends to be to advance their present-day political purposes. This chapter has explored some of the conflicting imperatives that have characterised the process of 'looking back' in relation to New Zealand's refugee policy and to building support for multiculturalism. It has outlined how, as well as looking backwards, political leaders and governments have from time to time glanced sideways—particularly towards Australia. In relation to the Tampa episode, for example, New Zealand has taken considerable pride in seeming to upstage its larger neighbour in the business of being humanitarian.

I would like to draw four main conclusions from the different, but not disparate, strands of the discussion. First, New Zealand has a mixed record in relation to refugee policy, with instances of compassionate generosity, such as the government's response to 'handicapped' refugees (of which the country is justly proud), and harsh restrictiveness, such as the response to Holocaust survivors at the end of World War II, which remains largely unacknowledged. Representations of the record as outstandingly generous to refugees for such a small country have sometimes served the purpose of justifying the acceptance of further groups of refugees. Representations of refugee policy as exceptionally humanitarian, regardless of the evidence in the record, have been in keeping with other myths held about New Zealand as an ideal society—such as the record of relations between coloniser and colonised, which is supposedly better than that of other countries. I have noted the possible connection between the idealisation of the humanitarian record in relation to refugees and the colonial legacy, suggesting that the former might serve the purpose of assuaging liberal guilt over the real record of exploitation of Maori.

Second, there has been a discrepancy between representations and the real record of New Zealand in relation to immigration policy and multicultural nation-building. Until the mid-1980s, the overwhelming majority of the population was of Anglo-Celtic origin, with immigration policy characterised by discrimination against those who did not hail from the British Isles. When policy became non-discriminatory on the basis of ethnicity from the end of the 1980s, however, New Zealand's immigration history was recast in a way that disguised the reality of past ethnic discrimination against non-British migrants. This was done to address a set of conflicting imperatives: the need to promote multicultural values of tolerance of diversity in order to facilitate the acceptance of comparatively substantial immigration from Asia and at the same time deal with the legacy of a discriminatory immigration history. Amnesia about the problematic past in the recast version of history contributed to the maintenance of New Zealand's self-image of being an ideal society with an almost unblemished record of excellent race relations, the only acknowledged stain being the nineteenth-century poll tax legislation directed at the Chinese.

Third, from time to time, acknowledging the problematic past has better served the purpose of multicultural nation-building than forgetting it. For example, it enabled the government to distance its new multicultural focus from the 'bad old days' and helped to persuade doubting members of the public of the benefits of moving towards multiculturalism. Acknowledging the problematic past has also been useful in enabling the harder line by the previous Labour-led government on detaining asylum-seekers to be seen, in comparison, in a fairly positive light.

Finally, Clark's 2002 apology to Chinese New Zealanders for past wrongs, particularly the poll tax legislation, was an example of the government both acknowledging and distancing itself from the past, with contrition and reconciliation used as a means of multicultural nation-building. The apology process showed the government addressing conflicting imperatives. In apologising, Clark had to deal with the tension between biculturalism (the New Zealand Government's focus on addressing the relationship between Maori and the Crown before addressing multicultural issues) and multicultural nation-building. The apology had the potential to devalue the Crown apology to Maori as a form of redress in *Treaty of Waitangi* settlements. The measure faced considerable dissent within the government and, as noted, Clark moved cautiously in a minefield of conflicting imperatives. Eventually, the government went ahead and apologised despite the risk. It was an instance of looking back as a way of moving forward, with saying sorry a convenient means of bridging the gulf between the troublesome past and the preoccupation with immigrant nation-building.

Acknowledgments

An earlier draft of this chapter was written for the Governing by Looking Back conference held in 2007 at The Australian National University. It was workshopped at a seminar at the Institute for Social Research, Swinburne University of Technology, in December 2007. The research for this chapter was funded by the Australian Research Council through a grant administered by Swinburne University of Technology. The views in the chapter are those of the author, not those of New Zealand government agencies.

Endnotes

1 Desai, Kiran 2006, *The Inheritance of Loss*, Grove, New York, p. 227.

2 Fairburn, Miles 1989, *The Ideal Society and Its Enemies: The foundations of modern New Zealand society 1850–1900*, Auckland University Press, Auckland.

3 Novitz, David and Willmott, Bill (eds) 1989, *Culture and Identity in New Zealand*, GP Books, Wellington.

4 Alessio, Dominic 2008, 'Promoting paradise: utopianism and national identity in New Zealand, 1980–1930', *New Zealand Journal of History*, vol. 42, no. 1, p. 22.

5 Ibid., p. 23.

6 Mitchell, Austin 1972, *The Half Gallon Quarter-Acre Pavlova Paradise*, Whitcombe & Tombs, Christchurch.

7 Speech from the throne, 8 November 2005, <www.beehive.govt.nz/?q=node/24330>

8 Alessio, 'Promoting paradise', p. 24.

9 Oliver, W. H. 1991, *Claims to the Waitangi Tribunal*, Waitangi Tribunal Division, Department of Justice, Wellington, p. 3.

10 Since the mid-1980s, both National and Labour-led governments have had a bicultural agenda, differing merely in its details. Labour held office from 1984 to 1990, National was in power from 1990 to 1999 and there was a Labour-led government from 1999 until the 2008 general election delivered a National-led government.

11 Department of Statistics 2000, *NZ Official Yearbook*, Department of Statistics, Wellington, pp. 134–5.

12 Beaglehole, Ann 2007, 'Refugees', *Te Ara—The encyclopedia of New Zealand*, updated 21 September 2007, <www.TeAra.govt.nz/NewZealandPeoples/refugees/en>

13 *Speech from the Throne*, 8 November 2005, <www.beehive.govt.nz/?q=node/24330>

14 Secretary of Cabinet to Minister of Immigration, 17 April 1973, Archives New Zealand [hereafter ANZ], ABKF 947 W5182 22/1/274 part 3.

15 '"Handicapped" Ugandan Asians are to be admitted here', *Evening Post*, 17 April 1973.

16 Beaglehole, 'Refugees'.

17 Lianne Dalziel, interviewed by Ann Beaglehole, 3 May 2007, Wellington.

18 For the history of restrictions on Chinese immigration, see, for example, Murphy, Nigel 2002, *The Poll-Tax in New Zealand: A research paper*, 2nd edn, Commissioned by New Zealand Chinese Association, Office of Ethnic Affairs, Department of Internal Affairs, Wellington. For restrictions on Jewish immigration, see Beaglehole, Ann 1988, *A Small Price to Pay: Refugees from Hitler in New Zealand, 1936–1946*, Allen & Unwin, Wellington.

19 For discussion on the ethnic biases involved in the selection of displaced persons, see Beaglehole, Ann 1986, 'A small price to pay: refugees from Hitler in New Zealand, 1936–1946', MA thesis, Victoria University of Wellington, pp. 124–7.

20 A. D. McIntosh to Acting Minister of External Affairs, 8 November 1956, ANZ, L1 22/1/189 part 1.

21 Binzegger, Anton 1980, *New Zealand's Policy on Refugees*, New Zealand Institute of International Affairs, Wellington, pp. 38–42; Beaglehole, Ann 'Hungarians', *Te Ara—The encyclopedia of New Zealand*, <www.TeAra.govt.nz/NewZealandPeoples/Hungarians/en>

22 Quoted in Department of Labour 1994, *Refugee Women: The New Zealand refugee quota programme*, Department of Labour, New Zealand Immigration Service, Wellington, p. 17.

23 Quoted in ibid., p. 20.

24 Statement by A. G. Malcolm, Parliamentary Under-Secretary to Minister of Immigration, at meeting on refugees and displaced persons in South-East Asia, Geneva, 21 July 1979, ANZ, ABKF 947 W5182 22/1/27/24 part 14.

25 Quoted in Gallienne, Robin 1991, *The Whole Thing Was Orchestrated: New Zealand's response to the Indo-Chinese refugees exodus 1975–1985*, Centre for Asian Studies, University of Auckland, Auckland, p. 200.

26 Aussie Malcolm, interviewed by Ann Beaglehole, 12 April 2007, Auckland.

27 Don McKinnon, written communication to Ann Beaglehole, 19 February 2007.

28 Marr, David 2006, 'The luck of the draw', *Dominion Post*, 26 August 2006.

29 Lianne Dalziel, Beyond Tampa, Speech notes, 16 May 2003.

30 Ibid.

31 Binzegger, *New Zealand's Policy on Refugees*, p. 49.

32 Quoted in Department of Labour, *Refugee Women*, p. 19.

33 Radio New Zealand, *Morning Report*, 6 December 2006.

34 Quoted in Small, Vernon 2007, 'High profile Iranian may have fresh appeal grounds', *Dominion Post*, 5 September 2007.

35 'Immigration: facts and fallacies', *Labour and Employment Gazette*, vol. 4, no. 3 (1954), p. 48.

36 Quoted in Department of Labour, *Refugee Women*, p. 35.

37 McKinnon, Malcolm 1996, *Immigrants and Citizens: New Zealanders and Asian immigration in historical context*, Institute of Policy Studies, Victoria University of Wellington, Wellington, pp. 66–71.

38 Kerry Burke, Minister of Immigration, 'Review of immigration policy August 1986', *Appendices to the Journal of the House of Representatives*, 1986–87, vol. 8, G42, p. 8.

39 Quoted in McKinnon, *Immigrants and Citizens*, p. 67.

40 Ibid., p. 67.

41 Ibid., pp. 66–9.

42 Lianne Dalziel, Launch of *Shifting Centres: Women and migration in New Zealand history*, 26 August 2002.

43 'Waka traditions' refer to the migration by canoe ('*waka*') of Maori ancestors from the original homeland, Hawaiki, to Aotearoa (New Zealand). The expression is also used to refer to the migration journeys of New Zealand's diverse settlers.

44 Dalziel, Launch of *Shifting Centres*, quoting Angella Wanhalla ('Maori women in waka traditions', in *Shifting Centres*, p. 15). '*Mana*' refers to authority and prestige.

45 Dalziel, Launch of *Shifting Centres*.

46 A Department of Internal Affairs recommendation to reintroduce naturalisation for Chinese who met certain conditions was approved and formalised in March 1951 by Cabinet as part of the government's review of immigration policy relating to the Chinese. Murphy, Nigel 2008, *Guide to Laws and Policies Relating to the Chinese in New Zealand 1871–1997*, New Zealand Chinese Association, Wellington, pp. 40–2.

47 Ibid. See also Wong, Gilbert 2003, 'Is saying sorry enough?', in Manying Ip (ed.), *Unfolding History, Evolving Identity: The Chinese in New Zealand*, Auckland University Press, Auckland, p. 278.

48 Wong, 'Is saying sorry enough?', p. 258.

49 Murphy, Nigel 2006, The role of apologies in international relations and domestic identity: the meaning of New Zealand's apology to the Chinese New Zealand community and Samoa, 2002, Unpublished paper, p. 2.

50 Prime Minister's speech to Chinese community, 12 February 2002, <www.ethnicaffairs.govt.nz/oeawebsite.nsf/wpg_url/Advisory-Services-Consultations-Prime-Ministers-speech-to-Chinese-Community>

51 Ibid.

52 Berry, Ruth 2002, 'Saying sorry and moving on', *Evening Post*, 2 June 2002, quoted in Murphy, The role of apologies in international relations and domestic identity, p. 17.

53 Statistics New Zealand 2002, 'Census snapshot: cultural diversity', *2001 Census, Key Statistics*, March 2002, p. 9, <www.stats.govt.nz/NR/rdonlyres/872D2D96-78A3-46E1-A419-E2CDCF3835D2/0/CenCulDiv.pdf>

54 Prime Minister's speech to Chinese community.

55 Murphy (The role of apologies in international relations and domestic identity, p. 19 n. 6) observes that '[a]n example of how the apology has potentially strengthened New Zealand's relations with China is shown by the response by a Chinese government official to a question relating to the apology in Singapore on 21 April 2004. The official responded that "we believe this gesture is good to strengthen social unity in New Zealand, it encourages Chinese participation in New Zealand's economic and social development and the Chinese government really appreciates it."' *Voice of America*, newsvoacom, retrieved via email conversation, 20 September 2006.

56 Goff, Phil 2003, The ethics of foreign policy, 27 June 2003, <http://www.beehive.govt.nz/node/17186>, quoted in Murphy, The role of apologies in international relations and domestic identity, p. 18.

[57] While there have been no further apologies to ethnic communities, there was one other recent apology outside the treaty settlement process: to Vietnam War veterans, on 29 May 2008. This apology recognised that the veterans were not treated fairly on their return home from Vietnam.

[58] Wong, 'Is saying sorry enough?', p. 275. Canada apologised to the Chinese in 2006, accepting 'moral responsibility' for 'these shameful polices of our past' and offering financial compensation. *Canada Online Newsletter*, 25 June 2006,
<http://canadaonline.about.com/b/2006/06/25/canada-gives-formal-apology-for-chinese>

[59] Wong, 'Is saying sorry enough?', p. 262.

[60] Hawkins, George 2002, Poll tax apology marks a new beginning, 12 February 2002,
<www.ethnicaffairs.govt.nz/oeawebsite.nsf/wpg_url/
Advisory-Services-Consultations-Poll-Tax-Apology-Marks-A-New-Beginning>

[61] Quoted in Wong, 'Is saying sorry enough?', p. 271.

[62] Ibid., p. 272.

[63] Ibid., p. 271.

[64] 'Apology fever: now it's Samoa's turn', *Evening Post*, 4 June 2002.

[65] Caution also needs to be exercised in making connections between representations of the relationship between the colonised and the coloniser and representations of the humanitarian legacy. The former is central to New Zealand identity; the latter is a somewhat marginal matter.

7. Testing times: the problem of 'history' in the Howard Government's Australian citizenship test

Gwenda Tavan

In 2007, the Howard Coalition Government introduced significant changes to Australian citizenship laws, including an extension of the residency requirements for applicants, a tightening of the English-language provisions and a test in which applicants needed to demonstrate their knowledge of Australian values and customs. According to the government, such measures were necessary to ensure the successful integration of migrants into the host society, to protect the Australian 'way of life' and to reinforce the fact that Australian citizenship was a privilege not a right. When Immigration Minister, Kevin Andrews, introduced the bill into Parliament, he claimed:

> The test will encourage prospective citizens to obtain the knowledge they need to support successful integration into Australian society. The citizenship test will provide them with the opportunity to demonstrate in an objective way that they have the required knowledge of Australia, including the responsibilities and privileges of citizenship, and a basic knowledge and comprehension of English.[1]

The proposals inspired significant public debate, particularly about the merits of a citizenship test. The government was no doubt buoyed by opinion polls suggesting a majority of Australians supported the introduction of a test.[2] Still, considerable public concern was expressed about its intent and possible effects. A summary of the written submissions in response to the government's discussion paper, which was released in September 2006, revealed that while a majority of *individuals* supported the implementation of the test, more than two-thirds of the *organisations* that responded were opposed to it.[3] Many of these were community groups involved in migrant welfare and settlement. They questioned the practicality of the test, arguing its complexity would inhibit rather than encourage migrants to apply for citizenship. Many critics interpreted the reforms as one more government attempt to wind the clock back to the bad old days of the White Australia Policy and the infamous 'dictation test'. In January 2008, less than three months after the citizenship test was formally introduced, and amid reports of high failure rates, especially among non-English-speaking migrants and refugees, the new Rudd Labor Government commissioned a review of the changes introduced by its predecessor.[4] In November 2008, it announced that it would dump the Howard version of the test, 'replacing it with a new, simpler test based on Australia's democratic values rather than obscure historical or sporting facts'.[5]

This chapter considers the role of history and memory in the introduction of the Howard Government's citizenship test. It identifies the processes of public, political and institutional remembering enacted in its construction, the interests and values this use of history serves and the practical and symbolic effects it has had. I argue that the test was a consciously constructed form of collective memory making that sought to reinforce a homogenous and undifferentiated view of Australian society and history in the pursuit of specific ideological and political interests. The 'memory politics' embedded in the test exemplify Brändström et al.'s warnings of the potentially 'constraining' use of history in public policy making when such a use serves to 'narrow' rather than 'broaden' a government's definition of the problem at hand (in this case, the presumed inadequacy of citizenship and integration policies in Australia) and the range of policy options it can draw on to deal with that problem.[6]

The Howard reforms: return to a cultural-normative model of citizenship

The Howard Government's citizenship reforms began on 1 July 2007 with the introduction of the *Australian Citizenship Act 2007*. Its provisions include, inter alia, a doubling of the residence requirements for citizenship to four years and new language requirements for employer-sponsored temporary business visas. The Australian Citizenship Amendment (Citizenship Testing) Bill 2007 followed, passed by Parliament on 12 September 2007. The test itself was formally implemented on 1 October 2007.[7]

The act provides that applicants for citizenship must successfully complete a test before making an application for citizenship to demonstrate that they meet the requisite criteria of an understanding of the nature of their application, a basic knowledge of the English language and an adequate knowledge of the responsibilities and privileges of Australian citizenship. The act allows exemptions for some people, including those under the age of eighteen or over the age of sixty, and 'those with a permanent physical or mental incapacity which prevents them from understanding the nature of the application'. Provision is also made for some people, who do not have the necessary literacy skills required, to sit a verbal rather than a written test.[8] The original test format was computer based, consisting of 20 multiple-choice questions randomly selected from a much larger pool. Questions aimed to test applicants' 'basic knowledge of English…knowledge of Australia and the responsibilities and privileges of citizenship'. Potential applicants were advised that the test would include questions on Australian history, geography, values, the Australian people and the system of government.[9]

The government justified the introduction of the test on the grounds that it would enhance the integration of immigrants and thereby contribute to meeting present and future immigration challenges. These challenges were always vaguely defined, though many critics linked them to the Howard Government's repeated public criticisms, after the 11 September 2001 terrorist attacks in the United States, of elements within the Muslim community for failing to integrate, and the government's longstanding belief that multicultural policies were a threat to national cohesion and stability. In its discussion paper, *Australian citizenship: much more than a ceremony*, released in September 2006, the government expressed the view that continuing large-scale immigration had significant implications for social stability and national identity:

> [T]he challenge we will face as a nation will be to ensure the effective integration of new migrants into the Australian community and to foster a strong commitment to and identification with Australia regardless of their background.[10]

Underlying this concern about migrant integration was the government's commitment to reaffirming a culturally normative model of Australian citizenship, centred on notions of shared values, a cohesive 'national identity' and allegiance to the nation-state. This was not a new commitment for the Howard Government. In August 1998, Immigration Minister, Philip Ruddock, had announced the formation of the Australian Citizenship Council. Its objectives were to provide advice on appropriate ways to mark the fiftieth anniversary of Australian citizenship, and to seek 'advice on how we can further enhance Australian citizenship as not only the unifying force but also the symbol at the very heart of what being Australian is all about'.[11] In its response to the council's 2001 report, *Australian Citizenship for a New Century*, the government reiterated its belief that 'more can be made of Australian citizenship, as a unifying concept, particularly by extending the focus to shared civic values in addition to the legal status of Australian citizenship'. 'Australian citizenship,' it reminded readers, 'is a common bond at the heart of a unified and inclusive Australia and it is our shared civic values that underpin Australian citizenship, in both the broad and legal sense and serve to unify us as a nation.'[12]

In the lead-up to the introduction of the test in 2007, the government affirmed the association of citizenship with issues of national identity and allegiance. According to the 2006 discussion paper, 'Australian citizenship is the single most unifying force…It lies at the heart of our national identity—giving us a strong sense of who we are and our place in the world.'[13] One of the principal stated aims of the reforms was to enhance the status and prestige of citizenship, and by implication that of the nation itself, by making it more difficult to attain.

Much of the campaigning surrounding the reforms focused on 'values', English language and integration into a 'way of life'. In the booklet *Becoming an Australian Citizen*, which potential citizens were encouraged to read carefully before sitting the test, the claim was made that modern citizenship 'rests on sentiments of nationhood and enduring attachment to what Australians hold in common'. With this in mind,

> new citizens are expected to have a basic knowledge of English. They are also expected to know something of Australia's history and heritage, our land and its people, and of the unique national culture which has evolved in Australia over time.[14]

This cultural-nationalist model proved to be problematic in a number of ways. It overshadowed the civic and democratic dimensions of Australian citizenship, as defined in the pages of the citizenship booklet on which the testing of applicants was based. Migrants were urged to embrace specific liberal democratic institutions and principles such as parliamentary democracy and the rule of law, as well as 'values' such as peacefulness, tolerance, compassion for those in need and freedom of religion, association and speech. These were presented, however, as uniquely 'Australian' characteristics rather than universal or civic principles. Notably absent was a discourse pertaining to the rights and responsibilities of 'free citizens' or the limits of the powers of the State in regard to those citizens. Rather, the citizenship bargain offered to prospective applicants comprised certain 'privileges' and 'responsibilities' to be bestowed by the State in return for settlers' declarations of loyalty and their ability to pass a test.[15] 'Allegiance' to the nation-state was a central feature of Australian citizenship policy and discourse throughout much of the twentieth century, giving way only gradually to a more civic definition during the 1980s and 1990s.[16] The introduction of the test, and Howard's broad package of citizenship reforms, aimed to reaffirm this allegiance model.

Another problem with the Howard model was that it encouraged an excessive reliance on self-referential, nebulous, highly contested and ultimately facile descriptors of national uniqueness. Their relevance and appeal to new settlers were always doubtful. For example, the citizenship booklet offered an extended discussion of the significance of various national symbols, including the flag, the national anthem, the national colours, Australia's floral emblem, the coat of arms and the national gemstone.[17] Critics rightly pointed out that 'good citizenship' depended on a lot more than due reverence for the wattle and the opal, or knowing which Australian was most famous for playing cricket.[18]

A similar self-absorption surrounded the discussion of national values and characteristics—for example, the importance of 'mateship':

> Australia has a strong tradition of mateship—where people help and receive help from others voluntarily, especially in times of adversity. A mate can be a spouse, partner, brother, sister, daughter, son or a friend. A mate can also be a total stranger.[19]

New settlers would be forgiven for expressing confusion about this most 'Australian' of characteristics—how it manifests itself in concrete, everyday terms, how such an attitude is learned or how it differs from Christian principles of charity or radical traditions of fraternity and egalitarianism.

Also questionable was the assumption that 'testing' applicants for knowledge of customs and values would tangibly improve people's commitment to those values as opposed to just extracting procedural obedience. This approach reinforces the administrative aspects of the reforms and the key role that immigration officials played in the introduction of the test, backed up by the Prime Minister's previously publicly stated concern about the absence of an 'institution or code [which] lays down a test of Australianness'.[20] In this respect, the introduction of the test can be interpreted as a statist-nationalist managerialist practice in which one group's ownership of the national and political space is asserted through its ability to control the behaviour and outlook of a group not considered to be part of the national community.[21] The physical 'act' of administrative compliance embodied in the test has been as significant as the content of the test itself in affirming the unequal power relationship that exists between the (foreign-born) 'out group' and the (white, British, Australian-born) 'in group', which has the power to demand obedience (the latter, of course, is not compelled to sit a test to prove its 'loyalty' and 'knowledge'). As a letter to the *Age* pointed out, 'The citizenship test should stay. This test is to find out how much people do know. Make it hard, keep it hard, a test is a test.'[22]

The citizenship test as a form of collective memory making (and forgetting)

History plays a fundamental role in nationalist discourse, creating the myths of origins by which national communities maintain a sense of unique identity and cohesion. This history, nevertheless, is always inherently contested, requiring selective forms of remembering and forgetting to maintain the facade of national homogeneity and cohesion. As Paula Hamilton puts it:

> [D]efining groups or nations always necessitates a dual process of inclusion and exclusion and remembering the past is a central mechanism of that process. Many have noted that forgetting is one of the most powerful forces that shape national remembering.[23]

Jeffrey Olick and Joyce Robbins reinforce this point, drawing on Renan's famous dictum, 'national identities combine remembering and forgetting, with greater emphasis on the latter: They forget that they are not inevitable and that their internal fissures may be as significant as their external boundaries'.[24]

This preoccupation with history and the highly contested narratives it gave rise to was duly manifested in the decision to test citizenship applicants on their knowledge of Australian history, and in the specific historical narratives that eventually emerged within the framework of the citizenship testing booklet. Prime Minister Howard was a fierce cultural warrior, defending the nation's conservative-liberal and British-imperial heritage and strongly criticising what he saw as a 'black-armband' view of history, which denigrated those achievements and overemphasised evidence of conflict, injustice and inequality in Australia's past. He strongly advocated a return to linear, narrative history to counter what he perceived as blatant (left-wing and progressive) ideological biases of thematic-based history.[25]

This intervention into cultural matters was not a new phenomenon, but continued a long tradition of prime ministerial concern with issues of national identity.[26] It also perpetuated the long-held belief in Australia that by virtue of their control of immigration and citizenship policies, bureaucrats and political leaders were the principal gatekeepers of the imagined national community. As Alastair Davidson observes:

> From its first formal statement of what it is to be a citizen in Australia, the Australian state has made it clear that its primary concern was to establish in a country of immigration that the newcomers show clearly that they have adopted a national identity, that they have joined the national family of British descent.[27]

Nevertheless, the Howard era was distinct for the extent of governmental interference in the cultural-nationalist arena, which included an (ill-fated) attempt to dictate the content of history teaching in schools.[28] It focused ultimately on the question of migration, citizenship and identity, and the development of the history section of the citizenship booklet, *Becoming an Australian Citizen*.

Howard and his supporters argued that knowledge of Australian history was fundamental to the social and cultural integration of new settlers. They did not acknowledge, however, that specific political and ideological interests, and highly selective forms of remembering and forgetting, shaped this history. In an illuminating article, eminent historian John Hirst reveals his involvement in the writing of the history section of the booklet, after challenging the government's original version, which he describes as 'appallingly bad'.[29] The basis for Hirst's claim was that the emphasis on narrative had led to

> all the standard events and developments [being]...present in chronological order but so severely compacted that they were often no more than a list. You could read right through it and have no sense of

the particular characteristics of Australian society; you would simply be overwhelmed by disconnected information…Quite strangely, for a book for newcomers, it frequently assumed knowledge of the subjects it treated—or rather mentioned.[30]

Hirst's offer to assist with the history section was accepted by officials within the Immigration Department, as was his recommendation that a themes-based approach be adopted. Ultimately, he professed 'little ground for complaint' with what eventually emerged, claiming that the Prime Minister's office 'signed off on a history which was not John Howard's, and was organised contrary to his declared preference for narrative'.[31] Hirst also admits, however, to a significant degree of interference by 'departmental, ministerial and prime ministerial players' in creating and approving the history. He criticises Howard, not for intervening, but for the fact that 'having intervened he did not know when to stop'.[32]

The manoeuvres surrounding the preparation of the history section attest to the ideologically and politically charged nature of the enterprise. Hirst's confidence about the quality of the finished work notwithstanding, it is difficult not to interpret it as a victory for Howard and his conservative-nationalist supporters. Its central themes and the discursive strategies of which it was constituted showed this narrative to have been much more than just a 'history for migrants' and a resource to assist integration. More significant was its function of providing powerful affirmation to an imagined (white, British) Australian-born audience, whose core identity was perceived to be under threat. This was manifested in the essentially monocultural and undifferentiated view of the national community it presented, privileging white, male, 'British-Australian' institutions, values and endeavours through a focus on issues such as convict settlers, 'a harsh country', diggers and the Anzac legend, the economy and politics, sport and the nation.

Such privileging served to marginalise the place of various groups in the national story, including women, the working class, Indigenous and non-Anglo Australians. They were reduced to bit players, the beneficiaries of white, British-Australian, masculine endeavour rather than historical agents in their own right, whose own unique experiences, identities and memories were integral components of the national narrative. Issues of difference, conflict and power between groups were suppressed or treated superficially to sustain the view of national homogeneity and stability. This was most evident in the citizenship booklet's account of Aboriginal people, which occupied a bare two pages (diggers and the Anzac legend received three pages), and where controversial issues such as land rights, the Stolen Generations, reconciliation and the military intervention in NT communities were downplayed.[33] Hirst himself admitted that officials removed some of his more sensitive comments regarding Indigenous–settler interactions on the frontier, the Stolen Generations and the plight of traditional people on their own lands in favour of more optimistic assessments.[34]

The suppression of the more problematic aspects of Australian history aimed to confirm the confident assertion in the citizenship booklet that Australia in the twenty-first century was 'a nation at ease with the world and with itself'.[35] There were audible silences nevertheless, conscious omissions that hinted at deep, continuing uncertainties about national identity and social cohesion. They reflect the continuing unsettling legacy of Australia's colonial heritage—in particular, the continuing failure of non-Indigenous Australia to come to terms with the dispossession and the continuing exploitation of Indigenous Australians. They belie repeated claims by the former government that during the Howard years Australians were finally 'relaxed and comfortable' about their identity and their past.[36]

There were other forms of historical forgetting at work in the citizenship test. One of the most troubling aspects was the decision to tighten English-language restrictions through formal testing. This was justified on the grounds that language skills were fundamental to good citizenship. It was also hoped this provision would provide 'incentives' for people to improve their English skills. Critics, in contrast, argued from the outset that the test would unfairly disadvantage people of non-English-speaking backgrounds and that too much emphasis was being given to English as a core requirement for citizenship (as opposed to a rights-based conception of citizenship that would privilege political knowledge and commitment to the body politic). While the centrality of English-language skills to structural integration is undisputed, it is difficult to see how a test in itself can possibly improve such skills. Claims of the commitment to improving English skills would have been more credible if they had been backed up with tangible efforts to improve funding and access to English classes.

The legitimacy of the new English-language requirements also depended on a fundamental act of historical amnesia. As Liberal MP Petro Georgiou—one of the few members within Coalition ranks to criticise the policies—pointed out, the language requirements were much tougher than anything Australia had in the past, and would be failed by thousands of people today, including the many native-born Australians who have poor literacy skills, and postwar immigrants from southern Europe with poor English who were nevertheless able to take out citizenship in the past.[37] The latter were the same people who were often lauded by the Howard Government as the type of exemplary citizens newer groups should try to emulate.[38] The self-evident contradictions of such claims were never openly addressed: that it is possible to be a good citizen and have poor English skills, and that non-English-speaking people have indeed played a fundamental role in the creation of the modern Australian nation-state.

A form of historical forgetting was also enacted in praising these earlier groups of migrants without acknowledging that they too had often been the focus of public derision for not assimilating well or fast enough. This fact did not fit well with popular narratives that celebrated the enormous success of the postwar immigration program, the basis for which lay partly, one suspects, in the need to justify the contemporary immigration program, the scale of which grew significantly during the Howard decade. They also suggest a desire to ignore the historical truth of migrant inequality and injustice during the much-idealised 'long boom' years of the 1950s and 1960s, and nostalgia perhaps, among social conservatives, for the cultural certainties of an earlier assimilationist era.

Finally, as I further discuss below, embodied in the citizenship test was a tangible neglect of flawed policy initiatives throughout the twentieth century that discriminated against specific racial and ethnic groups in the name of national cohesion and identity, and which served to inhibit rather than enhance the integration process for migrants despite the apparent best intentions of policy makers.

Historical analogies: citizenship policy in 'assimilationist Australia'

One of the most striking aspects of the Howard Government's citizenship policies and discourse was how closely they echoed the anxieties and concerns, and the failed policies, of an earlier era of immigration and citizenship history. It is by now well known that until the late 1960s Australian citizenship was an overwhelmingly cultural-racial model, conceptualised primarily in relation to (white) British-Australian culture and ethnicity, rather than civic and democratic values.[39] This manifested itself in a variety of racially exclusionary practices, including Australia's first officially sanctioned 'test' of assimilability, courtesy of the *Immigration Restriction Act 1901* and the dictation test.[40]

This cultural-racial model remained in place long after the introduction of mass European immigration in 1947. While non-English-speaking Europeans were eventually determined to be acceptable as immigrants, non-Europeans continued to face major restrictions on entry until the early 1970s. Entry for all non-Britons was premised on the principle that they would speedily assimilate into Australian society and culture. Blatant discrimination and inequalities continued to exist in relation to Australian citizenship, based on racial and ethnic/cultural criteria. The *Nationality and Citizenship Act 1948* defined an alien as 'a person who is not a British subject, an Irish citizen or protected person'.[41] British subjects did not have to take out Australian citizenship and were eligible to vote after six months' residence. European migrants could access voting rights only after becoming citizens and had to fulfil a five-year residency criterion. Non-Europeans were generally denied citizenship until 1956–57 and, after that, had to fulfil a 15-year residency criterion as distinct from the five-year rule for Europeans.

Indigenous Australians were British subjects and Australian citizens but were denied many basic rights, including voting rights, reaffirming the extent to which ideas of race and culture shaped assumptions of social membership.[42]

Because of the cultural assumptions that underpinned it, citizenship remained the most fundamental indicator of a migrant's successful assimilation into the national community. A lot of effort was expended during the postwar years in encouraging migrants to take up citizenship: through the creation of elaborate citizenship ceremonies, through direct appeals and through the annual Australian Citizenship Conventions, which brought bureaucrats and political and community leaders together to discuss how best to achieve assimilation and to sell the citizenship message. 'Every migrant a citizen' was a common catchphrase at such forums, confirming the belief of successive governments that migrant settlement should be permanent and required political as well as social and cultural integration. Migrants were constantly entreated to 'help make Australia great'. Citizenship education campaigns urged migrants to embrace the 'Australian way of life'.[43]

There were, nevertheless, strong tensions between successive governments' desire that immigrants settle permanently and embrace citizenship, and their belief that citizenship should be viewed as a privilege rather than a right—a prize that had to be earned rather than a cheap giveaway. Immigration officials actually contemplated the introduction of a formal test in 1945, on the grounds that it would

> ascertain whether an applicant had an adequate knowledge of English, had some acquaintance of Australian history, form of government etc, was favourably disposed to our ideals and outlook and was genuinely desirous of becoming a citizen of this country.[44]

Such a method, it was hoped, would 'tend to impress more strongly upon applicants the seriousness and importance of naturalisation'.[45]

A formal test was ultimately not adopted, most likely because of the enormous procedural complexities involved. Nevertheless, quite cumbersome administrative procedures for gaining citizenship existed. They included:

- a five-year residency criterion for Europeans (as opposed to one year for British subjects)
- lodgment of a Declaration of Intention to Apply for Naturalisation two years before the launch of the formal procedure for acquiring citizenship
- publication of an applicant's intention to become a citizen in two local newspapers
- three certificates of character written by Australian citizens
- knowledge of English (though that meant perfunctory knowledge only)
- renunciation of allegiance to the country of origin

- no formal test, but an informal one for English language and knowledge of Australian customs and institutions.

These procedures did little to encourage the embrace of citizenship. In 1952, only 29 000 of a possible 180 000 eligible adult migrants had taken out citizenship. Approximately only 52 per cent had applied by 1960.[46] Continuing research by the Immigration Department during the 1950s and 1960s revealed that the low take-up rate was attributable to a number of factors:

- prospective applicants, especially those with poor English skills, were discouraged by the complicated administrative procedures
- immigrants were not sure they wanted to stay permanently
- many immigrants were unwilling to renounce their allegiance to countries of origin
- citizenship was said to offer very few tangible benefits, other than voting rights and access to welfare
- some immigrants argued that citizenship would do little to enhance their social and economic position in society.

The message was clear. As Ann-Mari Jordens points out, citizenship for migrants involves an analysis of costs and benefits—a fact that postwar political leaders and bureaucrats were slow to realise. Despite the generous offer of citizenship, a sizeable proportion of migrants could discern no tangible advantage in making the leap.[47] The complex administrative arrangements did little to encourage take-up rates. Government leaders had likewise failed to confront a fundamental truth about assimilation: that it was a complex and contested process influenced by a range of personal, cultural and structural factors; that individuals possessed a measure of agency in regard to questions of identity, participation and belonging; and that state-driven approaches to these issues did not necessarily achieve the desired results. Clearly, the opportunity to participate in the 'Australian way of life' was not enough to counter the structural inequities and social marginalisation many migrants experienced during that period. Many were unwilling to renounce their own distinct former loyalties and 'collective memories' in pursuit of Australian national membership.[48] This included the many British migrants who failed to take up citizenship despite its ready availability to them.

Migrant resistance to assimilation and demands for a more equitable 'citizenship bargain', growing concerns about low citizenship take-up rates and increasing competition from other countries seeking migrants led over time to the liberalisation of settlement and citizenship policies. During the 1950s and 1960s, the most cumbersome procedural requirements were gradually removed. In the mid-1960s, the government initiated a shift away from assimilation policies towards an integrationist model that expanded provision of services for migrants.

The five-year residence requirement for Europeans was lowered to three years in 1973. Ethnic and racial discrimination in immigration policy was gradually abolished and the final phase of the ending of the White Australia Policy was enacted in 1973. Citizenship rights for British and other migrants were also equalised that year. The requirement that citizens renounce their former allegiance was abolished in 1986. Multicultural policies and discourses sought to address sources of migrant inequality and better integrate migrant settlers into the national story.

Altogether, these initiatives constituted a fundamental challenge to the once dominant cultural-racial and administrative model of Australian citizenship and signalled the emergence of a new regimen more closely attuned to issues of civic and democratic rights and responsibilities. Due largely to these initiatives, until recently, Australia could boast of some of the most inclusive and generous immigration and citizenship policies in the developed world. Citizenship rates during the 1990s were 'spectacular', according to social scientists Brian Galligan and Winsome Roberts, with the 2001 census recording that approximately 95 per cent of eligible permanent residents had become citizens, compared with about 50 per cent in the 1960s.[49] The significance of such numbers in terms of the wellbeing of migrants, Australia's social stability and its appeal as a destination for migrants should not be underestimated.

Policy constraints and the political uses of immigration history

There are a number of interesting parallels between Howard's citizenship test and the citizenship regime of the postwar assimilationist era. These include a definition of citizenship based on cultural absorption into an imagined homogenous social whole, the demand for allegiance to the nation-state and administrative complexity. Such parallels prompt the question of why the government and its supporters were so willing to pin their hopes on a model that had already proved to be a failure. Furthermore, why were they so disdainful of Australia's own proud, pioneering role in regard to citizenship policy from the late 1960s onwards?

It is not evident whether policy makers consciously knew of and ignored the precedents of the postwar period, including the doomed recommendation of the mid-1940s that formal testing be applied. Specific interests and values, however, clearly undermined any substantive engagement with this aspect of Australia's history, and thus any attempt to draw lessons from it. These interests related partly to the role of the bureaucracy in the reforms—that is, those members of the Department of Immigration whose brief it was to review Australia's citizenship provisions and who instigated an examination of international practices as part of that process. Much was made in the original discussion paper and subsequent related publications of the fact that 'many other countries' had formal testing procedures and were 'well ahead' in implementing their ideas.[50] The countries referred to most often were the United States, Canada, the United Kingdom and the Netherlands.

As Sue Wright points out, the practice of citizenship testing is growing in some parts of the world, raising important questions about the 'timing and scale' of this development—namely, why, when immigration is by no means a new phenomenon, so many states are formalising their citizenship arrangements and consolidating 'integration' efforts. No tangible evidence exists to prove that formal testing methods for citizenship achieve superior results in terms of assisting the integration process; testing content and procedures are not applied uniformly and many countries seem to manage quite well without formal testing.[51]

Various explanations have been offered to explain this apparent paradox, including the growth of anti-migrant and anti-Muslim sentiment and fears for national security in the post-11 September global environment, and popular resistance in developed economies to the contemporary scale of international migration. The renewed emphasis on citizenship and integration policies can be seen as part of a general tendency among sovereign states in the developed world to consolidate control over immigration intakes—legal and illegal—in the face of unprecedented global population movements, alongside stricter regulations of domestic entry, harsher sanctions against unauthorised entry and increased participation in international and intra-governmental arrangements to control migration flows.[52]

Another related factor is 'convergence', whereby strong similarities are increasingly evident in the policies of diverse states towards immigration and citizenship issues. The forces driving policy convergence are multifaceted but include the phenomenon of trans-governmentalism, whereby 'political networks are becoming more transnational and their members share knowledge and experience'.[53] The introduction of the Australian citizenship test suggests both the benefits and the limitations of trans-governmentalism. On the one hand, immigration officials' access to a wide diversity of ideas and practices in an international context has the potential to enhance efficiencies and equities in citizenship policy. On the other, officials clearly failed to invoke an institutional memory, forgetting or ignoring the positive Australian policy innovations of the previous three decades in their enthusiasm for achieving 'world's best practice'.

This failure of institutional memory in relation to immigration and citizenship policy also relates to the specific political and ideological preferences of the Howard Government. In reaching to the past, it sought only those aspects that conformed to its own essentially conservative, monocultural perspective of Australian society and history and the presumed perspective of its political constituency. That view precluded any consideration of Australia's rich, complex multicultural history,[54] of the political dangers of enacting policies that evoked memories of the racially exclusionary practices of the past, including the White Australia Policy and the dictation test, of the failures of assimilation policies during the 1950s and early 1960s and of the specific factors that facilitated the shift to multicultural policies and a more liberal approach to citizenship.

By ignoring that history, the Howard Government effectively narrowed its perception of the political problem at hand, thereby effectively creating a 'migrant integration' problem, which many commentators did not believe existed. After all, the government never offered any tangible reasons for the reforms. There was no evidence of declining citizenship rates. The reforms did not appear to be a response to specific examples of social dislocation and ethnic unrest, an unprecedented growth in unauthorised immigration or political demands from the community. On the contrary, the strong emphasis on skills and English-language competence in contemporary Australian immigration policy suggests that, generally, migrants today can be integrated more easily than at any other point in history.

It would seem that the reforms were the outcome of a set of attitudes and preferences of a government predisposed to view Australia's ever-increasing cultural plurality in negative terms, ideologically committed to winding back some of the social and policy advances of the past 30 years and sensitive to the domestic politics of immigration, which many critics believed the government consciously manipulated for electoral advantage during its almost 12 years in office. This was despite, and perhaps because of, the fact that immigration intakes increased dramatically during the Howard years, strengthening Australia's multi-ethnic character in the process.[55]

These preferences self-evidently constrained the scope for constructive policy solutions to the issues of migrant integration in the early twenty-first century: rather than look to Australia's proud record of immigration reform since the 1960s and build on earlier and present-day multicultural successes, the government chose to revive aspects of the assimilationist, administrative approaches of an earlier period. The danger of this approach was that it set in place a process with the potential to repeat some of the policy failures of that era, inhibiting rather than advancing the integration process for key groups by constraining their access to citizenship. This is borne out by the release of statistics on the early impact of the test. Between 1 October 2007 and 31 March 2008, almost 20 per cent of applicants failed on their first attempt. More troubling still was the wide disparity in success rates for skilled migrants, family reunion migrants and humanitarian entrants.[56] This was reinforced by a country-of-birth analysis, which showed that people from refugee-source countries and people of non-English-speaking background (from Afghanistan, Iraq, Sri Lanka and

Sudan) had much lower application rates and higher failure rates than those from other countries.[57] The reasons for the disparities are self-evident, reflecting the greater difficulties experienced by the most vulnerable among new settler groups, especially in relation to the English-language requirements.

Also significant was the evidence that citizenship applications 'plummeted' after the introduction of the test, down from 38 850 in March 2007 to 16 024 in March 2008.[58] Its complex requirements clearly had the potential to inhibit take-up rates, especially among the most vulnerable new settlers, further undermining the migrant integration process. This factor was undoubtedly crucial in convincing the Rudd Government to reassess the original test procedures, even though the Labor Party had supported its introduction.

Two final questions are raised by Howard's citizenship test, and my attempt here to contextualise the reforms within a broader history of Australian citizenship policy. To what extent did the government foresee the possibility that it would discriminate against specific groups, specifically refugees, the low skilled and people of non-English-speaking background, much as had occurred in the immediate postwar assimilationist period? If, as many critics suggested, the outcomes were predictable from the outset, did the government consciously set out to constrain access to citizenship rights and benefits for a significant minority of permanent settlers (and the most vulnerable of migrant groups), in contradiction of its stated objective that the aim was to enhance Australian citizenship and facilitate the integration process for all?

The possibility that citizenship laws function as a form of population gatekeeping, which regulates entry into the political community, with all its attendant benefits, if not the real physical national space, is not new, as this chapter has shown. It has, however, added salience in a world in which developed economies, including Australia, are competing for skilled and literate migrants, while attempting to limit the entry of low-skilled and illiterate or semi-literate people who are seeking better lives through emigration. This potential is reinforced in domestic and global environments in which elected governments remain preoccupied with the political consequences of their immigration policies and want to assure their electorates that they retain control of immigration intakes. Wright and others allude to this gatekeeping possibility in their recent work on citizenship tests in Europe:

> Adamo and van Oers show how a standardized test, rigorously applied, is likely to exclude weak individuals who do not possess the educational and linguistic prerequisites required to pass a test. There can be no interactive support, no leeway in a written test. The cards are stacked against those with limited literacy and only basic education. We have to wonder if this is not actually part of state policy, a desired effect of the test, even if it would never be publicly acknowledged as a

strategy…many European countries are moving towards the Australian/Canadian model of immigration, which encourages certain categories of well-qualified immigrants to fill clearly defined gaps in the skills base of the economy but bars those who would be less productive. If this is the case, tests for entry, settlement and naturalization aid European governments in encouraging literate and intellectually able citizens to migrate and settle definitively, while deterring the illiterate and the uneducated.[59]

If Wright is correct, what at first glance appears to have been the Howard Government's neglect of Australia's failed and discriminatory citizenship policies of an earlier era could in fact have been their wilful invocation. By 2006, the government was firmly caught between its neo-liberal commitment to large-scale economic migration and its much-touted social-conservative opposition to multiculturalism—and, likewise, between its repeated public pledge that immigration served an overwhelming economic good and the practical impossibility of completely excluding 'less-desirable' migrants such as refugees, the low skilled and the non-English speaking. In this context, the introduction of the citizenship test with its attendant emphasis on language skills, knowledge of core values and administrative complexity might have been intended to assert the privileged status of skilled, English-speaking migrants and, in a more practical sense, to discourage and inhibit the entry of less-desirable migrants into the Australian political community, even if their physical exclusion from the nation-state was not possible (or even desirable). It also aimed to send a powerful message to the electorate that the government retained firm control over the character of the national community, even if real control over immigration numbers had long ago been ceded.

Conclusion

The Howard Government's citizenship test reflected a deeply problematic model of citizenship that was always unlikely to achieve the desired result of enhancing the status of Australian citizenship and encouraging the integration process for all migrants. It relied on notoriously vague concepts such as 'the national community' and 'way of life' to sell the citizenship message. It embodied a monocultural, undifferentiated and exclusionary view of the Australian national community and Australian history that privileged white, male, 'British-Australian' institutions and endeavours and neither reflected nor responded adequately to Australia's multicultural, globalised reality. It set in place highly complex linguistic and administrative procedures that from the outset discriminated against the low skilled and those with poor English skills.

Despite the Howard Government's professed respect for the values and traditions of the past, the test embodied a highly selective form of social remembering that pointedly ignored the lessons of the past and had the potential to repeat some of the policy failures of an earlier assimilationist era. This chapter has raised the possibility that perhaps, after all, this was the government's true intention, using the citizenship test as a political tool to keep potentially disaffected voters onside, and also as a practical means of inhibiting entry into the political community of those people perceived as less-desirable settlers. It is too soon to say whether the Rudd Government's reforms will tangibly improve Australia's citizenship regime. In any case, the message is clear: if governments are serious about migrant rights and equity, they need to engage with Australia's past record on citizenship and migrant settlement, acknowledge and embrace the positive policy advances of the past four decades, look beyond merely cultural-nationalist and economic considerations in regards to citizenship and focus anew on questions of social justice, equity and respect for difference.

Acknowledgments

Versions of this paper were presented at a seminar at the Institute for Social Research, Swinburne University of Technology and the Governing by Looking Back conference at The Australian National University (both in December 2007). My thanks to Klaus Neumann and all participants for their valuable feedback.

Endnotes

[1] Kevin Andrews, *Commonwealth Parliamentary Debates* [hereafter *CPD*], Representatives, 30 May 2007, p. 6, <www.aph.gov.au/hansard/reps/dailys/dr300507.pdf>

[2] A Newspoll survey conducted on 22–24 September 2006 indicated that 77 per cent of respondents were in favour of the proposed citizenship test and 53 per cent strongly in favour (<www.newspoll.com.au/cgi-bin/polling/display_poll_data.pl>).

[3] Summary report on the outcomes of the public consultation on the merits of introducing a formal citizenship test, <http://pandora.nla.gov.au/pan/31543/20070124-0000/www.minister.immi.gov.au/parlsec/media/responses/citizenship-test/summary_report_citizen_test_paper.pdf>

[4] Butterly, Nick 2008, 'Migrants flunk citizenship tests', *Age*, 2 January 2008.

[5] Berkovic, Nicola 2008, 'Howard's migrant test to be dumped', *Australian*, 22 November 2008.

[6] Brändström, Annika, Bynander, Frederik and 't Hart, Paul 2004, 'Governing by looking back: historical analogies and crisis management', *Public Administration*, vol. 82, no. 1, pp. 191–210. See also Olick, Jeffrey K. and Robbins, Joyce 1998, 'Social memory studies: from "collective memory" to the historical sociology of mnemonic practices', *Annual Review of Sociology*, vol. 24, pp. 105–40.

[7] Department of Immigration and Citizenship, History of the citizenship test, <www.citizenship.gov.au/test/background/history.htm>

[8] *Australian Citizenship Act 2007*, s. 21, as amended by *Act No. 142 of 2007*.

[9] Commonwealth of Australia 2007, *Becoming an Australian Citizen*, September 2007, Reprinted with corrections November 2007, p. 43, <http://pandora.nla.gov.au/pan/53892/20081109-0018/www.citizenship.gov.au/test/resource-booklet/citz-booklet-full-ver.pdf>

[10] Commonwealth of Australia 2006, *Australian Citizenship: Much more than a ceremony*, 17 September 2006, p. 12, <http://pandora.nla.gov.au/pan/64133/20061005-0000/www.citizenship.gov.au/news/DIMA_Citizenship_Discussion_Paper.pdf>

[11] Ruddock, Philip 1998, Australian Citizenship Council announced, Press release MPS104/98, 7 August 1998, <http://www.multiculturalaustralia.edu.au/doc/immdept_1.pdf>

[12] Commonwealth of Australia 2001, *Australian Citizenship…A Common Bond: Government response to the report of the Australian Citizenship Council*, May 2001, p. 4, <http://pandora.nla.gov.au/pan/53892/20070509-0000/www.citizenship.gov.au/_pdf/0501report.pdf>

[13] Commonwealth of Australia, *Australian Citizenship: Much more than a ceremony*, p. 8.

[14] Commonwealth of Australia, *Becoming an Australian Citizen*, p. 1.

[15] The 'privileges' include the right to vote, to seek election to Parliament, to apply for a passport, consular assistance and employment in the defence services. The responsibilities include voting, serving on a jury and defending Australia should the need arise (ibid., pp. 3–4).

[16] Dutton, David 2002, *One of Us? A century of Australian citizenship*, UNSW Press, Sydney, especially chs 1 and 9.

[17] Commonwealth of Australia, *Becoming an Australian Citizen*, pp. 14–16.

[18] Tavan, Gwenda 2008, 'Multiple choice time for Labor', *Age*, 10 January 2008.

[19] Commonwealth of Australia, *Becoming an Australian Citizen*, p. 7.

[20] Howard, John 2006, Australia Day address to National Press Club, 25 January 2006, <http://pandora.nla.gov.au/pan/21243/20061016-0000/www.australianpolitics.com/news/2006/01/06-01-25_howard.html>

[21] Hage, Ghassan 1998, *White Nation: Fantasies of white supremacy in a multicultural society*, Pluto, Sydney, pp. 42–7.

[22] Judith Bond, 'Letter to the editor', *Age*, 3 January 2008.

[23] Hamilton, Paula 1994, 'The knife edge: debates about memory and history', in Kate Darian-Smith and Paula Hamilton (eds), *Memory and History in Twentieth Century Australia*, Oxford University Press, Melbourne, p. 23.

[24] Olick and Robbins, 'Social memory studies', p. 117.

[25] Macintyre, Stuart and Clark, Anna 2003, *The History Wars*, Melbourne University Press, Melbourne.

[26] Curran, James 2004, *The Power of Speech: Australian prime ministers defining the national image*, Melbourne University Press, Melbourne.

[27] Davidson, Alastair 1997, *From Subject to Citizen: Australian citizenship in the twentieth century*, Cambridge University Press, Cambridge, pp. 45–6.

[28] Taylor, Tony 2008, 'Howard's way fails school test', *Age*, 14 January 2008.

[29] Hirst, John 2008, 'Australia: the official history', *Monthly*, February 2008, p. 31.

[30] Ibid., p. 31.

[31] Ibid., p. 35.

[32] Ibid., p. 35.

[33] Commonwealth of Australia, *Becoming an Australian Citizen*, pp. 32–3.

[34] Hirst, 'Australia', pp. 34–5.

[35] Commonwealth of Australia, *Becoming an Australian Citizen*, p. 7.

[36] John Howard, quoted in Brett, Judith 2005, *Relaxed and Comfortable: The Liberal Party's Australia*, Black Inc., Melbourne, p. 29. See also Elder, Catriona 2007, *Being Australian: Narratives of national identity*, Allen & Unwin, Sydney, especially ch. 1.

[37] Georgiou, Petro 2007, Australian citizenship in the 21st century, Paper delivered to CO.AS.IT. Italian Assistance Association, 14 March 2007. An edited extract was published as 'A needless test for citizenship', *Canberra Times*, 16 March 2007. Reports of the speech were published in the *Age*, *Sydney Morning Herald*, *Australian* and *Herald Sun* on 15 March 2007. See also Petro Georgiou, *CPD*, Representatives, 8 August 2007, pp. 29–34, <www.aph.gov.au/hansard/reps/dailys/dr080807.pdf>

[38] Howard praised the Australian Greek community in 2006, citing it as an example of a community that had integrated well. The irony is that the Greek community has relatively low rates of English-language proficiency compared with other groups; see van Vliet, Peter 2006, 'Diversity is a fact, not a doctrine', *Age*, 29 November 2006.

[39] Dutton, *One of Us?*; Davidson, *From Subject to Citizen*.

[40] Holland, Alison (forthcoming), 'Australian citizenship in the twenty-first century: historical perspectives', in Christina Slade and Martina Mollering (eds), *From Migrant to Citizen: Testing language, testing culture*, Palgrave Macmillan, New York.

[41] Chesterman, John and Galligan, Brian (eds) 1999, *Defining Australian Citizenship: Selected documents*, Melbourne University Press, Melbourne, p. 62.

[42] Ibid., pp. 28–9, 32–6.

[43] Tavan, Gwenda 1997, '"Good neighbours": community organisations, migrant assimilation and Australian society and culture, 1950–1961', *Australian Historical Studies*, vol. 109, pp. 77–89;

Haebich, Anna 2008, *Spinning the Dream: Assimilation in Australia 1950–1970*, Fremantle Press, Fremantle, especially chs 3 and 4.

[44] Department of Immigration, 'Naturalization of aliens', 6 December 1945, National Archives of Australia, CP815/1, 29/021/53.

[45] Ibid.

[46] Jordens, Ann-Mari 1997, *Alien to Citizen: Settling migrants in Australia 1945–75*, Allen & Unwin, Sydney, pp. 175, 183.

[47] Ibid., p. 175.

[48] Davidson, *From Subject to Citizen*, p. 256.

[49] Galligan, Brian and Roberts, Winsome 2004, *Australian Citizenship*, Melbourne University Press, Carlton, p. 95.

[50] Commonwealth of Australia, *Australian Citizenship: Much more than a ceremony*, p. 9.

[51] Countries with citizenship tests today include the United States, the United Kingdom, Canada, Denmark, the Netherlands and Germany. Testing content and procedures vary widely. The United Kingdom, for example, has opted for a test that puts less emphasis on history and cultural integration and more on knowledge of practical day-to-day affairs. The Netherlands, in contrast, requires even prospective *residents* to formally pledge to uphold 'Dutch values' in its attempt to ensure maximum 'cultural assimilation'. Wright, Sue 2008, 'Citizenship tests in Europe—editorial introduction', *International Journal on Multicultural Societies*, vol. 10, no. 1, pp. 1–2, 5–7.

[52] Castles, Stephen J. and Miller, Mark J. 2003, *The Age of Migration: International population movements in the modern world*, 3rd edn, Guilford, New York, especially Introduction, chs 4 and 5 and Conclusion.

[53] Wright, 'Citizenship tests in Europe', p. 7.

[54] Hodge, Bob and O'Carroll, John 2006, *Borderwork in Multicultural Australia*, Allen & Unwin, Sydney, especially ch. 4.

[55] Annual immigration intakes rose from approximately 82 000 at the start of the Howard era in 1996 to 159 000 by its end in 2007.

[56] The percentage of applicants who passed the test on their first or subsequent attempt was 99 per cent for skilled stream clients, 91 per cent for family stream clients and 82 per cent for humanitarian program clients. An examination of the average number of tests per client shows that while skilled stream applicants average about 1.1 tests each, the figure is 1.2 for family stream and a significant 1.7 for humanitarian stream clients. Department of Immigration and Citizenship 2008, *Australian Citizenship Test: Snapshot report*, March 2008, pp. 3–5 (copy provided to the author by a private source).

[57] Ibid., p. 6.

[58] Topsfield, Jewel 2008, 'Citizenship test "spooks" many would-be Aussies', *Age*, 29 April 2008.

[59] Wright, 'Citizenship tests in Europe', pp. 4–5.

Afterword

Klaus Neumann

The contributions to this volume argue that Australian and New Zealand immigration, refugee and citizenship policies, and public debates about these policies, are marked by the absence of an informed assessment of past policies and practices. Glenn Nicholls, for example, suggests that those rewriting Australia's deportation policies since 1989 have ignored the knowledge built up by those administering past policies, while Amy Nethery shows that Australian debates about asylum-seeker policies refer to German concentration camps rather than to the local institutional predecessors of Port Hedland, Woomera and Baxter immigration detention centres.

How can such amnesia and disregard for historical analysis be explained? Policy makers and contributors to public debate might be convinced that new policies are self-evidently superior to old ones and that the present is infinitely more complex than the past. Those identifying current policies as being akin to policies adopted in the past often intend to draw attention to the supposedly retrogressive nature of the former. There is a tendency to perceive history as inherently progressive and progress as something that manifests itself in ever-increasing complexity. While immigration legislation enacted in either Australia or New Zealand in the early twentieth century usually consisted of a few short paragraphs, some of today's laws—such as New Zealand's Immigration Bill 2007, which is currently before Parliament—contain as much text as a novel. Because of a seemingly unprecedented level of complexity, even the mistakes of the past are rarely considered relevant.

Today's immigration legislation is indeed far more complex than that of 100 years ago. The amount of information available to us is far greater now than it was even a generation ago. We live in a globalised world and policy makers have to factor in an ever-increasing array of external influences. Such observations, however, could easily lead us to underestimate the past. Views of the past as a much simpler, less sophisticated and inherently inferior version of the present are evidence both of a certain degree of arrogance and of the propensity to view the past only through the lens of the present—that is, to adopt a Whiggish perspective, according to which only those aspects of the past count that have prefigured the present. By ignoring historical dead ends, those looking towards the past for guidance fail to appreciate the complexity that previous policy makers had to grapple with.

Any attempt to look to the past for guidance ought to be informed by the expectation that there is more to the past than what can be seen through a 'presentist' telescope. Nethery's argument that we are better able to understand the nature of Australian immigration detention centres if we explore the characteristics of civilian internment camps, quarantine stations and Aboriginal reserves, rather than liken detention centres to concentration camps, is convincing. Ideally, however, an analysis of the institutional predecessors of immigration detention would take into account their complex history, even if that seemingly made them less useable. When the Australian Army established internment camps at the beginning of World War II, they were initially known as 'concentration camps' (and listed as such in the public telephone book).[1] That was not because their creators saw any similarities between the Orange and Hay internment camps, on the one hand, and Dachau and Sachsenhausen, on the other, but because both the Nazi authorities and the Australian military used a term that had been coined by the British during the Second Boer War (1899–1902) to refer to camps for the confinement of non-combatants. And while the comparison with other forms of extrajudicial detention highlights some of the main features of today's immigration detention centres, it can also obscure the differences between Australian detention facilities that were operating some 50 years ago (such as Sydney's North Head detention centre, which was established in May 1959 in the grounds of a quarantine station) and the immigration detention centres at the turn of the twenty-first century.[2]

Philippa Mein Smith and Peter Hempenstall have recently drawn attention to Australians' striking lack of interest in and ignorance about New Zealand and New Zealanders' lack of concern for whatever has been happening in Australia. They point out that such disregard is surprising given the strong ties between the two countries.[3] These ties have extended to the area of policy making. As Ann Beaglehole discusses in her contribution, New Zealand's refugee policies have at times been influenced by Australian responses to refugees; there have also been instances in which Australian policy makers are highly attentive to a particular response to refugees adopted by New Zealand.[4]

In his chapter, Roderic Pitty demonstrates the fruitfulness of 'comparative insights' and advocates a process of 'mutual learning'. Australians and New Zealanders would do well to look beyond their own pasts and each other's presents. Given the similarities—and instructive differences—between the two countries, Australian policy makers could learn from the successes and failures of New Zealand citizenship, immigration and refugee policy in much the same way as New Zealand policy makers could let their decisions be informed by past developments on the other side of the Tasman Sea. In both countries, public debate about such policy would be richer if it drew on Australasian historical perspectives.

Thus, in 2001, Australian policy makers and public commentators would have been well advised to pay attention to the panic that led to the passing of New

Zealand's *Immigration Amendment (No. 2) Act 1999* on 16 June 1999, which provided the government with an opportunity to depart from the customary bipartisan approach to immigration matters. The law gave the New Zealand Government greater leeway in detaining unauthorised arrivals and prosecuting people smugglers. It had been prompted by news of a boat carrying 102 Chinese suspected asylum-seekers and heading for New Zealand, which journalists and politicians had interpreted as evidence that the country was about to be swamped by a tidal wave of illegal immigrants.[5] The 'boat people' never materialised. With the benefit of hindsight, it is now possible to see that the hysteria of late August and early September 2001, when the Australian Government introduced legislation supposedly designed to protect Australia from a large influx of asylum-seekers, was probably equally unwarranted. With the benefit of hindsight, it also seems apparent that the Labor Party gained little from supporting the government's position and that it might have been wise to follow the lead of the New Zealand Labour Party, which held firm and opposed the government's policy in 1999. Similarly, recent debates in New Zealand about the level of Asian immigration—perhaps best epitomised by the controversies about remarks by New Zealand First leader, Winston Peters—could have benefited from an informed assessment of similar debates in Australia in the first half of the 1990s, which were initiated by the historian Geoffrey Blainey, taken up by the Leader of the Opposition at the time, John Howard, and later reignited by Pauline Hanson.

While I would like to reiterate the argument put forward in all chapters—namely, that history *does* matter—I would also like to caution against overly simplistic expectations according to which histories are to save us from memories. The history that ought to inform policy making and public debate is necessarily in itself shaped by memories. It is always partial. While historians often claim that they are able to distinguish fact from fiction and that rigorous research allows them to arrive at accurate representations of historical developments, they too do not have unmediated access to the past. Policy makers who govern by looking back draw on a history, or on a range of histories, rather than on the past itself.

An appreciation of the making of memories and histories can therefore be as important for policy makers as a thorough understanding of the complexities of the past. Such an appreciation is particularly crucial when memories or histories have a constraining effect by favouring certain analogies and thereby limiting policy options. According to popular understandings of the country's historical response to refugees, which seem to be shared by many decision makers, Australia has been particularly generous and welcoming in the past. As Beaglehole's contribution shows, such understandings are equally prevalent in New Zealand. While it is important to critique such views where they are unfounded, it might be as important to explain why Australians and New Zealanders have imagined themselves as being the world leaders in humanitarianism.

Historical analogies are sometimes deliberately invoked to provide a narrow, simplistic or misleading view of the past and can be an effective means of propaganda. Former US President George W. Bush, for example, might not have lasted two terms in office if he had not been a master at invoking historical analogies to silence critical assessments of his policies.[6] In Australia and in New Zealand, the government has played an active role in propagating particular understandings of the past. Governments of various political persuasions have encouraged patriotic histories—that is, narratives about the past in which the nation's achievements are highlighted and its people are credited with a range of positive attributes. Thus, both New Zealand and Australia are said to have an excellent record in the reception and resettlement of refugees. The two examples most often cited in both countries concern the resettlement of Hungarians after the failed uprising in 1956 and of Indochinese after the end of the Vietnam War. Not only does the focus on Hungarian and Indochinese refugees distract from Australia's and New Zealand's miserly responses to refugee crises on other occasions, it emphasises the resettlement of Hungarians and Indochinese refugees. The emphasis on resettlement privileges the final result, rather than the process. In the case of Indochinese refugees, the narratives focus on the large number of refugees resettled and usually fail to mention that Australia did not open its doors until Malcolm Fraser took over from Gough Whitlam, and that New Zealand resisted playing a significant role in the resettlement of Indochinese refugees until 1979.[7]

Emphasising the status of Hungarian and Indochinese arrivals as refugees, these narratives do not mention that the criteria under which Hungarians were admitted to New Zealand and Australia from the end of 1956 have very little in common with the criteria that govern today's selection of refugees from camps in, say, Kenya or Thailand. The selection process in 1956 and 1957 differed from that in 2009 not least because Hungarians were perceived to be victims of the enemy in the Cold War, and because the Australian and the New Zealand economies needed additional labour. It would be hard to imagine that Burmese refugees being resettled in New Zealand today would ask to be repatriated because they 'fled' in search of adventure and are homesick—as happened in the case of some Hungarians resettled in New Zealand in the late 1950s.[8]

Arguing that the incoming Obama administration in the United States ought to make better use of historical analogies, Eric Stern observes: 'Just as keeping an eye on the rear view mirror is an essential part of driving an automobile, attending to the past is part of crisis navigation.'[9] Attending to the past ought to be an integral part of policy making and public debate about policy, irrespective of whether the policy is a response to a crisis. As, however, the motorist does not really see the cars behind her, but images of those cars in her rear-view mirror, we only ever see histories rather than the past itself. As the motorist who is keeping an eye on the rear-view mirror is able to see only some of the cars behind her, so commentators and policy makers tend to see only histories of a segment of the past. And as it is impossible for the motorist to see everything behind her, irrespective of how many mirrors she has in her car, we necessarily privilege some aspects of the past over others. Which aspects of the past are visible to us depend on a range of factors, such as the prisms that dominate public discourse and access to historical knowledge.

After the tragic events of 16 April 2009, when an explosion killed several people aboard a boat carrying asylum-seekers near Ashmore Reef (see Introduction), policy makers and commentators tried to make sense of the available policy options by referring to the Tampa crisis and the 'children overboard' saga in 2001. 'Suddenly, as if history is destined to repeat itself, Australia is facing a fresh divisive debate about asylum seekers,' Michelle Grattan, political editor of the Melbourne *Age*, wrote.[10] She and her colleagues, however, had only one particular history in mind. It was not the only obvious choice. They could have reminded their readers of the divisive debates in late 1977, when the then Labor Party President, Bob Hawke, criticised the Fraser Government for admitting Indochinese refugees, or of the arrival of asylum-seekers in 1989, when Hawke, as Prime Minister, called into question the motivations of Cambodian 'boat people'.[11]

I was reminded of Hawke when reading that Darwin residents had donated 'a pile of clothing' for the refugees who had been evacuated to Darwin after the explosion of 16 April 2009.[12] In 1977, Hawke had much support in Darwin. On 22 November 1977, the Waterside Workers' Federation called two two-hour strikes in Darwin 'in protest at the "preferential treatment" given to refugees, claiming concern about quarantine arrangements, adequacy of Australia's defences and questioning the status of the boat people as refugees'.[13] I could equally have remembered, however, that Darwin has a tradition of accommodating and supporting refugees, be it the East Timorese who arrived from late 1975 onwards or three Portuguese asylum-seekers in the early 1960s.[14]

The past is fascinating in its diversity, even if glimpsed only through a rear-view mirror. It is to be hoped that those making and debating immigration, refugee and citizenship policy in New Zealand and Australia develop a deeper appreciation of the benefits that can be gained from detailed historical analysis. This is not to say that such analysis ought to determine policy or that a consideration of precedents and analogies ought to come at the price of a comprehensive understanding of the issue at hand. Those studying the rear-view mirror too intensely will find themselves at the side of the road.

Endnotes

1 E. H. Bourne to R. H. Croll, Deputy Chief Publicity Censor, 6 January 1941, National Archives of Australia [hereafter NAA], SP109, 310/01.

[2] According to a letter drafted by the Department of Immigration for the Minister for Immigration in late 1958, the minister's 'sole objective in directing the establishment of such centres was to ensure that men (particularly young men) whose deportation I have had to order, solely because of their having entered or remained in Australia without proper authority, should not be thrown into gaols and there forced to associate with criminals, to the possibly great detriment of their characters'. T. H. E. Heyes to Director General of Health, 26 November 1958, NAA, A1658, 874/9/1 section 1.

[3] Mein Smith, Philippa and Hempenstall, Peter 2008, 'Rediscovering the Tasman world', in Philippa Mein Smith, Peter Hempenstall and Shaun Goldfinch (eds), *Remaking the Tasman World*, Canterbury University Press, Christchurch, pp. 13–30.

[4] See, for example, Neumann, Klaus 2004, *Refuge Australia: Australia's humanitarian record*, UNSW Press, Sydney, p. 43.

[5] Bain, Helen 1999, 'Law rushed to detain boatpeople', *Dominion*, 16 June 1999; 'Unwelcome by boat', *New Zealand Herald*, 17 June 1999; Shaw, Bob 1999, 'More boat people may be on the way', *Evening Post*, 17 June 1999.

[6] On Bush's use of historical analogies, see Noon, David Hoogland 2004, 'Operation enduring analogy: World War II, the war on terror, and the uses of historical memory', *Rhetoric & Public Affairs*, vol. 7, no. 3, pp. 339–66.

[7] Gallienne, Robin 1991, *The Whole Thing Was Orchestrated: New Zealand's response to the Indo-Chinese refugees exodus 1975–1985*, Centre for Asian Studies, University of Auckland, Auckland.

[8] See, for example, the correspondence in Archives New Zealand, IA 1 116/68 part 1.

[9] Stern, Eric K. 2009, 'Crisis navigation: lessons from history for the crisis manager in chief', *Governance*, vol. 22, no. 2, p. 191.

[10] Grattan, Michelle 1999, 'There and back again on refugees', *Age*, 17 April 1999.

[11] 'Hawke: return bogus refugees', *Australian*, 29 November 1977; Richards, Eric 2008, *Destination Australia: Migration to Australia since 1901*, UNSW Press, Sydney, p. 296. The response to the arrival of the first Indochinese 'boat people' in 1976 was also far more complex than is generally being remembered today; see Grant, Bruce 2009, 'After the exodus', *Inside Story*, 29 January 2009, <http://inside.org.au/after-the-exodus/>

[12] 'Darwin donates clothes, says prayers for asylum seekers', *ABC News Online*, 20 April 2009, <www.abc.net.au/news/stories/2009/04/20/2546899.htm>

[13] Viviani, Nancy and Lawe-Davies, Joanna 1980, *Australian Government Policy on the Entry of Vietnamese Refugees 1976 to 1978*, Centre for the Study of Australian–Asian Relations, Griffith University, Brisbane, p. 21.

[14] Neumann, Klaus 2005, '"Stayputs" and asylum seekers in Darwin, 1961–1962: or, how three Portuguese sailors helped to undermine the White Australia policy', *Journal of Northern Territory History*, vol. 16, pp. 1–25.

Select bibliography

Agamben, Giorgio 1998, *Homo Sacer: Sovereign power and bare life*, Translated by Daniel Heller-Roazen, Stanford University Press, Stanford.

Baubock, Rainer 1994, *Transnational Citizenship: Membership and rights in international migration*, Edward Elgar, Aldershot.

Beckett, Jeremy 1998, 'Aboriginality, citizenship and nation-state', *Social Analysis*, no. 24, pp. 3–18.

Binzegger, Anton 1980, *New Zealand's Policy on Refugees*, New Zealand Institute of International Affairs, Wellington.

Brändström, Annika, Bynander, Fredrik and 't Hart, Paul 2004, 'Governing by looking back: historical analogies and crisis management', *Public Administration*, vol. 82, no. 1, pp. 191–210.

Castles, Stephen 2005, 'Nation and empire: hierarchies of citizenship in the new global order', *International Politics*, vol. 42, pp. 203–24.

Chesterman, John and Galligan, Brian 1997, *Citizens Without Rights: Aborigines and Australian citizenship*, Cambridge University Press, Melbourne.

Davidson, Alastair 1997, *From Subject to Citizen: Australian citizenship in the twentieth century*, Cambridge University Press, Cambridge.

Department of Labour, 1994. *Refugee Women: The New Zealand refugee quota programme*, Department of Labour, New Zealand Immigration Service, Wellington.

Dutton, David 2002, *One of Us? A century of Australian citizenship*, UNSW Press, Sydney.

Fischer, Gerhard 1989, *Enemy Aliens: Internment and the homefront experience in Australia 1914–1920*, University of Queensland Press, St Lucia.

Gallienne, Robin 1991, *The Whole Thing Was Orchestrated: New Zealand's response to the Indo-Chinese refugees exodus, 1975 to 1985*, Centre for Asian Studies, University of Auckland, Auckland.

Galligan, Brian and Roberts, Winsome 2004, *Australian Citizenship*, Melbourne University Press, Carlton.

Hage, Ghassan 1998, *White Nation: Fantasies of white supremacy in a multicultural society*, Pluto, Sydney.

Halbwachs, Maurice 1992, *On Collective Memory*, Translated by Lewis A. Coser, University of Chicago Press, Chicago.

Holland, Alison (forthcoming), 'Australian citizenship in the twenty first century: historical perspectives', in Christina Slade and Martina Mollering (eds), *From Migrant to Citizen: Testing language, testing culture*, Palgrave Macmillan, New York.

Jayasuriya, Laksiri, Walker, David and Gothard, Jan (eds) 2003, *Legacies of White Australia: Race, culture and nation*, University of Western Australia Press, Crawley.

Johansson, Jon 2004, 'Orewa and the rhetoric of illusion', *Political Science*, vol. 56, no. 2, pp. 111–29.

Latham, Suzie and Goddard, Chris 2008, *Human Rights Overboard: Seeking asylum in Australia*, Scribe, Melbourne.

Liu, James H. et al. (eds) 2005, *New Zealand Identities: Departures and destinations*, Victoria University Press, Wellington.

Maglen, Krista 2005, 'A world apart: geography, Australian quarantine, and the mother country', *Journal of the History of Medicine and Allied Sciences*, vol. 60, no. 2, pp. 196–217.

Mares, Peter 2002, *Borderline: Australia's response to refugees and asylum seekers in the wake of the Tampa*, UNSW Press, Sydney.

Marr, David and Wilkinson, Marian 2003, *Dark Victory*, Allen & Unwin, Crows Nest.

McKinnon, Malcolm 1996, *Immigrants and Citizens: New Zealanders and Asian immigration in historical context*, Institute of Policy Studies, Wellington.

McMaster, Don 2001, *Asylum Seekers: Australia's response to refugees*, Melbourne University Press, Carlton South.

Mein Smith, Philippa, Hempenstall, Peter and Goldfinch, Shaun (eds) 2008, *Remaking the Tasman World*, Canterbury University Press, Christchurch.

Nagata, Yuriko 1996, *Unwanted Aliens: Japanese internment in Australia*, University of Queensland Press, St Lucia.

National Inquiry into the Separation of Aboriginal and Torres Strait Islander Children from their Families 1997, *Bringing Them Home: Report of the National Inquiry into the Separation of Aboriginal and Torres Strait Islander Children from their Families*, Human Rights and Equal Opportunity Commission, Sydney.

Neumann, Klaus 2004, *Refuge Australia: Australia's humanitarian record*, UNSW Press, Sydney.

Neumann, Klaus 2006, 'Guarding the flood gates: the removal of non-Europeans, 1945–1949', in Martin Crotty and David Roberts (eds), *The Great Mistakes of Australian History*, UNSW Press, Sydney, pp. 186–202.

Neumann, Klaus 2006, *In the Interest of National Security: Civilian internment in Australia during World War II*, National Archives of Australia, Canberra.

Neumann, Klaus 2007, 'Been there, done that?', in Dean Lusher and Nick Haslam (eds), *Yearning to Breathe Free: Seeking asylum in Australia*, Federation Press, Annandale.

Neustadt, Richard E. and May, Ernest R. 1986, *Thinking in Time: The uses of history for decision makers*, Free Press, New York.

Nicholls, Glenn 2007, *Deported: A history of forced departures from Australia*, UNSW Press, Sydney.

Nobles, Melissa 2008, *The Politics of Official Apologies*, Cambridge University Press, New York.

Olick, Jeffrey K. and Robbins, Joyce 1998, 'Social memory studies: from "collective memory" to the historical sociology of mnemonic practices', *Annual Review of Sociology*, vol. 24, pp. 105–40.

Pearson, David 2004, 'Rethinking citizenship in Aotearoa/New Zealand', in Paul Spoonley, Cluny Macpherson and David Pearson (eds), *Tangata Tangata: The changing ethnic contours of New Zealand*, Dunmore Press, Southbank, pp. 291–314.

Phillips, Jock et al. (eds) 2006, *Settler and Migrant Peoples of New Zealand*, David Bateman, Auckland.

Rothman, David J. 1971, *The Discovery of the Asylum: Social order and disorder in the new republic*, Little, Brown and Company, Boston.

Rubinstein, Kim 2000, 'Citizenship and the centenary—inclusion and exclusion in 20th century Australia', *Melbourne University Law Review*, vol. 24, pp. 576–608.

Rubinstein, Kim 2002, 'Citizenship, sovereignty and migration: Australia's exclusionary approach to membership of the community', *Public Law Review*, vol. 13, pp. 102–9.

Saunders, Kay and Daniels, Roger (eds) 2000, *Alien Justice: Wartime internment in Australia and North America*, University of Queensland Press, St Lucia.

Tavan, Gwenda 2005, *The Long, Slow Death of White Australia*, Scribe, Melbourne.

Viviani, Nancy 1996, *The Indochinese in Australia, 1975–1995: From burnt boats to barbecues*, Oxford University Press, Melbourne.

www.ingramcontent.com/pod-product-compliance
Lightning Source LLC
Chambersburg PA
CBHW041119280326
41928CB00061B/3444